A
SHARED
SPIRITUAL
JOURNEY

A
SHARED
SPIRITUAL
JOURNEY

Lutherans and Catholics
Traveling toward Unity

*Susan K. Wood and
Timothy J. Wengert*
FOREWORD BY
Martin E. Marty

Paulist Press
New York / Mahwah, NJ

Library of Congress Cataloging-in-Publication Data
Names: Wood, Susan K.
Title: A shared spiritual journey : Lutherans and Catholics traveling toward unity / Susan K. Wood, Timothy J. Wengert ; foreword by Martin E. Marty.
Description: New York : Paulist Press, 2016. | Includes bibliographical references and index.
Identifiers: LCCN 2015033772 (print) | LCCN 2015035119 (ebook) | ISBN 9780809149797 (pbk. : alk. paper) | ISBN 9781587685958 (ebook)
Subjects: LCSH: Catholic Church—Relations—Lutheran Church. | Lutheran Church—Relations—Catholic Church.
Classification: LCC BX8063.7.C3 W66 2015 (print) | LCC BX8063.7.C3 (ebook) | DDC 280/.042—dc23
LC record available at http://lccn.loc.gov/2015033772

ISBN 978-0-8091-4979-7 (paperback)
ISBN 978-1-58768-595-8 (e-book)

Published by Paulist Press
997 Macarthur Boulevard
Mahwah, New Jersey 07430

www.paulistpress.com

Printed and bound in the
United States of America

Contents

Foreword

Whoever regularly passes a bulletin board on a campus or in a church can expect to see a dazzling and probably bewildering mix of notices, invitations, and pleas. It is often difficult to sort through them mentally and to determine what will count in the mind of any particular individual or group of believers such as readers of this book. One can picture encountering such a group of bulletins in the small city of Wittenberg, or a short time later, in Mainz, Germany, on a day half a millennium ago and being drawn to a proposed debate. In such cases, a professor or monk would suggest a thesis for debate, as scholars did then and still do. A debate, as we all know, takes the form of an argument, after which there is a winner and a loser. This means that the defense of the thesis has been judged to have been successful by the standards and intentions of someone else. Or, conversely, the debater may have been unsuccessful and unconvincing.

NOT A DEBATE BUT A DIALOGUE, A CONVERSATION

This book is not a debate, though it elaborates on and traces the destiny of earlier ones. In the present case, it commemorates, first, not *one* thesis but, famously, *ninety-five* of them. Readers will find that instead of a *debate*, this is a *conversation* and even is called a dialogue. A conversation, be it noted, is based not on answers but on questions. Debates like those that grew out of a

vii

challenge issued in autumn of 1517 demanded a response. But the conversations chartered or informed by this book and others like it will be more free-form. The participants will be expected to listen and to respect "the other," and to be ready to expect and realize change.

Note how Professors Wengert and Wood treat their topics and their readership. They deal with accepted facts about old debates, they helpfully explore historical accounts about them, and they appraise proposed outcomes. As the title of this book has it, they are on a journey, and they invite others to walk with them toward a goal, which in this instance, is the realization of more unity among Protestants and Catholics within Christ's Church.

DETERMINING THE MAIN THEMES THAT ARE STILL AT ISSUE

This journey may be arduous: every step taken earlier has been complex. The record suggests that those who deal with questions about the journey will not have an easy time of it. But they and the people about whom they write—and whom they *now* invite for a larger conversation—have to agree on some terms and goals if they want to progress. Finding themes for the exchanges should not be difficult since the dialogue, in this case between a Lutheran and a Catholic, deals with a five-century controversy of great note among Christians. A surprise, however: it will be quite difficult to define the issues. It was so in October 1517, and as one will soon read here, the efforts remain so now.

No one pretends that all the debates of long ago are over, that there is little to be exercised about in a new era of peace. In everyday life and through access to a whole world made accessible by media, it is obvious that controversies remain. The problem results from the tangle inherited from past debates and is complicated by the passing of time and historical changes. Put most simply, the goal of realizing Christian unity across old boundaries and barriers, which the debate of 1517 left as burden and legacy, relates to constants within Christian life and practice. But the cultures and worldviews of participants keep changing significantly. For example, the Wittenberg story was developed by many who could assume that everyone around them was culturally and officially Christian however much they sinned and failed to live within the Christian story. Of course, people in any period live with guilt and seek ways to deal with it. But those ways are by no means confined to paths worn smooth by monks, priests, and penitents in Christian Europe of old.

Thus, it is often pointed out, if the listeners to debates issuing from Wittenberg were wrestling with the desperate question, "Is God gracious?" their distant heirs today are more likely to ask "Is God?" meaning, "Is there a God?" Five hundred years ago, those concerned spoke readily of their sin as part of their common search for any meaning at all to life. The Theses from October 1517 reflected an assumption that *meaning* was all too real, since it was imparted and defined by a God who readily, even eternally, might punish them for their shortcomings. Now it is the task of theologians, pastors, and spiritual leaders in general in the twenty-first century to join with and learn from the journeyers who struggled from the sixteenth to the twenty-first century in vastly differing cultures. It is the gift of the Wengert/Wood dialoguers that they both revisit the debate "then" and make it available for "now."

Fortunately for readers, the coauthors know that the people of 1517 were not all eager to hear formal theology discussed as they tried to make sense of their lives and to see their spiritual life improved. The prime "reformer" in this book, Martin Luther, himself knew the problem and confessed that he dreaded the task of preaching to townspeople about the central aspect of the Reformation, which we have codified as "justification by grace through faith." He complained that when he did treat that doctrine, people did anything but pay attention. They slept, or left the church. So? To hold attention and to preach the truth, Luther enlivened the theme and expounded the biblical truth to which it pointed by telling stories, which meant that he avoided abstractions and dealt with daily-life themes in concrete and vivid terms.

THE FIRST IMPETUS: MOMENTUM FROM VATICAN II

The authors of this book are assigned the task not of preaching sermons but of clarifying the issues still at stake in the main themes of the Reformation heritage. Professors Wood and Wengert show their gratitude and awaken ours to the spiritual ancestors who have helped those on the journeys today. They acknowledge, for example, what the Second Vatican Council of 1962–65 did to advance the steps toward unity. They can assume that millions of Catholics and Protestants, especially since the Council, no longer regard their fellow travelers as enemies or subjects of suspicion, but as colleagues, teammates, partners. As such, they do not need to be imprisoned by the remembrance of clashes that have now become obsolete and irrelevant.

On the other hand, it is clear that in the face and heritage of some agreements noted in this book, neither the Catholic nor the Protestant participant believes that dialogue has to be bland and that hoped-for agreements have to be crowd-pleasing efforts, wishy-washy and shallow. They simply and gratefully send a figurative card of thanks to Vatican II's participants as well as both the Catholic and Protestant biblical scholars and theologians who have cleared many obstacles and set up new signposts for the journey.

THE SECOND IMPETUS: AN AGREEMENT IN 1999

The other main signpost for which the attention in this book is much to be appreciated is the set of dialogues by authorized leaders in Catholicism and the Protestantism in the Wittenberg lineage, which in this case means Lutheran communions (in the Lutheran World Federation). After decades of dialogue, they produced in 1999 a "Joint Declaration" on the enduring and central issue, which is code-named "the Doctrine of Justification." While there is assumed agreement on the document by formal Catholic leadership, there has been protesting by some among Lutheran theologians. My calling on these pages is simply to write this foreword and not to try to enter the debates that ensued after the dialogues were publicized. The assignment is to move the dialogue forward by indicating the importance of what has been achieved so far and then to join the company of those millions of Christians who hope for more creative steps and results in a future informed, for some of them, not only by books *like* this one, but by *this* book!

When the document of 1999 first met criticism, many theologians took up a new challenge and reframed the dialogue, also accepting the great gifts they had received. It was hard for the critics who raised theological points that meant "unfinished business" to carry things back to the "bad old days" of debate apart from dialogue, of contest instead of consensus. Enduring conflicts called to mind a story told by Winston Churchill. It featured the response of a mother whose little boy had just been rescued from drowning. She accosted the man who had risked his life to save "Johnny" and who had thereupon presented the boy back to his mother. She barked a question, "Where's Johnny's cap?" The years ahead will find Catholics and Lutherans doing more than finding and parading Johnny's cap; as this book shows, the years before and after 1999 have been times of significant achievement and encouragement for more dialogue and searching for agreements.

Chapters on the Scripture, the sacraments, church, and ministry spell out many of the issues still to be faced. The two partners in the dialogue formally accept baptism across the lines of the communions. But, as Professor Wood's chapter demonstrates, that formal agreement does not mean that there are no plaguing differences in the implications of baptism. In the case of the Eucharist or holy communion, the work still to be done is even more complicated. In most cases, members of the Body of Christ in Catholicism do not affirm the right of Protestants to share the table—and, to some extent, vice versa. Having the issues so clearly outlined here will be an asset in continuing conversation.

Similarly, church and ministry signal areas in which there have been great gains in mutual understanding. But Catholics do not accept the ministerial "orders" of any Protestants; most Protestants are uneasy with many concepts of priestly ordination and practices. Appointed committees and task forces of experts to advance the dialogue are crucial for effecting change toward greater expressions of unity, but how the mass of believers are instructed, what they confess, and how they practice the faith offer both problems and hopes for those on the journey. They will welcome the directions indicated in this book and will be helped in finding more of the way with partners from other communions at their side. They know that they are not free to abandon the search for the unity Christ has promised, and they can face the meanings of 1517, 1999, and other moments with fresh knowledge and inspiration.

Martin E. Marty
The Fairfax M. Cone Distinguished
Service Professor *Emeritus*
The University of Chicago

Preface

The year 2017 marks the 500th anniversary of the Reformation, a watershed event in the lives of Western Christians. For Lutherans, the anniversary evokes their determination to proclaim the gospel with purity and their efforts to live a reformed ecclesial life even if this eventually led to a break with the Roman Church of Luther's time. Viewed in this light, 2017 is a celebration of the gospel message of God's free gift of justification in Christ and its reception in faith. Catholics, perhaps, experience the commemoration of 2017 more painfully as a break in communion, as a schism in the church.

This bifurcated account of differing perspectives on the anniversary of the Reformation fails to account, however, for the past fifty years of patient, intense, and collegial dialogue between Lutherans and Catholics and the deep friendships forged between them in the process. The commemoration of the Reformation can occur for the first time within an ecumenical context that reflects the progress toward reconciled unity that has been achieved through these many years of dialogue.

The project began with Christopher Bellitto's proposal from Paulist Press for a book that would explain to Catholics and Lutherans the history of our shared spiritual journey, starting with Luther, then explaining the path to the Joint Declaration of 1999 and what it means, the *status quaestionis* of the various topics of dialogue, and future possibilities for a reconciled unity. It was most fitting that the book be coauthored by a Lutheran and a Catholic so that the story would be told jointly, the two coauthors modeling the dialogue they recounted.

Timothy J. Wengert, historian of the Reformation period, is the primary author of chapters 1 and 3 and coauthor of chapter 7. Susan K. Wood is the primary author of chapters 2, 4, 5, and 6, and coauthor of chapter 7. Both authors exchanged chapters, making corrections and substantial additions where helpful, and both signed off on the entire text. Christopher Bellitto, Paulist Press editor, was an engaged conversation partner throughout the process.

Timothy J. Wengert is the emeritus Ministerium of Pennsylvania professor of Reformation History and the Lutheran Confessions at The Lutheran Theological Seminary at Philadelphia. Wengert, an ordained pastor of the Evangelical Lutheran Church in America, has served his church in various capacities, including as a member of the ELCA–United Methodist dialogue team and as a member of the Task Force for ELCA Studies of Sexuality. He also served on a Lutheran World Federation team in conversation with the Mennonite World Churches. He now serves on the North American Lutheran/Roman Catholic dialogue and on an international team of scholars producing an ecumenical commentary on the *Ninty-five Theses* of Martin Luther.

In addition to his published dissertation on Philip Melanchthon's interpretation of John's Gospel, Professor Wengert is coeditor (with Robert Kolb of Concordia Seminary, St. Louis) of the English edition of *The Book of Concord*. His translation of Luther's Small Catechism is widely used throughout the Evangelical Lutheran Church in America. With Gordon Lathrop, he wrote a book on Lutheran ecclesiology, *Christian Assembly: The Marks of the Church in a Pluralistic Age* (Fortress, 2003). In 2006, he published a practical commentary on the Formula of Concord, *A Formula for Parish Practice: Using the Formula of Concord in Congregations* (Eerdmans). In 1997 and 1998, he published three books on Philip Melanchthon. One, *Human Freedom, Christian Righteousness* (Oxford University Press), investigates Melanchthon's relation to Erasmus. In 2007, he edited *Centripetal Worship: The Evangelical Heart of Lutheran Worship* (Augsburg Fortress); in 2008, he published *Priesthood, Pastors, Bishops* (Fortress); and in 2009, he published a book on Luther's catechisms. In 2012, Mohr Siebeck of Tübingen published his study of the Osiandrian controversy of the 1550s, *Defending Faith*, and in 2013, Baker Books published *Reading the Bible with Martin Luther*. In February 2000, the city of Bretten,

Germany (Melanchthon's birthplace), honored him as the first American recipient of the Melanchthon Prize. In addition to producing two volumes of essays for the *Lutheran Quarterly* book series, *Harvesting Martin Luther's Reflections on Theology, Ethics and the Church* and *The Pastoral Luther: Essays on Martin Luther's Practical Theology* (Eerdmans, 2004 and 2009), he is general editor of a Fortress Press project of six volumes of "The Annotated Luther" and the general editor of Baker Academic's *Dictionary of Luther and the Lutheran Traditions*.

Susan K. Wood is professor of theology at Marquette University in Milwaukee, Wisconsin. Very active in ecumenical work, she serves on the US Lutheran-Roman Catholic Dialogue (1994–present), the North American Roman Catholic-Orthodox Theological Consultation (2005–present), the conversation between the Roman Catholic Church and the Baptist World Alliance (2006–10), and the International Lutheran-Catholic Dialogue (2008–present). She has also participated in consultations on baptism, theological anthropology, and the nature and purpose of ecumenical dialogue sponsored by Faith and Order of the World Council of Churches and the Joint Working Group.

Wood is an associate editor of *Pro Ecclesia* and serves on the editorial advisory board of the journal *Ecclesiology*. Most of her writing explores the connections between ecclesiology and sacramental theology as well as reflecting her continuing interest in the theological movement of the *nouvelle théologie* and the theology of Henri de Lubac. In addition to numerous articles, she has published *One Baptism: Ecumenical Dimensions of the Doctrine of Baptism* (Liturgical Press, 2009), *Spiritual Exegesis and the Church in the Theology of Henri de Lubac* (Eerdmans, 1998), and *Sacramental Orders* (Liturgical Press, 2000), translated into Spanish (Barcelona, 2008) and is the recipient of the second place book award in the category of liturgy from the Catholic Press Association, May 25, 2001. She is the editor of *Ordering the Baptismal Priesthood* (Liturgical Press, 2003) and coeditor, with Alberto Garcia, of *Critical Issues in Ecclesiology: Essays in Honor of Carl. E. Braaten* (Eerdmans, 2011). Wood served as President of the Catholic Theological Society of America (2014–15).

We express to Paulist Press and especially Christopher Bellitto, editor for the project, our sincere gratitude for the invitation to tell this story of a shared spiritual journey between Lutherans and Catholics. Participation in the ecumenical movement is one of the great graces in our lives. We are mindful of the ecumenical giants from both traditions who have gone before us and on whose shoulders we stand as we reap the results of fifty years of dialogue statements. We pray that this work for church unity will bear abundant fruit in the Spirit. In addition, gratitude goes to Marquette University for the year sabbatical given to Susan Wood, which enabled her to devote substantial time to its completion.

The collaboration reflected in this volume also forms an invitation to ecumenically minded Christians everywhere to listen once again to their brothers and sisters in Christ as together we bear witness to the savior of the world.

Susan K. Wood
Timothy J. Wengert
Feast Day of the Apostles Philip and James, 2015

Part I

THE
ECUMENICAL
JOURNEY

Chapter One

Martin Luther, the Reformation, and Ecumenical Conversation

In his biography of Martin Luther, Heiko Oberman calls what we label simply the Reformation "the unexpected Reformation" and contrasts it to the many pressures for reform swirling around late-medieval central Europe in the early years of the sixteenth century.[1] For a variety of reasons, Oberman argues, people *were* expecting reform of: (1) the political system of the Holy Roman Empire of the German Nation, (2) the way the late-medieval church was financed and run (in line with the conciliar movement of the fifteenth century and its call for reform of the church in head and members [i.e., curia and clergy]), and (3) learning (among other things, a reflection of shifts in the intellectual milieu as a result of the continuing Renaissance with its humanist support for good letters and ancient sources). But no one, least of all Martin Luther, set out to start what we now know as the Reformation.

THE *NINETY-FIVE THESES*

One well-known, but often misunderstood, event may help explain the rather ambiguous beginnings of this unexpected Reformation. On October 31, 1517, Martin Luther wrote a letter to Albrecht, archbishop of Mainz, outlining his deep distress at the

3

preaching of the "Peter's Indulgence," a plenary indulgence given in exchange for support for the rebuilding of St. Peter's Basilica in Rome—the architectural results of which are still on breathtaking display in Vatican City today.[2] With that letter, he enclosed a copy of the *Ninety-five Theses*, in order to demonstrate just how confusing the theological underpinnings for such indulgences and their preachers' claims were.[3] Scholars debate whether at Evening Prayer that same day Luther affixed these theses to the door of the Castle Church in Wittenberg.[4] Unquestionably, however, given that Luther's original letter to Albrecht still exists, Luther "posted" these theses in the mail, so to speak, to the religious primate of the Holy Roman Empire. Moreover, in that letter, Luther reiterated the objective of the *Theses* themselves: to protect common folk from bad preaching and teaching.

Yet Luther's intention has often been obscured by subsequent historiography from the extremes of the ecumenical divide in his day and ours. One side viewed Luther's action as revolutionary and subversive, a calculated attempt to undermine the authority of church and papacy. Another side depicted Luther as breaking the shackles of the church of the Dark Ages and bursting into the splendid new age of individual freedom and Scriptural authority. Whether Luther is portrayed as traitor or hero, neither extreme captures the unexpected nature of the events in Wittenberg and Rome from 1517 and beyond.

On the one hand, by taking Luther at his word concerning his motives for writing the *Ninety-five Theses*, one discovers that especially his pointed criticisms of the indulgence preachers and their extreme claims found a receptive audience—even among some of his later opponents. Thus, Johannes Eck, who debated Luther in Leipzig in 1519 and opposed Luther throughout his career, welcomed Luther's sharp criticism of the indulgence preachers, though not his understanding of penance.[5] The bishop of Merseburg seems to have suggested that the *Ninety-five Theses* should be posted in his diocese.[6] Luther's immediate ordinary, the bishop of Brandenburg, simply warned Luther about the radicalism of the *Theses* without banning them, and the following year, he even permitted Luther's publication of their defense.[7]

On the other hand, given that Luther's pointed remarks curtailed papal authority regarding indulgences, it becomes clear both that this document contained propositions seldom heard in contemporary academic debates on the subject and that defenders of papal authority would doubtless see the *Ninety-five Theses* as challenging the church's God-given order. Thus, Archbishop Albrecht, fearing that Luther was teaching "new doctrine" (a sure sign of heresy), immediately submitted the *Theses* to his theological faculty at the University of Mainz and to the pope in Rome. For those convinced that the church's practice was as trustworthy as its doctrine, Luther's questioning indulgence sales and limiting papal authority were tantamount to heterodoxy, a position reflected in one of the earliest responses to the *Ninety-five Theses*, penned by the papal court's theologian, Sylvester Prierias.[8]

Subsequent history places another formidable obstacle in the way of understanding the unexpected nature of the Reformation. One needs remarkable historical imagination to recover a Christian world in the Latin West *before* the Council of Trent (1545–63) or the Vatican I Council (1869–70), where issues about the doctrine of justification and papal authority were clarified, and *before* the presentation of the Augsburg Confession (1530), the publication of *The Book of Concord* (1580), and the subsequent twists and turns in the development of Lutheran Churches and their theology. On the one hand, certain theological and practical trajectories, already present in late-medieval Christianity, provided the impetus for subsequent events during the Reformation and beyond. On the other hand, none of the participants knew what those trajectories were or where they were headed. Thus, a proper, balanced telling of the story of these early years demands a certain fair-mindedness to all sides in the dispute and a careful attempt *not* to rush to judgment.[9]

FROM DISPUTANT TO HERETIC AND OUTLAW: MARTIN LUTHER FROM 1517 TO 1521

After Luther distributed the *Ninety-five Theses* to friends in Nuremberg, Erfurt, and elsewhere, they appeared in print in Nuremberg, Leipzig, and Basel.[10] In addition to the condemnation by the Mainz faculty in December 1517, Johannes Tetzel, one of the Peter Indulgence's chief promulgators, and Conrad Wimpina, professor at the University of Frankfurt/Oder, published a series of theses against the *Ninety-five Theses*—a typical reaction in late-medieval academia.[11] Luther was by this time busy with his defense of the *Theses* and responded to some of his opponents' objections in a document published later in 1518, the *Explanations of the Ninety-five Theses*.[12]

Not only had Luther's friends in Nuremberg published the *Theses* in Latin, they also produced a German translation.[13] In lieu of publishing that version, Luther produced a twenty-point summary in German, titled *Sermon on Indulgences and Grace*, which appeared in March or April 1518.[14] It was this document, rather than the *Ninety-five Theses*, that turned Luther into a best-selling author. Printed twenty-four times between 1518 and 1520, it brought the gist of Luther's argument about indulgences to the common people. By contrast, when Tetzel published his German refutation of the *Sermon*, no one reprinted it.[15] Clearly, Luther had touched a nerve among the German-speaking public. This sermon, unlike the *Ninety-five Theses*, contained no comments about the papacy directly, a further indication of Luther's intention to restrain the preaching and sale of indulgences that, he argued, rested on shaky theological foundations and prevented Christians from performing true good works, especially care for the poor.[16]

Meanwhile, a chorus of opponents took offense not just to Luther's challenge to the prevailing attitude toward indulgences but also to his surprising comments restricting papal authority vis-à-vis indulgences. While at the end of the *Ninety-five Theses* Luther posed questions and objections as if formulated by a sharp layperson, his critical readers realized that arguments throughout the *Theses* limited papal authority in granting indulgences to the lifting of ecclesiastical penalties in this life, and not of punishment for sin in the life to come (in purgatory). His opponents pointed out that Luther did not have the authority to make such arguments, despite the fact that many of the theses reflected the ongoing debate over the nature of indulgences. Moreover, they argued, presuming to teach the church was itself an indication of heresy.

Within this early phase of the dispute, Luther's audience with Cardinal Cajetan in October 1518 was crucial.[17] Here Luther appeared before the papal legate. Despite having instructions from Pope Leo X to cart Luther off to Rome for trial, as a courtesy to Luther's prince, the Saxon elector Frederick the Wise, Cajetan engaged Luther in formal, if somewhat truncated, conversation. On the one hand, Cajetan—steeped in an Augustinian piety that insisted the penitent must never presume (out of pride) that the absolution in the sacrament of penance would certainly be applied to him or her—objected to Luther's claim in his *Explanations to the Ninety-five Theses* that the one confessing ought to believe firmly that their sins were in fact forgiven.[18] Here Cajetan was questioning a central aspect of Luther's theology, namely, that one could trust with certainty in God's divine promise of forgiveness and life and thereby be justified by faith in God's promise alone. Luther's response revealed the pastoral side of the debate, in that Luther, whose *Theses* had in part been written to instruct and protect the faithful, now begged Cajetan to have pity on his bound conscience and not "cast his soul into hell" by forcing him to give up on the sure promises of God.[19]

On the other hand, Cajetan, assuming that Luther was not familiar with some of the later additions to canon law (when, in fact, he was), attacked thesis 58 of the *Ninety-five Theses* by referring to a decree of Clement VI from 1343, stating that the treasury out of which indulgences derived their worth was indeed the merits of Christ and the saints. In thesis 58, Luther had stated that this could not be the case since already without papal authority these merits "work grace for the inner person and cross, death and hell for the outer." By contradicting a papal decree, Luther opened himself up to the charge of novelty and thus the suspicion of heresy. When Cajetan dismissed Luther's defense (that Clement's decree contradicted the teaching of the church and thus should be rescinded), Luther responded after the hearing by formally appealing to a pope "better informed." When Pope Leo X immediately reaffirmed earlier positions on indulgences, Luther then appealed to a general council, an appeal that many of his opponents, who supported a curialist position on papal authority, claimed was *ipso facto* proof of heresy.[20] It should be noted that the conversation with Luther provoked Cajetan into researching and writing on indulgences, producing a work that stands yet as one of the most complete treatments of the doctrine and the practice, both not well defined formally in the early sixteenth century.[21]

One of Luther's most formidable adversaries was Johannes Eck, theologian at the University of Ingolstadt. When Luther got hold of Eck's refutation of the *Ninety-five Theses*, called the *Obelisks*—handwritten copies of which were circulating among Eck's friends—he published it with his response, titled *Asterisks*. Eck subsequently challenged first Luther's colleague, Andreas Bodenstein aus Karlstadt, and then Luther himself to a debate, which after complicated negotiations, finally was held at the University of Leipzig in the summer of 1519. It is sometimes thought that the highlight of these debates came when Eck forced Luther to admit that councils (and not just popes) could err. However, more recent research has shown that this somewhat misconstrues what actually happened. Luther only admitted that the Council of Constance, in condemning certain teachings of Jan Hus (the Czech reformer burned at the stake as a result of the council's decision), had contradicted Catholic teaching on the nature of the church. Here Luther thought he was on particularly solid ground, since the council's teaching did indeed seem to contradict earlier conciliar, to say nothing of patristic, understanding of the church.[22]

After the encounter in Leipzig, Eck made his way to Rome and helped draft a bull of excommunication (*Exsurge Domine*), published in June 1520, which he and the papal legate, Jerome Aleander, then attempted to promulgate throughout the Holy Roman Empire. At the same time, Luther continued to develop and express quite different views of church and papal authority as he sought to work out more clearly the consequences of justification by faith alone for doctrine and life. In particular, that year he published four tracts: *On Good Works*, an exposition of the Ten Commandments; *Address to Christian Nobility*, a plea to the imperial estates to reform the church now that Pope Leo X seemed to have refused; *The Babylonian Captivity of the Church*, an in-depth analysis of the seven sacraments of the church in which Luther reduced the number to two (baptism and the Lord's Supper) while still retaining the practices of private confession (as daily return to the promises of baptism), ordination (for proclaiming the gospel), and marriage;[23] and *The Freedom of a Christian*, his most exhaustive description of justification by faith alone and its relation to preaching law and gospel and doing good works. To this final work, Luther added a preface to Leo X, demonstrating at the same time obedience to ecclesial authority (as Luther understood it) and freedom in Christ.[24]

Luther's "official" excommunication, however, did not stop the political negotiations, so it was agreed that Luther would appear before the imperial diet (parliament) meeting in the imperial city of Worms in the spring of 1521. When simply asked to recant all of his writings, Luther first delayed and then separated out those to which his opponents had never objected. In the end, he refused to contradict his conscience and his understanding of Scripture, claiming that his opponents had not proved him wrong. Most scholars now believe that Luther's famous line, "Here I stand; I can do no other. God help me!" which was already found in the first published account of the proceedings at Worms, was most likely his confession of faith added to the written document and did not express exactly what he actually said. We can be fairly certain, however, that he did say the following in concluding his address to the diet:

> Unless I am convinced by the testimony of the Scriptures or by clear reason (for I do not trust either in the pope or in councils alone, since it is well known that they have often erred and contradicted themselves),[25] I am bound by the Scriptures I have quoted and my conscience is captive to the Word of God. I cannot and I will not retract anything, since it is neither safe nor right to go against conscience.[26]

As Scott Hendrix has shown in his book on Luther and the papacy, Luther never advocated for a position often labeled as *sola Scriptura* (Scripture alone).[27] Even here, he made clear that he gave pope and council some authority but, because of apparent contradictions, could not trust them *alone*. Instead, like other humanists of his day whose cry was *ad fontes* (to the [earliest] sources), Luther insisted on returning to the oldest and most reliable sources for theology. For him, the Scripture was the sole ultimate authority, but he also took very seriously the secondary, hermeneutical authority of ecumenical creeds, councils, and church fathers. Moreover, he also always allowed an important place for reason, that is, logical arguments. As he had in Augsburg with Cajetan and also in Worms, Luther insisted that his conscience must be shown the truth from Scripture before he could possibly change his mind—already an important aspect in medieval assertions of truth. This assertive invitation to serious dialogue also marked much of the debate in the ensuing years and still constitutes an indispensable first step in all useful ecumenical dialogue.

FROM WORMS, 1521, TO AUGSBURG, 1530

At Worms, despite misgivings among some princes, no one objected publicly to the diet's decision to declare Luther an outlaw of the empire. Despite this, Emperor Charles V honored his promise of safe passage, and Luther safely left Worms. On the journey back to Wittenberg, Elector Frederick staged a kidnapping in order to place Luther in protective custody at the Elector's Wartburg Castle in Thuringia. From the relative safety in "the region of the birds," Luther continued to publish—not only answering opponents (e.g., *Against Latomus*)[28]—but also providing pastoral resources (a commentary on appointed Sunday texts for Advent and Christmas [his *Christmas Postil*] and a translation of the New Testament) and addressing other theological questions, including the binding nature of monastic vows.[29]

At the same time, pressure for changes in the liturgy and other church practices was building in Wittenberg. A reform party at the University, which included Luther's closest colleagues (Nicholas von Amsdorf, Philip Melanchthon, Justus Jonas, and Karlstadt), was pressing for an elimination of the sacrificial language in the canon of the Mass, for communion in both kinds (bread and wine), and for an end to certain fast days and to celibacy for priests. Around the New Year 1522, Karlstadt celebrated the Mass at St. Mary's (the city church) in German, distributing both kinds and refusing to wear vestments. He also married. At the same time, mendicant friars were vilified, Latin Masses interrupted, and some statues and paintings were stripped from Wittenberg's churches and destroyed. Despite opposition from the conservative canons of the All Saints' Foundation, the reform party successfully lobbied Wittenberg's city council to approve many of these changes.

After the Elector rejected such alterations and the congregants in Wittenberg begged Luther for his opinion, Luther took it upon himself to leave the Wartburg without the prince's permission or protection, and on Invocavit Sunday 1522 (the first Sunday in Lent), he appeared back in his pulpit at St. Mary's, where he preached eight days in a row (March 9–16) against the changes. Although he admitted that many of the changes reflected suggestions from his own writings and were consonant with his understanding of justification by faith alone, still he insisted that by legislating such things and, for example, by forcing people to receive communion in both kinds and placing the bread in their hands, the reform party had neglected love and patience in order to defend right doctrine.[30]

This "Wittenberg Unrest" has sometimes been interpreted as evidence for Luther's conservatism and Karlstadt's eventual abandonment of the university as indication of a power struggle, which Luther (allegedly as a toady of the prince) handily won. In fact, it marks a crucial aspect of Luther's understanding of reform, which continues to shape Lutheran witness to the gospel up to the present. For Luther, pastoral authority had always to bend to the weak, so that they could hear and believe the gospel not under coercion but freely. His concern for bad preaching in the *Ninety-five Theses*, his appeal to Cajetan and Pope Leo X to have regard for his own conscience, his stand at Worms, and now his behavior in 1522 reflected this basic premise, which Luther had already discussed at some length in the 1520 Latin version of *Freedom of a Christian*.[31] Wittenberg's reform party, which with the exception of Karlstadt, all came around to Luther's point of view, had assumed that church reform was centrally a matter of legislating proper practice—a stance that echoed late-medieval impulses for reform and would later find far more fertile ground among Reformed theologians and churches. Luther, on the contrary, insisted (consistent with his own theological method) that the Word of God, preached and celebrated in the sacraments, had to do the reforming *before* changes in practice could be legislated. Only when a practice directly endangered the hearing of the gospel did Luther think change unavoidable. Every practice—old or new—had to be measured by the message of God's unconditional forgiveness, life and salvation in Christ. This attitude is a key feature of the unexpected Reformation.

Thus, Lutherans were never iconoclasts, as were members of Reformed Churches related to Ulrich Zwingli in Zürich, John Calvin in Geneva, or John Knox in Scotland. As a result, to this day, many Lutheran Churches in Europe contain a rich variety of late-medieval statues, murals, and paintings, and in the subsequent centuries, Lutherans added their own decorations to them.[32] Things like fasting, making the sign of the cross, and praying at certain times of the day continued to shape Lutheran worship in many territorial churches. While eliminating prayers to the saints and sacrificial language from the canon of the Mass in his Latin and German revisions of the liturgy from 1523 and 1526, respectively, Luther nevertheless kept the basic structure of the Western rite—in the German version, simply replacing certain traditional Latin chants (the *Gloria in excelsis*, the Nicene Creed, the *Sanctus*, and the *Agnus Dei*) with German-language hymns.[33] Indeed, in 1536, as reformers in Strasbourg and Augsburg reached agreement with Wittenberg on the matter of Christ's presence with the bread and wine in the Supper, an eyewitness from Augsburg wrote home in shock at how traditionally the Wittenbergers celebrated the Lord's Supper, complete with Mass bells and the elevation.[34]

This conservational approach to teaching and preaching shaped Wittenberg's way of doing theology. While theological debates continued—in 1525 alone, there were disputes over free will with Erasmus; over the presence of Christ in the Lord's Supper with the Swiss reformers, Ulrich Zwingli, and Johann Oecolampadius; and (in 1528) against Anabaptists over the baptism of infants—questions of church authority also loomed. With the death of Elector Frederick in 1525 and the accession of his brother John the Steadfast, a staunch supporter of Luther, changes were made to the university curriculum and to liturgical practices, but the problem of the oversight of congregations in Saxony and elsewhere remained an open question.

Electoral Saxony was now protecting an open heretic of the church and outlaw of the empire, so its relations with the ordinary bishops had almost completely broken down. In the 1520s, no bishop in good stead with Rome could give the Saxons any official sanction for ecclesiastical changes. (This contrasted, for example, with the Landgraviate of Hesse, where Landgrave Philip, an outspoken supporter of the Reformation, received permission from the archbishop of Mainz to conduct his own official visitation of the congregations and monasteries in his realm.)[35] Given the chaos following the Peasants' War of 1525 (which had come as far north as Thuringia) and the uncertainties brought about by the Reformation itself, there was great confusion concerning the staffing and finances of parishes, the oversight of monasteries, and a host of other practical matters—to say nothing of Luther's chief concern: proper preaching and teaching. As a result, early in 1527, the Elector decreed his own visitation of churches, to be carried out by a team consisting of two representatives of the court, a professor of law from the university (Jerome Schurff) and a teacher of theology (Philip Melanchthon, elected by the theology faculty at Luther's insistence).

From his experience as a visitor in the summer of 1527, Philip Melanchthon wrote theological instructions in Latin for Saxony's pastors and preachers, which Luther, Johannes Bugenhagen (head pastor at Wittenberg's city church, St. Mary's, and later, general superintendent), and Melanchthon painstakingly translated into German and published in early 1528 under the title *Instructions of the Visitors for the Parish Pastors of Germany* and under the coats of arms of Luther and Melanchthon.[36] In the preface, Luther traced the practice of visitation back to Elijah in the Old Testament and Paul in the New, yearned for the days when bishops performed this duty properly, and compared Elector John's action in assembling visitors at the Saxon Church's request with Constantine's calling of the Council of Nicea in AD 325.

At nearly the same time and for many of the same causes that marked the origin of the 1528 *Instructions*, Martin Luther also set out to write simple explanations of the basic parts of the Christian faith, using the traditional "catechism" (Ten Commandments, Apostles' Creed, and Lord's Prayer) as a model, and adding sections on sacraments (baptism, the Lord's Supper and, later, confession, which in other venues, the reformers preferred to call the Sacrament of Absolution, derived directly from baptism). The Small Catechism contained simple explanations suitable for use in household and school. The Large Catechism was meant especially for instruction of simple German pastors.[37]

THE AUGSBURG CONFESSION, 1530

This very public act of officially visiting churches helped to propel the unexpected Reformation into a confrontation with authorities in church and empire. While Elector John argued that he was following the guidelines of the first diet of Speyer in 1526 (at which, in the absence of Emperor Charles V, each sovereign territory and city promised to behave in such a way as could be justified before God and emperor), the second diet of Speyer in 1529 rescinded the earlier diet's actions and prepared the way for the Diet of Augsburg in 1530. There, Emperor Charles, newly victorious over the French and the Pope and now officially crowned emperor by the latter, came prepared to solve the religious strife in the empire and to muster a united effort against the invading Turkish Sultan, who the previous year had besieged Vienna before having been forced to withdraw.

In preparation for that diet, the emperor had instructed the various imperial estates to prepare statements of faith. Three such statements exist. One was the private confession of Ulrich Zwingli, which was not considered at the diet. A second, the *Confessio Tetrapolitana*, was presented by four imperial cities (Lindau, Memmingen, Constance, and Strasbourg) and written by two Strasbourg reformers, Martin Bucer and Wolfgang Capito.[38] The third was the Augsburg Confession (CA). Drafted in large part by Philip Melanchthon and signed by representatives of two imperial cities (Nuremberg and Reutlingen) and princes from five territories (Saxony, Brandenburg-Ansbach, Braunschweig-Lüneburg, Anhalt, and Hesse), this document summarized the heart of Wittenberg's faith (CA I–XXI) and defended the ensuing changes in religious practice (CA XXII–XXVIII). It became *the* basic confession of faith among Lutherans ever since.

The document itself fulfilled several different goals of the Evangelical party gathered in Augsburg.[39] In the first place, in line with Charles V's demand for an accounting of theology and practice, the Augsburg Confession represented just such a summary of the faith, especially in matters over which the parties at Augsburg and within the empire disagreed. Second, that very summary strove to present the Evangelical position as catholic, consonant with the teaching of the whole church. Third, the document was also a defense of civil disobedience, since changes in ecclesiastical practice in Saxony and elsewhere (especially the marriage of priests, the general amnesty for monks breaking their vows, the ending of private masses and, above all, the Saxon Visitation) also entailed breaking imperial law.[40]

Alongside these differing goals, the confession in Augsburg occurred on several different levels.[41] First and foremost, the Augsburg Confession was an event that took place on June 25, 1530, when the German version was read aloud at the diet and the princes and cities that signed the confession staked lives and lands on the act of confessing their faith.[42] Thus, preaching at Elector John's funeral in 1532, Luther could even say that John had already died in Augsburg and that his physical death was a mere *Kindersterben* (child's [or childish] death).[43] Beyond that, especially in light of the opponents' response, the Augsburg Confession stood as a benchmark for such confessing and thus very quickly became a standard to which others also subscribed, so that in 1537, for example, some of the most well-known Evangelical theologians subscribed to it.[44] Already in 1533, the statutes for the University of Wittenberg singled out the Augsburg Confession as the basis for subscription by candidates for the doctorate in theology. Third, the Augsburg Confession finally became a fixed norm or doctrinal standard. Later confessions of faith by Evangelicals (such as the Saxon Confession of 1551 or the Formula of Concord published in 1580) referred back to the Augsburg Confession as such a standard—in the words of the Formula of Concord, "our creed [*symbolon*] for this age."[45] As such, the Augsburg Confession became imbedded in larger theological systems that were being produced at this time to explain and defend Evangelical theology.

Several documents provided sources for the language and theology of the Augsburg Confession: Martin Luther's personal confession of faith from 1528 contained in his attack on Ulrich Zwingli's denial of Christ's presence in the Lord's Supper (*Confession Concerning Christ's Supper*); the Schwabach and Marburg confessions of faith from 1529; the *Instructions of the Visitors* mentioned above; and a series of memoranda drawn up by the Evangelical theologians meeting in early 1530 at the Torgau Castle in Saxony.[46] This last set of documents formed the basis for the defense of changes in practice (CA XXII–XXVIII). The others provided material for the theological articles. Because Luther, as an outlaw of the empire, could not appear in Augsburg and was holed up instead in the Feste Coburg, the elector's castle nearest Augsburg, Melanchthon took over the bulk of the work of drafting. Several articles, especially one on the relation between faith and works (CA XX), was written *de novo* in Augsburg as a response to a particularly pugnacious tract penned by Johannes Eck and rolling off Augsburg's presses at the very time the Evangelical party arrived. These *404 Articles* contained a pastiche of statements gleaned from the writings of Luther and others that Eck declared were completely heretical. His intent was to force the imperial diet into simply condemning the Evangelicals as heretics. At various points in the first twenty-one articles of the CA, the drafters took into account Eck's challenge, changing language from the previous confessions to answer his objections and prove the catholicity of the Evangelicals' faith.

CA I–XXI never mentioned the papacy, purgatory, or indulgences, even though much of the original case against Luther had highlighted these issues. Instead, it attempted to present a catholic (i.e., universal) confession of the Christian faith—albeit from a strongly Evangelical viewpoint—to which all Christians could not but agree. Thus, at the transition between articles I–XXI and XXII–XXVIII, Melanchthon described both how the confessors were conscience-bound to confess these articles and how these same articles corresponded with the Christian faith. The German version reads, "This is nearly a complete summary of what is preached and taught in our [the signers'] churches for proper Christian instruction and the comfort of consciences....For we certainly wish neither to expose our souls and consciences to grave danger before God by misusing the divine name or Word."[47] In both the German and Latin versions, the catholicity of the confession was stressed (here quoting the Latin): "As can be seen, there is nothing here that departs from the Scriptures or the catholic church, or from the Roman church, insofar as we can tell from its writers."[48]

CA I and III (on God and Christ) referred to the Nicene and Apostles' Creeds and rejected ancient trinitarian and christological heresies.[49] CA II and IV–VI dealt with hotly disputed topics between the Evangelicals and their opponents: original sin, justification by faith through the Word, and good works. Original sin (CA II) was defined not merely in terms of concupiscence but as a lack of fear of God and faith in God, thus setting up the article of justification by faith (CA IV), namely, that "we cannot obtain forgiveness of sin and righteousness before God through our merit, work, or satisfactions, but that we receive forgiveness of sin and become righteous before God out of grace for Christ's sake through faith."[50] CA V continued the article on justification by focusing on the "office of preaching," that is, the means of grace (Word and sacraments) that the Holy Spirit uses to create and strengthen justifying faith.[51] Finally, CA VI insisted that such faith "should yield good fruit and good works" but that a person must "not place trust in them as if thereby to earn grace before God."[52] This final article used for the first time that much-disputed phrase "through faith alone"—not as a direct statement by the Evangelicals but as a quote from an ancient source ascribed to Ambrose of Milan.[53]

Of course, there were other important differences between the two parties beyond but related to justification. Thus, CA VII–VIII discussed the nature of the church as the assembly of believers (visibly) marked by Word (the preaching of the [law and] gospel) and the proper distribution of the sacraments. Having described this "Word" in CA I–VI, the document then outlined the three sacraments (baptism, the Lord's Supper, and confession [CA IX–XII]) and their effects (CA XIII), the public office of ministry (CA XIV), and ecclesiastical rites (CA XV). Articles XVI–XIX and XXI dealt with other important issues. CA XVI made clear (over against certain Anabaptist but also monastic practices) the breadth and limits of Evangelical obedience to secular government and involvement in the world; CA XVII opposed millenarian views of Christ's return that had recently resurfaced; CA XVIII and XIX defined the Evangelical position on free will and the cause of sin in light of recent fights between Erasmus and Luther; CA XXI examined "the cult of the saints."

Because Johannes Eck's *404 Articles* had particularly accused the Evangelicals of forbidding good works, CA XX, by far the longest and most pointed of the doctrinal articles, repeated much of what was said in CA IV and VI (and CA XV), rejecting an exclusively religious definition of good works in favor of the Christian life lived out in various callings in the world. Not only did the CA for the first time take up as their own the language "faith alone" (now not quoting a patristic source),[54] but Melanchthon also went out of his way to define faith as not simply "knowledge, such as the ungodly have, but as trust that consoles and encourages terrified minds."[55]

On the basis of these twenty-one articles, the Augsburg Confession then turned its attention to specific disputed changes in practice: communion using both bread and wine (CA XXII), the marriage of priests (CA XXIII), rejection of the sacrifice of the Mass (CA XXIV), the abolition of compulsory private confession (CA XXV), the ending of certain fasting regulations (CA XXVI), and a critique of the binding nature of monastic vows and their relation to baptism (CA XXVII). CA XXVIII, which one important modern commentator has argued was the central article of the Confession,[56] dealt with the question of episcopal power and tried to distinguish between the secular power of the prince-bishops in the empire and their divinely authorized calling as pastors and ministers of the gospel and sacraments. This article, by stating that "bishops do not have the power to institute or establish something contrary to the gospel,"[57] echoed the early debates over the *Ninety-five Theses*.

We know from other sources that these final eight articles contained the gist of the negotiating position of the Saxon court and its theologians. If the bishops and the imperial diet would allow the Evangelical party communion in both kinds, married priests, and an end to private Masses (and the associated theology of sacrifice) and would not prohibit them from preaching and teaching according to the gospel (i.e., according to the "catholic" confession in CA I–XXI), then for their part, the Evangelicals would accept the oversight of the imperial bishops (in communion with Rome). We find this basic proposal reflected in at least one tract published by Luther at the time,[58] in the correspondence and negotiations undertaken by Philip Melanchthon,[59] and in certain documents of the Saxon court itself.[60] No wonder Melanchthon used these words to conclude CA I–XXI: "Since, then, there is nothing unfounded or deficient in the principal articles and since this our confession is godly and Christian, the bishops should in all fairness act more leniently even if there were a deficiency in regard to tradition—although we hope to offer solid grounds and reasons why some traditions and abuses have been changed among us."[61]

FROM AUGSBURG IN 1530 TO LUTHER'S DEATH IN 1546

Church historians have debated when the Evangelicals' "break with Rome" occurred. In one way, this is an anachronistic, even unfair question, since the Wittenberg reformers never saw themselves as breaking with the church. However, if understood more neutrally, then it could perhaps be argued that the *Ninety-five Theses* themselves contained the seeds for the break, although this is frankly more a matter of "twenty-twenty hindsight" than proper historical analysis. More helpful might be to see the break occurring with the 1520 papal bull declaring Luther a heretic or with the 1521 decision of the Diet of Worms to declare Luther an outlaw of the empire. But even those events did not result immediately in an irreparable break. More recently, some have tried to argue that the Augsburg Confession itself marked the birth of the Lutheran Church as it ceased formally to be an evangelical proposal to the church catholic and became a separate confession of faith. However, an equally if not more important event might be the Confutation of the Augsburg Confession offered by the Evangelicals' opponents in August 1530 and accepted by the emperor as legally binding before the diet's dissolution, giving the princes and cities six months to pledge their allegiance to it.[62]

Yet the events leading up to the reading of this document at the diet (it was not published until many years later) also indicate the stress that both sides placed on conversation and careful listening to one another's arguments. Charles V and his advisors rejected out-of-hand a first attempt at a refutation of the Augsburg Confession because it failed to distinguish between articles on which there was agreement and articles where the sides were truly divided. Sent back to the drawing board, the imperial theologians produced a far more nuanced document, which accepted many articles outright, specifically rejected only certain aspects of other articles and, at the same time, dismissed completely the changes defended in CA XXII–XXVIII. Despite negotiations throughout August 1530, the diet could broker no lasting compromise to avoid political and religious division within the empire.

In August 1530, Melanchthon also started working on a defense (labeling it with the Greek word *Apologia*) of the Augsburg Confession over against the *Confutatio*. When the emperor refused to allow its presentation, he continued to expand it, publishing the Latin version of the *Apology of the Augsburg Confession* in May 1531 along with an "official" (though somewhat expanded) Latin version of the Augsburg Confession. In September or October 1531, a second edition appeared that remained the official version (along with its German translation) until 1584 when the first (Latin) edition came to be included in the official Latin *Book of Concord*.[63]

In any case, the *Apology* was the first and most important interpretation and defense of the Augsburg Confession, a position confirmed by its inclusion in various Evangelical confessional standards leading up to and including *The Book of Concord* of 1580. It defended Evangelical understandings of original sin, justification by faith alone, and the relation between faith and good works. In addition, it insisted on Christ's real presence in the Lord's Supper while rejecting the notion that sacraments were effective by their mere performance (*ex opere operato*). On the question of the church, Melanchthon defended the Evangelical definition (that *church* is the assembly of believers of every time and place) and stressed that God provided the church with certain visible markings (*notae ecclesiae*) by which people could recognize it, namely, preaching of the Word and administration of the sacraments. The *Apology* also insisted on the necessity of oversight in the church, while specifically holding the bishops in communion with Rome responsible for the break in the church.

Besides the *Confutation* and the *Apology*, several important events from 1531 until Luther's death in 1546 shaped Wittenberg's theology. In 1535, four years after the deaths of Ulrich Zwingli and Johann Oecolampadius, their erstwhile supporter Martin Bucer worked out an agreement with Wittenberg's theologians over the presence of Christ in the Lord's Supper. This "Wittenberg Concord" (so named because it was signed there) insisted that Christ was present "with" the bread and wine, avoiding the prepositions *in* or *under* (where especially the latter smacked of the doctrine of transubstantiation to which Bucer objected strenuously). Although not accepted by all Reformed churches (especially Zurich), it provided the basis for an agreement that lasted until the 1550s, when John Calvin distanced himself from the Concord by entering into an agreement with Zwingli's successor in Zurich, Heinrich Bullinger.[64]

At nearly the same time, Pope Paul III called for a church council to meet in Mantua in 1536. Although delay resulted in the council first meeting in 1545 and then in Trent, this invitation matched earlier calls by Evangelicals, first by Luther and then in the preface to the Augsburg Confession itself, for a free, general council of the church.[65] The pope's call weakened the electoral Saxon legal case and caused the Elector John Frederick to ask Luther for a response, which Luther understood as setting the agenda for the Smalcald theologians to use at the council. Given Luther's failing health (despite his living another ten years), the resulting Smalcald Articles, as published in 1538, became a kind of theological last will and testament for Luther and was signed by many Evangelical theologians meeting in the town of Smalcald in 1537.[66] While noting agreement between Rome and Wittenberg on the ancient trinitarian and christological doctrines, Luther focused in the second part on the work of Christ and justification, contrasting justification by faith alone to the sacrifice of the Mass and other Roman practices, as well as to the papacy itself. In the third part, by contrast, Luther insisted that articles on original sin, law and gospel, repentance, church, and the sacraments could be discussed among open-minded people.[67]

At nearly the same time, Philip Melanchthon wrote an addendum to the Augsburg Confession, *The Treatise on the Power and Primacy of the Pope*, which attacked papal claims to superiority among the bishops. This, too, was signed by a number of theologians. Published most often in conjunction with the Smalcald Articles, its origins quickly slipped into obscurity, so that by the time both documents were included in the 1580 *Book of Concord*, few realized that Melanchthon's Latin version was the original, a confusion first rectified in 1584 with the publication of a Latin version of *The Book of Concord*. The Smalcald Articles gained a higher level of authority among Lutherans after Luther's death, as disputes over justification and Christ's presence in the Lord's Supper flared up and Luther's defense of the real presence was appealed to over against language viewed as compromising the Evangelical position. From its inclusion in certain collections of confessional documents in the 1550s, it then became a part of *The Book of Concord*.

In the face of delays in convening a church council, a final attempt was made to solve the religious divisions in the Holy Roman Empire. In 1540, theologians from both parties were called first to Worms (where the question of original sin was debated) and then in 1541 to Regensburg, where a series of articles were discussed, including justification. On the one side was that chief antagonist of the Evangelicals, Johannes Eck, and on the other sat Philip Melanchthon. Excluded from direct negotiations, but playing an important role in discussions with the Roman Catholics, was Cardinal Gasparo Contarini.

In preparation for the colloquy, Melanchthon set about to rewrite the Augsburg Confession (most likely with the full agreement of the princes of the Smalcald League and perhaps even Luther). This edited version (later called the *Variata*) reflected more closely the language of the Wittenberg Concord on the Lord's Supper but also contained expanded explanations of justification by faith in line with Melanchthon's own developing theological language.[68] At this time, one could say that among Evangelicals, the Augsburg Confession functioned more like a "mission statement" than like a fixed, secondary authority. Melanchthon brought copies of this version with him to Worms and insisted that the debate center on it. However, after reaching a tentative agreement on original sin, the colloquy was moved to Regensburg where, instead of using the Augsburg Confession, the collocutors were presented a document secretly composed by members of both sides (including Martin Bucer of Strasbourg). Based upon this *Regensburger Book* but in large part due to the colloquy itself, a tentative agreement was reached on the doctrine of justification. Despite the ringing of church bells commanded by the emperor, who was in Regensburg for an imperial diet, the compromise language of a kind of "double justification" did not please either side. When Elector John Frederick asked Luther and Johannes Bugenhagen for their opinion, they expressed their dissatisfaction at the way the two positions had been sewn together into one statement.[69] They also insisted on making a distinction between what a Christian becomes or is (justified by faith alone) and what that one does (good works, the fruits of the justified faith).[70] Pope Paul III also rejected this compromise. In the twentieth century, as we shall see, some of the language from these conversations helped orient conversations around justification between Lutherans and Roman Catholics.

Far more difficult matters than justification arose in connection with discussions over the Lord's Supper. Melanchthon and especially Bucer objected to language that referred to transubstantiation. When the two sides agreed to speak of Christ's presence without using that language, Cardinal Contarini strongly objected, since Lateran IV council and the pope had approved the doctrine. Any deviation from that language, he argued, could only be understood as undermining the authority of council and pope. A related issue arose over the *Regensburger Book*'s definition of *church*. An early article seemed to agree with the language of the Augsburg Confession, but when a later article on the authority of bishops came up, it became clear that the earlier definition implied that bishops and churches had to be in communion with Rome.[71]

Despite the continuation of talks into the summer, the colloquy finally collapsed and the pressures toward a military solution continued to build on both sides, culminating in the Smalcald War of 1547. The war pitted Electoral Saxony and Hesse, above all, against the emperor and his allies, including the Evangelical Saxon duke, Maurice, who rightly saw the defeat of John Frederick as the vehicle for getting the electorship transferred to his side of the Wettin family.

TURNING LUTHERAN: 1546 TO 1580

Meanwhile, in February 1546, Martin Luther died in Eisleben, where he was born, while on a diplomatic mission to make peace among the feuding counts von Mansfeld. Given the popularity of Max Weber's theory about the "routinization of charisma" in religious and political social systems, one could probably without contradiction depict the years following Luther's death among Evangelicals in terms of their inevitable adjustments to this loss.[72] However, such speculation ignores several important facts. For one thing, theology in Wittenberg was carried out more through conversation and subscription than through fiat or coercion. By the 1530s, it was the university's entire theology faculty that, not unlike the University of Paris in an earlier era, issued official memoranda and offered judgments on difficult theological cases. Other Evangelical universities followed their lead. For another, the churches in Electoral Saxony, like churches in other Evangelical territories of the empire (especially Württemberg) and, in the ensuing years, like those in certain sovereign lands (e.g., Denmark and Sweden), had developed and refined church governance—not wholly unrelated to late-medieval structures—with general superintendents[73] overseeing superintendents in major cities, and with consistories comprised of various secular and ecclesiastical authorities overseeing regular visitations and the practical running of parishes.[74]

This is not to say that theological battles did not arise among the Evangelicals. By this time, various forms of Evangelical theology had spread to territories throughout the empire. Even with Philip of Hesse and Elector (now Duke) John Frederick under arrest with a sentence of death hanging over them and Spanish and imperial troops throughout the region, the Evangelical party continued to function. With John Frederick's cousin, Duke Maurice, named the new elector, the Evangelicals in Wittenberg were more or less assured of an Evangelical prince and went about reconstituting the university under the aegis of their new prince.

When the victorious emperor Charles V called for a diet to meet in Augsburg (from 1547–48), Elector Maurice thought the religious integrity of his expanded Evangelical territories was protected. However, when imperial theologians, aided by Luther's former student and advisor to the elector of Brandenburg, Johann Agricola, composed a solution to the religious divisions to be used until the reconvening of a general council (hence called the Augsburg Interim), the new elector and his theologians, including Philip Melanchthon, objected.[75] (Practically speaking, it allowed the Evangelicals little more than married priests and communion in both kinds.) In the fall of 1548, Melanchthon and other theologians from Wittenberg and Leipzig entered into negotiations with Julius Pflug, the newly designated Roman bishop of Naumburg-Zeitz, to work out a compromise that, over against the Augsburg Interim, insisted on a somewhat clearer exposition of Evangelical theology while allowing for the reintroduction of neutral practices (called *indifferentia* [undifferentiated matters] in Latin or, using the Greek equivalent, *adiaphora*). This compromise, nicknamed by its opponents the Leipzig Interim (because, in December 1548, it had been presented but not agreed to by the territorial Saxon estates gathered in that city), finally pleased no one, except perhaps Johann Agricola, who publicly claimed it vindicated his participation in writing the Augsburg Interim.

Other theologians,[76] most of whom lived in Magdeburg (a city that did not finally capitulate to Elector Maurice until 1550) and who thus had free access to Magdeburg's printing presses, objected to the reintroduction of such undifferentiated practices, not because they denied the existence of adiaphora but because, they argued, in a situation of persecution such as existed in the aftermath of the Smalcald War, such matters *ipso facto* demanded clear confession of faith so that adiaphora was no longer adiaphora. When Maurice of Saxony and other princes became aware of Emperor Charles V's intentions to subdue all imperial estates under his direct rule, there followed the successful Princes' Rebellion that led first to the Treaty of Passau in 1552 and finally to Peace of Augsburg of 1555, when certain rights to exercise religion were allowed to Evangelical princes, Imperial cities, and their subjects.[77] At Elector Maurice's death from battle wounds, his brother, Augustus, became elector.

Nevertheless, tensions that had flared up over the Interims among Evangelical theologians continued unabated.[78] Melanchthon and Wittenberg's leadership and authority were put in question, as fights arose over not only adiaphora but also the necessity of good works for salvation, the role of the law, the nature of original sin, and the limits of free will. In 1552, a conflict with Andreas Osiander, the former Nuremberg pastor who had fled after the Smalcald War to become professor of theology at the University of Königsberg in East Prussia, arose over the nature of justification by faith itself. Here, finally, was a topic on which both Melanchthon and his supporters (nicknamed Philippists) and the party labeled by Melanchthon and others "genuine Lutherans" (gnesio-Lutherans) could agree. Rejecting Osiander's claim that the believer's righteousness consisted of the indwelling of Christ's divine nature, Evangelicals insisted ever more clearly on the declarative nature of forgiveness and righteousness. This imputed righteousness later would be labeled "forensic" justification, not only because this declaration took place *in foro*, that is, in the divine courtroom, where the sinner was declared righteous, but also because it emphasized the act of speaking, pronouncing the sinner forgiven.[79] For these Evangelicals, questions of ontology (expressed by Osiander in terms of indwelling and participation) were instead always tied to God's creative and re-creative Word and the way that Word effected faith and righteousness without human works.

In part, these disputes could take place because of the relative independence of each territorial church and university in Evangelical lands. Except where generally banned from publishing, theologians could prosecute their cases quite openly with little fear of reprisal. Although some individuals might be banned from one territory, they could often set up shop in the neighboring one. Yet, rather than leading to the complete fragmentation of the Evangelical message and its churches, this relative freedom of the theological press led these leaders and their churches to search for new ways to foster unity. Not only did the controversy with Osiander provide an opportunity for disputants in other matters to express their unity on the central doctrine of justification,[80] but a variety of formal disputes, meetings, and negotiations during this period also attempted to restore peace.

Later controversies over the Lord's Supper, however, brought these divisions to a crisis point. By the time of Philip Melanchthon's death in 1560, some Lutherans, especially in Hamburg and Bremen, had already objected in print to the Zurich Consensus, signed by Heinrich Bullinger and John Calvin, which seemed to herald Calvin's abandonment of the Wittenberg Concord.[81] Moreover, in late 1559, Melanchthon wrote a memorandum to the Elector of the Palatinate in which he attacked the understanding of Christ's presence in the Lord's Supper held by several other Lutherans, including Tilemann Hesshus, a Wittenberg-trained theologian on the faculty in Heidelberg. In part on the basis of this memorandum, the Palatine elector removed Hesshus and put in his place two Reformed theologians, Caspar Olevianus and Zacharias Ursinus, whose famous Heidelberg Catechism served Reformed churches up and down the Rhine River valley for centuries.[82] In the 1560s, debate revolved around two interrelated matters: the real presence of Christ's body and blood with the bread and wine and the union of Christ's natures that allowed the one seated at God's right hand to be simultaneously present in the elements of the Supper. Alongside attacks on the Heidelberg theologians by Johannes Brenz and other Evangelical theologians from Württemberg, Martin Chemnitz, a student of Luther and Melanchthon, wrote several important tracts defending Christ's presence in the Supper and defining more precisely the character of the communication of attributes (*communicatio idiomatum*) between the divine and human natures in the one person of Christ that allowed Christ's human nature to participate in the omnipresence of the divine.

In the 1570s, the faculty of the University of Wittenberg itself became divided over the question of the real presence, where one group was perceived by Evangelical opponents there and elsewhere in the empire as having abandoned Luther's understanding of Christ's real presence in the Lord's Supper for a more Calvinist position. Because this group held this position secretly, they are often called crypto-Calvinists, although they themselves thought they were upholding certain teachings of Melanchthon and might better be labeled crypto-Philippists. When their presence (and their disdain for Elector Augustus and his spouse) became public, some were arrested (for treason) and others were dismissed. Theologians from other territories, such as Martin Chemnitz, then worked to restore the Wittenberg faculty.

In the wake of these uncertainties among German-speaking Evangelicals, a group of theologians emerged who attempted to unite these disparate churches and theologians. Throughout the unrest of the 1550s and 1560s, calls had already come from various quarters (even from Melanchthon) for assembling a general council of Evangelical theologians to solve these disputes. This mirrored not only ancient and medieval practice but also the perspective of Erasmus of Rotterdam and the experience both with the Marburg Colloquy in 1529 and with the moderately successful Wittenberg Concord of 1536. All such attempts at general discussions, however, had failed by 1570, at which time the second-generation reformer and successor to Johannes Brenz in Württemberg, Jakob Andreae, published a series of "sermons" (better: essays) that attempted to describe these earlier disputes and suggest solutions to the debates.[83] On the basis of this first proposal, small groups of theologians from different parts of the empire met during the 1570s and began working on a text, or formula, for concord, basing their work upon the Augsburg Confession, other documents described above (as well as Luther's catechisms), and other writings by Luther. Three drafters—Andreae, Chemnitz, and David Chytraeus (professor at the University of Rostock and devoted student of Melanchthon)—provided the bulk of the text, although in the later stages, Andreas Musculus of the University of Frankfurt/Oder also contributed. The most recent English translation of the text has reconstructed this varied conversation over the Formula's topics, which included original sin, free will, justification, good works, law and gospel, third use of the law, adiaphora, and predestination, as well as three articles on the recent Lord's Supper controversy (including the Lord's Supper, Person of Christ, and the Descent into Hell).[84]

A nearly completed draft was submitted to some of the Evangelical princes, who insisted that a condensed version be prepared as well. This *Epitome*, written by Jakob Andreae, took its place alongside the longer *Solid Declaration* to provide a new basis for Evangelical unity within the empire: the Formula of Concord. It was subscribed to by over eight thousand pastors, superintendents, deacons, and teachers in Evangelical territories of the empire. The Formula did not so much advertise itself as a new confession of faith but as "a thorough, clear, correct, and Final Repetition and Explanation of Certain Articles of the Augsburg Confession on Which Controversy Has Arisen."[85]

After more negotiation over the preface, three of the four secular electors of the empire from Saxony, Brandenburg, and the Palatinate subscribed to *The Book of Concord*, along with many other Evangelical princes and cities.[86] All told, about two-thirds of Lutheran territories subscribed.[87] *The Book of Concord* consisted of the three ecumenical creeds, the Augsburg Confession and Apology, the Smalcald Articles and Treatise, Luther's Large and Small Catechism, and the entire Formula of Concord. To bolster further their arguments about Christology, reflected in Chemnitz's earlier writings, a collection of texts from Scripture and the church fathers were added to some editions.[88] The names of the more than eight thousand signers were also published, broken down by territory and superintendency.

At the same time Lutheranism was being shaped by its internal disputes, actions by others also molded the religious landscape of central Europe and beyond. The Council of Trent, which began to meet in 1545, after initial hesitation decided to take up doctrinal matters. While there can be no doubt that the anathemas to articles on, for example, justification had a variety of Protestant theologians and churches in mind, they also clearly rejected the most egregious forms of works-righteousness that had dominated late-medieval theology and practice. Some of the very abuses of indulgences to which Luther had objected came under attack. Thus, even though Luther and the Evangelicals could be viewed as the target for Trent's decrees, the debates of the Reformation also positively influenced the council's language. With Thomas Aquinas emerging as *the* theologian of Trent, the Nominalist approaches of William of Occam and Gabriel Biel (whose work Luther had studied thoroughly and rejected as Pelagian)[89] fell into disrepute.

Moreover, when the Smalcald War interrupted the Council, in its reconstituted sessions (again in Trent) Evangelical observers were invited. Thus, Johannes Brenz attended some sessions, and Philip Melanchthon was on his way to Trent (he made it as far as Nuremberg) when the Princes' Rebellion abruptly ended his travels.[90] After the Peace of Augsburg in 1555, any level of participation by Evangelicals was deemed superfluous by both sides. Neither the Smalcald War nor other religious conflicts, however, stopped theological debate among the various parties. As a result, one of the most influential writings of Martin Chemnitz remains his *Examination of the Council of Trent*, where he painstakingly reviewed all of the council's decrees and refuted them along Evangelical lines. Some of his work is reflected in sections of the Formula of Concord, which addressed not only internal disputes but also major differences between Lutherans and the Council of Trent. Although one could easily rush to judgment and imagine that such mutual condemnations spelled an end to all conversation, the opposite was more likely the case. That is, these condemnations showed just how seriously the opposing sides were listening to one another.

Even if, in the end, these condemnations did not fairly characterize the opposition, they set a standard for theological discourse across the Reformation divide. Indeed, one of the unanticipated results of the unexpected Reformation was a heightened awareness of and respect for true differences that divided Christians who on other matters were united.

The other major religious force to be reckoned with in the sixteenth century was the Reformed churches, which traced their origins back to Reformations in Zurich, Basel, and Strasbourg and who broke with Wittenberg theologians over the question of Christ's presence in the Lord's Supper. From these churches came such important teachers as Ulrich Zwingli, Johann Oecolampadius, and Martin Bucer of the first generation and John Calvin and Heinrich Bullinger, among others, of the second. The Reformed churches, the Presbyterian churches, and (at least until the nineteenth century) the Anglican Church (and by extension the Methodist movement and churches) can best be understood as comprising this important branch of Christianity. In the sixteenth century, dialogue between these churches and their teachers on the one side and Evangelicals on the other often collapsed over the Lord's Supper and Christology, although matters related to predestination occasionally played a role. Thus, the Formula of Concord also took aim at some teachings of the Reformed, arguing that they were not adherents of the Augsburg Confession and, thus, should not be accorded the legal rights guaranteed to Evangelicals in the Peace of Augsburg.[91]

Although accorded great interest by social historians and some modern theologians, the role of Anabaptists and their successors in shaping the theological discourse of the sixteenth century was slight. The reformers often did not understand the variety of groups practicing believers' baptism and would thus lump them together under blanket condemnations. Not only the religious practice of believers' baptism but their withdrawal from sixteenth-century society and criticism of its practices made Evangelical, Reformed, and Roman Catholic theologians prone to reject them out-of-hand as seditious and heretical, a tendency heightened by the rebellion in Münster in 1535.[92] Thus, Reformed, Lutherans, and Roman Catholic areas persecuted Anabaptists and put hundreds of them to death. This behavior has only recently become the object of ecumenical discussions, where the "lifting of condemnations" has also entailed (for Lutherans at any rate) asking for forgiveness for acts of persecution committed in the past and condoned by Luther and Melanchthon, among others, sometimes even on the basis of adherence to the Augsburg Confession.[93]

LOOKING TO THE FUTURE (1580–PRESENT)

By 1580, adherents to the Augsburg Confession and, hence, heirs of Martin Luther's unexpected Reformation had spread throughout Europe. In some cases, as in sixteenth-century France, the Netherlands, Scotland, or England, the direct influence of Wittenberg's theology was eventually overshadowed by Reformed theologians, especially those influenced by John Calvin in Geneva and by Ursinus and Olevianus in Heidelberg. Yet even here Luther's heritage played a special role, as these Christians often wrote catechisms and confessions that borrowed in a variety of ways from the Augsburg Confession and Luther's catechisms.

In northern Europe, Lutheranism rapidly spread to Denmark, Sweden, Finland, and their territories (e.g., Iceland and Norway), as well in East Prussia, Latvia, and other Baltic nations and cities. In these places, like in the Holy Roman Empire itself, adherence to the Augsburg Confession and use of Luther's Small Catechism became central doctrinal standards for clergy and laity alike. Pockets of Luther's supporters also thrived in Slovakia, Hungary, and parts of what is now Poland.

The religious settlement of the Peace of Augsburg in 1555, often summarized by the Latin slogan *"cuius regio, eius religio"* (to whom the region [belongs], his the religion), stopped the spread of Evangelical theology into the traditional princely bishoprics and, above all, into the archbishoprics of Cologne, Trier, and Mainz, where the ecclesiastical rulers were also counted among the seven electors of the Holy Roman Emperor.[94] This imbalance made the slogan somewhat inaccurate, with the Evangelical territories and cities always holding a slightly lower status in the empire than their Roman Catholic counterparts.

At the same time, a Roman Catholic Church reinvigorated by the Council of Trent and by the Society of Jesus, among other orders, made some headway in shoring up traditionally Roman Catholic lands and in reclaiming previously Evangelical areas of the empire and beyond. A vigorous application of the Inquisition in the Italian peninsula and Spain meant that the small pockets of Evangelical and Reformed theology that existed south of the Alps and Pyrenees eventually disappeared. Yet it must not be imagined that, despite the highly charged polemical and political situation (which pitted Protestant against Catholic, Lutheran theologians against Reformed ones, and left Mennonites and other Anabaptists often fleeing for their lives), no conversations took place among the various Christian confessions in western Europe.

Not only were there occasional formal colloquies,[95] but theologians were carefully reading their opponents' works. In the seventeenth century, one of the most interesting conversations involved Robert Bellarmine, SJ (1542–1621), and Johann Gerhard (1582–1637), professor at the University of Jena.[96] Bellarmine's work provided strong defense of Roman Catholic, Tridentine doctrine and seriously challenged Evangelical alternatives. Gerhard's chief work, a multivolume *Loci communes theologici*, showed careful attention to Bellarmine's writings and tried to provide answers to his most trenchant objections. Although both theologians were apologists—by no stretch of the imagination ecumenists—they represented an important first phase in ecumenical rapprochement: careful listening to the arguments of the other side. Even though the conversations ended in condemnation, the fact that such exchanges took place at all signaled to their age and ours just how important divisions in the church were for them.

At various times throughout the intervening 350 years, other important conversations took place across the Lutheran-Roman Catholic ecumenical divide. In the late nineteenth century, stimulated by a revival of interest in especially the earliest sources of Luther's theology (his lectures on the Psalms, Romans, Galatians, and Hebrews from 1513–18) that became known as the Luther Renaissance, Roman Catholic scholars like Hartmann Grisar and Heinrich Denifle, while not abandoning their own staunch opposition to Luther's theology, forced Lutheran historians to revisit and relearn late-medieval theology and Luther's great debt to the entire Catholic tradition.[97] This careful reading of the sources, coupled with a growing convergence in the historical-critical exegetical method among biblical scholars, paved the way for new ways to view Luther and the unexpected Reformation that he started. This movement will be the subject of the following chapters.

Chapter Two

The Path to the Joint Declaration on the Doctrine of Justification

Representatives of the Lutheran World Federation and the Catholic Church signed the *Joint Declaration on the Doctrine of Justification* (JDDJ) in Augsburg on October 31, 1999. The signing signifies that the mutual condemnations of the sixteenth century do not apply to the understanding of justification expressed in the document. For the first time, the Roman Catholic Church and the Lutheran World Federation declare "in a binding manner that an understanding has been reached on a question of faith and doctrine which has been divisive for centuries." This declaration constitutes official ecclesial reception of decades of dialogue on this topic and represents the first official reception by the Catholic Church of the results of dialogue with ecclesial communities issuing from the Protestant Reformation.

The significance of this event becomes evident when one realizes that a "doctrinal condemnation" is the highest degree of escalation in a theological controversy within a church or between churches. Doctrinal condemnations are the confirmation and seal of church division, the authoritative declaration that a difference with regard to a particular teaching is of such grievous nature that it divides the church. Conversely, the declaration of nonapplicability of a doctrinal condemnation means that the ecumenical dialogue has reached a point where the difference with regard to a particular teaching has lost its cutting edge so that this difference is no longer church-dividing.

This inapplicability of condemnations does not mean that we erase our history or change the doctrinal definitions of the Council of Trent or the Lutheran Confessions. However, it does mean that the two faith communities do not today hold the positions that are condemned in the way that they were condemned in the sixteenth century. Historical research and present dialogue have exposed misunderstandings of the past and allowed the faith communities to deepen their current understandings so that the remaining differences are transcended by a common confession of belief.

The groundwork leading to the JDDJ was laid by the ecumenical commitments of both Catholics and Lutherans, theological research by theologians of both groups, the results of earlier dialogues, and by work that synthesized and assessed the achievements of the previous thirty-five years.

ECUMENICAL COMMITMENTS OF CATHOLICS AND LUTHERANS

Lutheran Ecumenical Engagement

Protestant churches have been involved in ecumenism since the event credited with giving rise to the ecumenical movement, the 1910 World Missionary Conference of Edinburgh, where the participants discussed impediments to their missionary endeavors including the disunity among Christian churches. The next step toward cooperation was the formation of the International Missionary Council in 1921, comprised of Protestant national missionary councils and councils of churches from Africa, Asia, and Latin America. The World Conference on Faith and Order, which focused on the theological basis for church unity, met in Lausanne, Switzerland, for the first time in 1927 with representatives of the major Christian traditions with the exception of Catholics. Two other organizations that had emerged by the mid-twentieth century were Life and Work, which promoted joint social service and action, and the World Council of Christian Education. In 1948,

Faith and Order came together with Life and Work in the founding of the World Council of Churches, which originally defined itself as "a fellowship (*koinonia*) of churches which confess the Lord Jesus Christ as God and Savior." This was amended in 1961 to add trinitarian, doxological, and scriptural emphases with the phrase "according to the scriptures and therefore seek to fulfill together their common calling to the glory of the one God, Father, Son, and Holy Spirit."[1] Although the Catholic Church is not a member of the World Council of Churches, it has been a member of the Faith and Order Commission since 1968 and collaborates in programs sponsored by the council. Many Lutheran churches around the world were founding members of the World Council of Churches.

In addition to the collaborative and multilateral work of the World Council of Churches, confessional traditions engage in ecumenical work on behalf of their own tradition. The Lutheran World Federation (LWF) acts as the instrument of Lutheran churches in global ecumenical dialogue. Its Web site states, "For us, Christian ecumenism is not a choice: it is our mission to witness together with and in Christ, and it is a gift we receive from God through the Holy Spirit."[2] The 1984 assembly of the LWF adopted the following understanding of unity, consisting of a communion that admits of diversity and multiform confessions of the one faith:

> This unity is expressed as a communion in the common and at the same time, multiform confession of one and the same apostolic faith....It is a communion where diversities contribute to fullness and are no longer barriers to unity....The diversity present in this communion rises out of the differing cultural and ethnic contexts in which the one church of Christ lives out its mission and out of the number of church traditions in which the apostolic faith has been maintained, transmitted, and lived throughout the centuries. In recognizing these diversities as expressions of the one apostolic faith and the one catholic church, traditions are changed, antagonisms overcome, and mutual condemnations lifted. The diversities are reconciled and transformed into a legiti-

mate and indispensable multiformity within the one body of Christ.[3]

This statement, often cited as an expression of what is called "reconciled diversity," demonstrates a potential openness to what would be the methodology of differentiating consensus of the JDDJ.

Individual member churches also engage in national or regional dialogues. In the United States, the Evangelical Lutheran Church in America (ELCA) and its predecessor bodies enjoy a long history of ecumenical commitment and engagement. Many North American Lutherans were in committed ecumenical partnerships as early as 1950. At its eleventh biennial convention in 1982, one of the ELCA's predecessor bodies, the Lutheran Church in America, approved as its official ecumenical position the document, "Ecumenism: A Lutheran Commitment." This statement became a charter for a deliberate program of ecumenical study and activity. Three years later, the church council of a second predecessor body, The American Lutheran Church, approved a similar document titled, "Ecumenical Perspective and Guidelines." The Evangelical Lutheran Church of America was formed by the union of these two church bodies and the Association of Evangelical Lutheran Churches in 1988. The statement "The Vision of the Evangelical Lutheran Church in America" comprehensively presents the ecumenical commitment and vision of the ELCA.[4] There the ELCA describes itself as "evangelical," "catholic," and "ecumenical," stating, "Its confessional character is not opposed to its ecumenical commitment, but necessitates it as a consequence of the Gospel."[5]

Catholic Openings to Ecumenical Engagement

The Second Vatican Council marked the formal entrance of the Catholic Church into the ecumenical movement. Pope John XXIII, in his announcement of the Council at the close of the Week of Prayer for Christian Unity (January 25, 1959), said that he desired "to invite the separated Communities to seek again that unity for which so many souls are longing in these days throughout the world."[6] In his address to open the Council, he once again mentioned other faith communities:

To this chorus of prayers we also invite all Christians of Churches separated from Rome, so that the Council may also be to their advantage. We know that many of these children are eager for a return of unity and peace, in accordance with the teaching and the prayer of Christ to the Father. And we know that the announcement of the Council was not only received by them with joy, but that more than a few of them have already promised to offer their prayers for its success and hope to send representatives of their communities to follow its work at close hand. All of this is for us a cause of great comfort and hope and it is precisely to facilitate these contacts that we established some time ago a Secretariat for this precise purpose.[7]

Pope John XXIII died between the first and second sessions of the Council and was succeeded by Pope Paul VI. In his address to the opening of the second session of the Council, he spoke of his "deep sadness" at the "prolonged separation" of the communities of the non-Catholic observers and the Catholic Church, saying, "If we are in any way to blame for that separation, we humbly beg God's forgiveness and the pardon too of our brethren who feel they have been injured by us." He continued, "For our part, we willingly forgive the injuries which the Catholic Church has suffered, and forget the grief endured during the long series of dissensions and separations. May the heavenly Father deign to hear our prayers and grant us true brotherly peace."[8] Paul VI enumerated four objectives of the Council: the awareness of the church, its reform, the bringing together of all Christians in unity, and the dialogue of the church with the contemporary world. For both John XXIII and Paul VI, the ecumenical agenda was intrinsic to the Council. The first document to be promulgated by the Council, the Constitution on the Sacred Liturgy (*Sacrosanctum Concilium*), in its very first paragraph cites ecumenical unity as one of the goals of the Council when it says that one of the Council's intentions is "to encourage whatever can contribute to the union of all who believe in Christ" (*Sacrosanctum Concilium* § 1).

A number of Protestants were invited as observers to the sessions of the Council and influenced its development and improvements through their suggestions to the Secretariat for Promoting Christian Unity. John Radano's history notes three major contributions of their presence mentioned by Paul VI in his statements to observers during the third and fourth sessions. First, their presence helped to keep the ecumenical question before the Council, both with respect to the Catholic Church's understanding of separated Christians and for the renewal within the Catholic Church itself. Second, their presence contributed to the development of new attitudes toward their separated communities. Third, Paul VI encouraged the continuation of reciprocal contacts and changed relationships with separated Christians.[9]

Three documents of the Council directly contributed to Catholic ecumenical engagement: the Dogmatic Constitution on the Church (*Lumen Gentium*, November 21, 1964), the Decree on Religious Freedom (*Dignitatis Humanae*, December 7, 1965), and, most fully, the Decree on Ecumenism (*Unitatis Redintegratio*, November 21, 1964).

The first, the Dogmatic Constitution on the Church, states that the Church of Christ "subsists in" the Catholic Church, although "outside its structure many elements of sanctification and of truth are to be found which, as proper gifts to the church of Christ, impel toward catholic unity" (LG § 8). This means that the Catholic Church claims to have all those elements necessary for salvation and to be Christ's Church, but it also acknowledges the presence of some of these elements outside of its visible boundaries. Some of the most notable of these elements would be the Sacred Scriptures, baptism, and the confession of faith contained in the Nicene-Constantinopolitan and Apostles' Creeds. This statement represents a development from the papal encyclical of Pius XII, *Mystici Corporis*, which simply identified the Church of Christ with the Roman Catholic Church (§ 13).[10] Although there has been much theological discussion since the Council about the meaning and intent of the phrase "subsists in," the Congregation for the Doctrine and the Faith confirmed that it means that the Church of Christ "continues to exist in" the Catholic Church.[11] *Lumen Gentium*'s formulation, however, means that ecclesiality does not simply coincide with the Catholic Church, but that other Christian traditions are also truly ecclesial. Some separated groups the Catholic Church explicitly recognizes as churches, especially in the Christian East. The exact understanding of the communities issuing from the Reformation remains a topic of ecumenical conversation. Nevertheless, the Council's description of them as "ecclesial communities" must mean that they have an ecclesial character as communities. The mutual acknowledgment of ecclesial elements provides an important basis for ecumenical dialogue.

The Decree on Religious Freedom presents three doctrinal tenets: "The ethical doctrine of religious freedom as a human right (personal and collective); a political doctrine with regard to the functions and limits of government in matters religious; and the theological doctrine of the freedom of the Church as the fundamental principle in what concerns the relations between the Church and the socio-political order."[12] This eliminates a previously assumed double standard by which the church enjoys freedom when it is a minority and exercises intolerance when it is a majority.[13] It thus elicited new confidence in ecumenical relationships.

The Decree on Ecumenism marked the beginning of a new era in the relationship of Christian churches to one another. The Catholic attitude toward ecumenism up to that time had been most explicitly articulated by Pius XI, who wrote in his letter *Mortalium Animos* (1928): "It is clear why this Apostolic See has never allowed its subjects to take part in the assemblies of non-Catholics: for the union of Christians can only be promoted by promoting the return to the one true Church of Christ of those who are separated from it, for in the past they have unhappily left it" (§ 10). Twenty years later, in 1949, Pius XII authorized the participation of Catholics in ecumenical meetings with other Christians. These meetings prepared the way for Vatican II by providing opportunities for growth in mutual knowledge and trust as well as the discovery of how much Christians from various traditions share in common.

The Decree on Ecumenism positively recognizes other Christians, echoing *Lumen Gentium* § 8 when it says, "Moreover some, and even most, of the significant elements and endowments which together go to build up and give life to the church itself, can exist outside the visible boundaries of the catholic church: the written word of God; the life of grace; faith, hope and charity, with the other interior gifts of the holy Spirit and visible elements too" (UR § 3). Furthermore, the document asserts, "Our separated brothers and sisters also celebrate many sacred actions of the Christian religion. These most certainly can truly engender a life of grace…and must be held capable of giving access to that communion in which is salvation" (UR § 3). It concludes this thought saying, "It follows that the separated churches and communities as such, though we believe them to be deficient in some respects, have by no means been deprived of significance and importance in the mystery of salvation" (UR § 3). In some measure, through these shared elements, the one Church of Christ is present and operative in these separated Christian churches and communities, albeit imperfectly.[14] The Church of Christ extends beyond the visible boundaries of the Catholic Church. These groups participating in the one Church of Christ are in varying degrees of ecclesial communion with one another. It is the task of ecumenical work to achieve fullness of unity (UR § 4).

In addition to this opening to other churches and ecclesial communities, the Decree on Ecumenism emphasizes the need for a spiritual ecumenism. This includes fidelity to the church's own calling, continual renewal and purification, repentance for sins against unity, and above all, a change of heart through a deeper conversion to Christ. The foundational principle of spiritual ecumenism is that the more Christians live holier lives according to the gospel, the better they will practice Christian unity, for the closer their union to Father, Word, and Spirit, the more deeply they will be able to grow in mutual love (UR § 7).

The ecumenical initiatives of the Council bore fruit. A joint working group between the Catholic Church and the Lutheran World Federation came into existence in 1965, the same year as the conclusion of the Second Vatican Council.

Theological Research

Among several works of Catholic scholarship, the work of Otto Hermann Pesch (1931–2014) was particularly instrumental in paving the way for the JDDJ.[15] A lifelong ecumenist, his many contributions included the identification of common ground between Aquinas and Luther on the subject of justification,[16] his synthesis of other Catholic theologians on justification such as

Hans Küng and Karl Rahner,[17] and his hermeneutic of identifying the Thomistic world view as sapiential and the Lutheran world view as experiential.[18] Attending to this distinction between two different thought forms or world perspectives governing the outlook of Catholics and Lutherans paved the way for the methodology of a differentiated consensus employed in the JDDJ. A "sapiential" theology attempts to view the relationship between God and human beings from an objective distance. Even though it presupposes the personal act of faith, it does not consider the relationship from the perspective of personal faith, but rather as if from the perspective of an objective bystander observing the relationship between God and a human being. Thomas as a "sapiential" theologian presents the work of divine wisdom in the total plan of creation. In contrast, the Lutheran "experiential" perspective addresses how God encounters the person by speaking words of promise, command, and consolation and engages human lives in a gracious and saving way. It is the perspective of God's direct address and a person's response in faith. These two perspectives provided a way of understanding how Catholics and Lutherans viewed the process and results of justification in different ways, one not necessarily negating the other, even though at first they may seem to be incompatible and even contradictory. Such hermeneutics helped to navigate the apparent contradictions between a Catholic theology of states of sinfulness and grace and the Lutheran teaching on *simul iustus et peccator*, and between the difference between the Lutheran *sola fide* and the Catholic *fides caritate formata*. In spite of their helpfulness for understanding differences between Lutherans and Catholics, Pieter de Witte argues that the two perspectives are asymmetrical, with the Catholic position more open to incorporating an experiential perspective along with the sapiential in certain contexts of prayer and worship, while the Lutheran perspective fears corruption by a sapiential perspective.[19]

On the Lutheran side, scholars such as Wilfried Joest and Peter Brunner prepared the way to the JDDJ by showing that what Trent condemned in topics like "faith alone" and in the notion of forensic righteousness did not correspond to Lutheran teaching. Additionally, much of what Trent proposed with respect to a person's free response to prevenient grace and on merit or reward for good works was not subject to Lutheran condemnation.[20]

The Finnish School of Lutheran theology, consisting of

the work of Tuomo Mannermaa and his students, provided an important bridge to Catholic theology.[21] Inspired by the dialogue between the Lutheran Church in Finland and the Russian Orthodox Church, the Finnish School explored the concept of *theosis* and divinization in Luther's writings as a key to understanding Lutheran notions of justification by faith, law, and grace and the Christian as simultaneously righteous and sinner. The patristic concept of divinization has the advantage of avoiding the modern contrast between personalistic, relational, and ethical aspects of salvation in some Lutheran theologies of justification and the ontological soteriologies operative in the Roman Catholic Scholastic concept of habitual grace.[22] Another contribution of the Finnish School is its correction of an overly one-sided emphasis on the forensic character of justification to the neglect of salvation as regeneration and vivification.[23] This imbalance is often traced to a neo-Kantian influence that, in theologians like Albrecht Ritschl, deprived Christ's presence in faith of its metaphysical objectivity in favor of a dynamic and relational interpretation wherein Christ's presence is only considered from the perspective of God's effects on the believer.[24] The divine reality (the noumenal) remains inaccessible behind God's actions (the phenomenal) on the believer. The result is that "the possibility of a real ontological presence of Christ in faith—and a real union of the believer and Christ—is thereby excluded."[25] The Finnish interpretation of the Lutheran concept of justification is much closer to the Roman Catholic interpretation of salvation. It also challenges the traditional opposition between Lutheran "dynamic" thinking and Catholic "substance" thinking.

Results of Ecumenical Dialogues

Already at an early stage in official dialogues, Lutherans and Catholics recognized substantial convergence on the doctrine of justification. In 1972, the first dialogue document of the international Lutheran-Roman Catholic joint commission, *The Gospel and the Church*, the so-called Malta Report on account of the location of its final meeting, determined that "a far-reaching consensus is developing in the interpretation of justification."[26] The core of the consensus lies in its statement,

> Lutherans and Catholics share the conviction that we
> owe our salvation exclusively to the saving act of God
> accomplished once for all in Jesus Christ according to
> the witness of the Gospel. (§ 48)

The document corrected traditional misperceptions of the dialogue partners when it spoke of the Catholic view of salvation as
"unconditional as far as human accomplishments are concerned"
and the Lutheran view as emphasizing "that the event of justification is not limited to individual forgiveness of sins," and not
"a purely external declaration of the justification of the sinner"
so that "the righteousness of God actualized in the Christ-event
is conveyed to the sinner through the message of justification as
an accompanying reality basic to the life of the believer" (§ 26).
The participants of the dialogue agreed that the issue of justification need no longer divide their respective churches.[27] The Malta
Report became the foundation of further dialogue, a fact acknowledged in the foreword to the report of the third phase of the dialogue.[28]

Similarly, the statement of the second phase of the Lutheran-
Roman Catholic international dialogue, "All under One Christ,"
produced for the 450th anniversary of the Augsburg Confession
in 1980, asserted:

> A broad consensus emerges in the doctrine of justifica-
> tion, which was decisively important for the Reforma-
> tion (CA IV): it is solely by grace and by faith in Christ's
> saving work and not because of any merit in us that we
> are accepted by God and receive the Holy Spirit who
> renews our hearts and equips us for and calls us to good
> works. (§§ 14–15)[29]

Meanwhile, the American Lutheran-Catholic Dialogue began
work on justification in 1978, issuing its document, *Justification
by Faith*, in 1983.[30] The introduction to the document presents
the statement as a response to the Malta Report's statement that
"a far-reaching consensus is developing," but that "a further treatment of the subject and its implications is needed" (§ 2).

The material convergences between Lutheran and Catholic

positions on justification include Christ as the central source, center, and norm of Christian life; righteousness as the prerequisite of final salvation; the universal need of justification as a consequence of original sin; the lack of human capacity to turn to God without divine help; justification as both being declared and made righteous; Scripture, proclamation of the Word, and sacraments as means to awaken and strengthen justifying faith; justifying faith as a trustful, self-involving response to the gospel; justifying faith as not possible apart from hope and love; sin no longer reigning in the justified even though they remain subject to sinful inclinations and are capable of losing justification; eternal reward promised to the righteous as gift; recompense given to the good works of the justified; the priority of God's redeeming will over every human action according to the classic doctrine of predestination (§ 156).

The document acknowledges several remaining differences due to "differing concerns" and "differences in thought structures" (§ 154). These include forensic and effective justification, the sinfulness of the justified, the sufficiency of faith, the meritorious nature of good works, the freedom and goodness of fallen human beings, and satisfaction and justification as "a" or "the" critical principle in the church.

In spite of remaining difference, the document articulates a fundamental affirmation on the nature of trust or assurance of salvation and on the fundamental experiential attitude of the justified in relation to God: "Our entire hope of justification and salvation rests on Christ Jesus and on the gospel whereby the good news of God's merciful action in Christ is made known; we do not place our ultimate trust in anything other than God's promise and saving work in Christ" (§ 157). Nevertheless, the document acknowledges that this affirmation "is not fully equivalent to the Reformation teaching on justification according to which God accepts sinners as righteous for Christ's sake on the basis of faith alone" even though it expresses a central concern of that doctrine, and that it "does not exclude the traditional Catholic position that the grace-wrought transformation of sinners is a necessary preparation for final salvation" (§ 157).

A third international document of the Lutheran-Roman Catholic Joint Commission, *Church and Justification* (September 11, 1993), also citing the Malta Report as the foundation for further dialogue, had as an aim in the original mandate given to the commission to test the "far-reaching consensus" on justification by dealing with the question of the church in light of sacramentality and justification.[31] This arose from the conviction that justification needed to be proved ecclesiologically because of the mutual relationship between everything believed and taught about the nature of the church, the means of salvation, and the church's ministry, on the one hand, and justification-faith as the way in which the salvation-event is received and appropriated, on the other hand (§ 2). In submitting its report, the Joint Commission asked whether, taken together with the documents of the second phase of the dialogue—namely *The Eucharist*, *The Ministry in the Church*, *Ways to Community*, and *Facing Unity*—there was sufficient consensus to enable the churches "to embark upon concrete steps toward visible unity."[32]

Assessments of the Achievements of Dialogue

A Joint Ecumenical Commission (1981–85) comprising Lutheran, Reformed, and Catholic participants (*Gemeinsame Ökumenische Kommission*) was established in Germany after the visit of Pope John Paul II to Mainz in 1980 to address practical problems such as improved ecumenical cooperation with regard to Sunday services, Eucharistic fellowship, and mixed marriages. This commission, realizing that these practical problems could not be addressed adequately until fundamental theological questions were solved, entrusted the task of studying the mutual doctrinal condemnations of the sixteenth century to an already existing standing committee, the Ecumenical Study Group of Protestant and Catholic Theologians (*Ökumenische Aerbeitskreis evangelischer und katholischer Theologen*, also known as the "Jaeger-Stählin Group").

Bishop Lohse and Cardinal Ratzinger described the task to the chairmen and scholarly directors of the study group in 1981:

> During the discussions in Munich, it once again became clear that our common witness is counteracted by judgments passed by one church on the other during the sixteenth century, judgments which found their way into the Confessions of the Lutheran and Reformed churches

and into the doctrinal decisions of the Council of Trent. According to the general conviction, these so-called condemnations no longer apply to our partner today. But this must not remain a merely private persuasion. It must be established by the churches in binding form.[33]

The work of the study group was not restricted to a historical study of the sixteenth-century condemnations, but also included an assessment of the results and reception given to ecumenical convergence documents.

Three subgroups involving over thirty theologians worked on the themes of justification, sacraments, and ministry, submitting an extensive report to the Joint Ecumenical Commission in 1985. The commission then issued a Final Report, which was sent to the German Episcopal Conference and the Evangelical Church in Germany (*Evangelische Kirche in Deutschland*—EKD) along with the study of the ecumenical working group. The study, the report, and some background documents were published under the title *The Condemnations of the Reformation Era: Do They Still Divide?*[34] Because this study outlined the traditional oppositional positions of the Reformers and Catholics on the topic of justification, identified new insights and the paths leading to them received since the Reformation, and explained why the sixteenth-century condemnations need no longer apply to our partner today, the story of the path to the JDDJ merits a close consideration of this study to see how some of the traditional differences were reconciled.[35] In what follows, the principal opposing positions are listed followed by a brief explanation of why the study group concluded that they no longer apply today.

1. Reformers teaching the complete depravity of human nature, and Catholic doctrine insisting that human nature is not entirely depraved.[36]

    Catholic doctrine is in agreement with the Reformers' judgment about the radical depravity of the unredeemed human being. However, when Catholics recognize some good in the sinner, this is seen as the work of grace in the event of justification, which renews God's work through the power of his grace.

The justified person is not "replaced" by God's grace, but is awakened to a new life, thereby witnessing to the continuity between creation and redemption. For Catholics, Christian liberty issuing from the power of grace is not with respect to God, but rather with regard to the things of this world. This is the liberty from which issue the works done based on justification. Both sides are subject to misunderstanding—the Protestant view to the interpretation that God justifies a person without that person being affected, and the Catholic view to the presupposition that human cooperation is necessary for baptismal grace.[37]

2. Reformers considering concupiscence to be sin, and Catholics considering it to be an inclination to sin but not sin in the proper sense in the justified.[38]

The principal issue here is the definition of *sin*. Lutherans consider concupiscence to be a sin because it is against the will of God, signifies the desire to be like God, and therefore is part of original sin. Catholics consider it in the justified not to be sin in a proper sense, but an inclination to sin, because it does not engage the will. Even at the time of the Reformation, there was agreement that "original sin has been removed 'formally' but remains 'materially.'"[39] Lutherans and Catholics agree that original sin and concupiscence are in contradiction to God, that concupiscence is the object of the lifelong struggle against sin, and that after baptism, concupiscence is "controlled sin" (Lutheran understanding) or "no longer sin in the real sense" (Catholic understanding).[40]

3. Reformers teaching the complete passivity of human beings toward God, and Catholics insisting that human beings cooperate with God when touched by God's justifying grace.[41]

While the word *cooperation* is certainly open to misunderstanding, Lutherans and Catholics agree that "there can be 'cooperation' *only* in the sense that in faith the heart is involved, when the Word touches it and creates faith."[42] Both agree that "before the face of God, human beings cannot in any way cast a sideways glance at their own endeavors—not even 'partly,' and not even after their regeneration through the Holy Spirit, and on the basis of that regeneration."[43]

4. Reformers teaching that justifying grace is a reality on God's side alone, identical with God's forgiving love and his ever-new commitment, and Catholics saying that justifying grace is a reality in the soul of the human being.[44]

This is a clear difference between Lutherans and Catholics, although both positions can claim a biblical basis. The Protestant position can point to 1 Corinthians 1:30, which speaks of God making Christ righteousness for us. The Catholic view can refer to Romans 5:5, which describes grace as "poured into" the soul. Taken together, one arrives at the indissoluble connection both between "uncreated" and "created" grace and between "forensic" and "effective" justification.

The study group concluded that canon 11 of Trent's Decree on Justification, in condemning the doctrine that grace is merely the favor of God, does not truly capture the Lutheran position. Luther's distinction between "grace" and "gift" preserves the insight "that 'external' grace touches and claims the person of the believer."[45] By the same token, Protestant theology cannot say that the notion of grace as a *habitus* is equivalent to loving God by means of one's own natural powers. Scholarship shows that although the Council of Trent *expressed* itself in terms of the *habitus* doctrine, it did not *define* justification as *habitus*. Positively, Catholics and Lutherans both embrace the personal character of grace (a Protestant emphasis), and the creative and renewing character of God's love (a Catholic emphasis). They both avoid what the other fears, namely, "grace as an objective 'possession,'" (a typically Protestant fear), and "God's impotence toward a sin which is 'merely' forgiven in justification but which is not truly abolished in its power to divide the sinner from God" (a more typically Catholic fear).[46] The study group concluded that the mutual rejections on this point applied, even in the sixteenth century, to "indistinct and misleading *formulations.*"[47]

5. Reformers stressing that human beings receive the gift of justification through faith alone, that is, solely through trust in the mercy of God, while Catholics insisting that faith and trust justify only if united with hope and love and "joined by a corresponding active cooperation with God's grace."[48]

The fathers of the Council of Trent primarily understood faith in an intellectualist manner as the assent of the mind to the revealed Word of God and the "objective" belief expressed in creed and doctrine. From this perspective, they interpreted the Protestant phrase "by faith alone" as excluding the necessity of sacraments, good works, and a binding creed. The Reformers, on the other hand, primarily understood faith as "trust in the promise" and as "the forgiveness and fellowship with Christ effected by the word of promise itself."[49] Once again, both sides can claim a scriptural basis for their position, Protestants pointing to Paul in Romans 3:21—4:24 and Galatians 2:14—3:29, and Catholics appealing to Paul in 1 Corinthians 13:13. Taken as a whole, the New Testament witnesses to the connection between confession of faith (Rom 10:9), love of God (1 Cor 8:3), and love of neighbor (Gal 5:6).

Luther's insistence on justification "by faith alone" and his rejection of justification on the basis of "faith formed by love" (*fides caritate formata*) was due to his fear of incorporating something humanly ethical in the justification process, that is, a love of God accomplished by one's own powers. Ultimately, though, Luther's understanding of "faith" includes what Catholics understand as faith, hope, and love and term "justification through grace."

A difference, nonetheless, remains between the

Lutheran and the Catholic formulation in both concerns and emphases. In the Protestant interpretation, "the faith that clings unconditionally to God's promise in Word and Sacrament is sufficient for righteousness before God, so that the renewal of the human being, without which there can be no faith, does not in itself make any contribution to justification."[50] Catholic doctrine, on the other hand, while also emphasizing that the renewal of the human being does not "contribute" to justification, stresses the renewal of the human being through justifying grace. This renewal accomplished in faith, hope, and love is "nothing but a response to God's unfathomable grace."[51]

6. Reformers holding that justifying faith creates the assurance of salvation, while Catholics insisting that because of human weakness, Christians can never be certain whether they are really in a state of grace or be assured of justification simply by believing themselves to be justified.[52]

Catholic doctrine teaches that objectively one may be completely certain of the forgiveness of God from the perspective of the effect of the sacrament. However, the recipient of the sacrament can subjectively never be certain whether he or she has been sufficiently open to the efficacy of the sacrament. Luther says we should never avert our eyes from God's promise of forgiveness pronounced in the objective efficacy of the words of absolution. To look at our sin, our doubt, and ourselves is to take our eyes off Christ. Since we can never subjectively meet the demands of the law, faith relies on the objectivity of the divine promise and confidently trusts Christ. Luther's Catholic opponents, especially Cajetan, thought that this assurance of salvation was based on the believer's subjective conviction or even feelings, but this was not the case. Luther's assurance was based on the objectivity of Christ's promise, and he explicitly rejected an assurance of faith that had its foundation only in subjective conviction rather than in Christ. Thus, both the Council of Trent and the Reformers rejected security and self-conceit about one's own position and stressed the reliability of God's promise.[53]

7. Reformers teaching that "although good works performed out of faith in God's grace are certainly the consequence and fruit of grace, they are in no way a 'merit' in the sight of God," while Catholics insisting that "the good works of those who are justified, performed in the power of grace, are in the true sense meritorious before God, not because of the human achievement as such, but by virtue of grace and the merits of Christ."[54]

The Council of Trent clearly taught that the first grace of justification is never merited, and that gaining eternal life is based on the gift of grace through membership in Christ.[55] Whatever merits we have are themselves gifts. The concept of merit expresses the responsibility of human beings, a responsibility not denied by the Reformers. The study finds that many antitheses could be overcome if "merit" were to be viewed through the biblical terms *wage* or *reward*, admitting that the term *merit* has been used in an unbiblical form in Catholic theology, pastoral care, and spirituality. With these clarifications, the study finds that the relevant condemnatory pronouncements no longer apply today.[56]

The study concluded, "Where the interpretation of the justification of the sinner is concerned, the mutual sixteenth-century condemnations...no longer apply to our partner today in any sense that could divide the churches."[57] Historical investigations showed that even in the sixteenth century, many of the condemnations did not touch the opponent's real intention. Nevertheless, not all the differences were simply due to misunderstandings or different modes of expression. Remaining differences on the doctrine of justification include the question of forensic or transformative justification, that is, whether *the essence of grace or righteousness before God is defined on the one hand as an objective reality* on

God's side '*outside ourselves*,' and on the other hand as *a reality in the human soul*, a 'quality' intrinsically 'adhering' to the soul;"[58] the question of the sufficiency of faith for justification when contrasted with the Catholic stress on the necessity of the renewal of the human being through justifying grace;[59] and various uses of the concept of merit, not all of which are biblical.[60]

Further Steps toward Affirming Consensus

The work of the German Joint Ecumenical Commission and the Ecumenical Study group was published in German in 1986. The first volume was translated into English and published in 1990 to facilitate the reception process. Both Lutherans and Catholics at this point were trying to find a way forward toward reception.

The ELCA considered the possibility of officially affirming the results of the study, even if unilaterally, in 1992 and 1993.[61] However, Bishop Pierre Duprey, from the Pontifical Council for Promoting Christian Unity (PCPCU), and Harding Meyer, from the Strasbourg Institute for Ecumenical Research, in addressing the 1993 ELCA Bishops' Conference, stressed first, that reception of the consensus needed to be reciprocal, and second, that reception should not be limited to the question of the applicability of the condemnations of the Reformation era, but should also address the possibility of a common expression of the doctrine of justification.[62]

At the worldwide level, two events opened a way forward toward reception. First, at its Eighth Assembly in 1990, the LWF changed its constitution to describe itself no longer as "a free association of Lutheran churches" (Constitution 1984), but as a "communion of churches which are in pulpit and altar fellowship," with a constitutive obligation "to serve Christian unity throughout the world" (Constitution 1990, III).[63] Second, the LWF and the PCPCU together formed a joint staff group that produced a working paper, *Strategies for Reception*.[64] The reception process would have to be very different for Catholics and Lutherans on account of their differing ecclesiastical structures and self-understanding. *Strategies* notes that although "the Lutheran churches are autonomous bodies, in the Lutheran World Federation they have an expression of their communion and an instrument for common action," which positions it "to play a crucial role in the official reception of international dialogue results."[65] The challenge in ascertaining a Lutheran consensus involved both receiving responses from individual Lutheran churches and reflecting the character of the communion as a whole. Consequently, a simple tally of individual responses from the churches was deemed inadequate. A yet unidentified further step would be necessary.[66]

In 1993, the LWF and the PCPCU initiated a process intended to lead to a declaration about the condemnations on justification in 1997 on the occasion of the 450th anniversary of the Tridentine decree on justification. A small working group produced a draft of a joint declaration on justification, the first of what would eventually be four texts (March 1994, September 1994, June 1996, January 1997), the later texts the work of an expanded working group. Three of these were sent out for review by sponsoring bodies to Lutheran member churches of the LWF and Catholic bishops' conferences in countries with a large Lutheran presence, and to theologians. Proposals had also come from a joint working group of the PCPCU and the Congregation for the Doctrine of the Faith. The final text, drafted in 1997, took into account proposals for revision from the Congregation of the Doctrine of the Faith and the German National Committee of the LWF.[67]

The Text of the *Joint Declaration on the Doctrine of Justification*

The final text of the JDDJ has this structure:[68]

Preamble (§§ 1–7)
1. Biblical Message of Justification (§§ 8–12)
2. The Doctrine of Justification as Ecumenical Problem (§ 13)
3. The Common Understanding of Justification (§§ 14–18)
4. Explicating the Common Understanding of Justification:

    4.1 Human Powerlessness and Sin in Relation to Justification (§§ 19–21)

Section 15 states the consensus expressing the common understanding of justification:

> In faith we together hold the conviction that justification is the work of the triune God. The Father sent his Son into the world to save sinners. The foundation and presupposition of justification is the incarnation, death, and resurrection of Christ. Justification thus means that Christ himself is our righteousness in which we share through the Holy Spirit in accord with the will of the Father. Together we confess: By grace alone, in faith in Christ's saving work and not because of any merit on our part, we are accepted by God and receive the Holy Spirit, who renews our hearts while equipping and calling us to good works.

The seven affirmations of what Lutherans and Catholics confess together regarding justification follow a methodology of differentiating consensus. Each positive statement of common confession is followed by a paragraph clarifying the Catholic understanding and another clarifying the Lutheran understanding. These two paragraphs allow the differences within the two traditions to stand even as they are subsumed under a broader agreement. These differences

55

do not destroy the consensus regarding basic truths.[69] Thus, this document presents a reconciling diversity rather than a uniformity of the Lutheran and Catholic positions.

In summary, the seven statements are the following:

1. "All persons depend completely on the saving grace of God for their salvation." "Justification takes place solely by God's grace" (§ 19).
2. "God forgives sin by grace and, at the same time, frees human beings from sin's enslaving power and imparts the gift of new life in Christ" (§ 22). Here Lutherans understand "that the sinner is granted righteousness before God in Christ through the declaration of forgiveness and that only in union with Christ is one's life renewed." They understand that "justification remains free from human cooperation" (§ 23).
3. "Sinners are justified by faith in the saving action of God in Christ. By the gift of the Holy Spirit in baptism, they are granted the gift of salvation which lays the basis of the whole Christian life" (§ 25).
4. "In baptism the Holy Spirit unites one with Christ, justifies, and truly renews the person," who "must all through life consistently look to God's unconditional justifying grace" and who is "not exempt from a lifelong struggle against the contradiction to God within the selfish desires of the old Adam" (§ 28). Lutherans understand this condition as being "at the same time righteous and sinner." However, on account of the merit of Christ, this sin "no longer brings damnation and eternal death" and is "no longer a sin that 'rules' the Christian for it is itself 'ruled by Christ' with whom the justified are bound in faith" (§ 29). "Catholics hold that the grace of Jesus Christ imparted in baptism takes away all that is sin 'in the proper sense' and that is 'worthy of damnation'" (§ 30). However, "an inclination (concupiscence) understood as the inclination that comes from sin and presses toward sin" remains (§ 30).
5. "Persons are justified by faith in the gospel 'apart from works prescribed by the law' (Rom 3:28)" (§ 31).

56

6. "The faithful can rely on the mercy and promises of God" (§ 34).
7. "Good works—a Christian life lived in faith, hope, and love—follow justification and are its fruits" (§ 37).

Remaining differences between Roman Catholics and Lutherans, which are subsumed under the consensus statements, include these:

1. Catholics speak of "cooperation" with God's grace, while Lutherans stress the "passivity" of human beings in the event of justification (§§ 20, 21).
2. Lutherans understand the grace of God especially as "forgiving love," while Catholics stress becoming justified, or the inner renewal of the human being through the reception of grace (§§ 23, 24).
3. Lutherans understand justification "by grace alone," while Catholics speak of the inner reception of the grace of justification in "faith, hope, and love" (§§ 26, 27).
4. For Lutherans, the justified person remains "at the same time righteous and sinner," while for Catholics, the inclination remaining in the baptized person toward evil (concupiscence) is not sin in an authentic sense (§§ 29, 30).
5. According to Catholic teaching, the good works of the justified—although a gift of grace—are at the same time merited, while on the Lutheran side, the "merit character" of these good works is denied (§§ 38, 39).
6. For Lutherans, trust in the promise of God's salvation includes the "certainty of salvation"; the Catholic Church rejects such a certainty of salvation (§§ 35, 36).
7. Lutherans distinguish between law and gospel, and Catholics stress the binding validity of the law for the justified (§§ 32, 33).

Affirmation of the JDDJ

The LWF sent the text to its member churches and national committees asking two questions: (1) whether the JDDJ shows "that a consensus in basic truths of the doctrine of justification exists between Lutherans and Catholics," and (2) whether "the condemnations in the Lutheran Confessions do not apply to the teaching of the Roman Catholic Church presented in this Declaration." At the time, there were 124 member churches of the LWF. Of these, 89 churches, representing 95 percent of the world LWF membership, responded: 80 with a "yes," and 5 with a "no." The remaining four answers were difficult to categorize.[70]

The Council of the LWF affirmed the *Joint Declaration* on June 16, 1998, by adopting a recommendation presented in the Report of its Standing Committee for Ecumenical Affairs.[71] Regarding the authority of the process, the report stated that the Lutheran affirmation of the *Joint Declaration* "is a result of a process involving both the action of the affirming churches and the action of the LWF Council."[72] It further recommended that "the agreements regarding the doctrine of justification as presented in the 'Joint Declaration' be affirmed, and that, on the basis of these agreements the doctrinal condemnations in the Lutheran confessional writings regarding justification be declared not to apply to the teaching of the Roman Catholic church as presented in the 'Joint Declaration.'"[73]

In spite of the overwhelmingly positive response of the churches, many German Lutherans, especially academic theologians, were highly critical of the document.[74] According to the 141 Protestant professors from both Reformed and Lutheran traditions who published an opinion in the *Frankfurter Allgemeine Zeitung,* the text of the JDDJ fails to do justice to these Protestant positions: the "decisive insight that belief is assurance of salvation," sin in the justified, the meaning of works after justification, the relationship of law and gospel, and the status of the doctrine of justification within church teaching. They also criticized the lack of Old Testament texts in the JDDJ and objected to the lack of any immediate ecumenical impact such as the recognition of the Lutheran churches as proper churches by the Catholic Church. Furthermore, the professors worried that the JDDJ is a step toward subsuming all Evangelical office holders into the Roman hierarchy. Thus, in their judgment, the text fails to reach a consensus.[75]

The official Catholic response was released June 25, 1998, nine days after the LWF's official affirmation of the central statements of the JDDJ. It also affirmed that a consensus on justification had been reached.[76] The "Catholic Response" consists of a two paragraph declaration affirming a "consensus on basic truths on the doctrine of justification" demonstrating "a high level of agreement," followed by six paragraphs of "Clarifications" and two paragraphs of "Prospects for Future Work." Unfortunately, the "Catholic Response" sent an ambiguous message regarding how much consensus had been achieved.

An assessment of the import of the "Catholic Response" must take into account three documents: the *Joint Declaration* itself; the press conference statement by Cardinal Edward Cassidy, then president of the Pontifical Council for Promoting Christian Unity; and the text of the "Catholic Response." Cardinal Cassidy's statement represents the most direct response of the Roman Catholic Church to the *Joint Declaration* when he says, "It is for me a pleasure and source of much satisfaction to present today a document declaring that a consensus on fundamental truths regarding the doctrine of justification has been reached in the dialogue between the Catholic Church and the Lutheran World Federation (§ 1)."[77] He adds, "The present joint declaration has this intention: namely, to show that on the basis of their dialogue the subscribing Lutheran churches and the Roman Catholic Church are now able to articulate a common understanding of our justification by God's grace through faith in Christ. It does not cover all that either church teaches about justification; it does encompass a consensus on basic truths of the doctrine of justification and shows that the remaining differences in its explication are no longer the occasion for doctrinal condemnations" (§ 6). Thus, Cardinal Cassidy announces that (1) a consensus has been reached and (2) on the basis of our common understanding of our justification, the remaining differences in its explication are no longer the occasion for doctrinal condemnation.

Although the "Catholic Response" asserts "a consensus on basic truths of the doctrine of justification" in the "Declaration" section, there is no mention of the nonapplicability of condemnations.[78] To the contrary, there is a conditional sentence stating, "If, moreover, it is true that in those truths on which a consensus has been reached the condemnations of the Council of Trent no longer apply, the divergences on other points must, on the contrary, be overcome before we can affirm, as is done generically in No. 41, that these points no longer incur the condemnations of the Council of Trent."[79] This sentence seems to indicate uncertainty whether the condemnations of the Council of Trent apply or not. This sentence's location in the "Clarifications" section of the response rather in the "Declaration" section is significant. Cardinal Ratzinger, in a letter to the *Frankfurter Allgemeine Zeitung* published on July 11, 1998, pointed out that only the "Declaration" is to be considered strictly as a response to the questions raised in the *Joint Declaration*. Thus, there was to be no question but that "there is a consensus in basic truths of the doctrine of justification." Nevertheless, this sentence more than any other in the "Catholic Response" seemed to negate the declaration of nonapplicability of the condemnations.

The primary issues raised by the "Clarifications" include (1) the meaning of *simul justus et peccator*, (2) the question of merit, (3) the doctrine of justification as sole criterion, (4) whether human beings are passive or whether they cooperate with grace, and (5) the authority of the consensus reached by the Lutheran World Federation.[80]

Because of its tone, the "Catholic Response" gives the impression of refuting what has been affirmed in the *Joint Declaration*. However, the criticisms of the "Catholic Response" do not always correlate directly with assertions in the *Joint Declaration*. For example, the "Catholic Response" states, "We cannot yet speak of a consensus such as would eliminate every difference between Catholics and Lutherans in the understanding of justification." The *Joint Declaration* itself acknowledges such differences, but affirms that these differences "are no longer the occasion for doctrinal condemnations" (§ 5). In fact, the very structure of the declaration, which consists of a positive common confession followed by two paragraphs of confessional understanding of the teaching, underlines the differences between the two churches. In a similar vein, the "Catholic Response" seems to understand that according to the *Joint Declaration*, these differences are merely of emphasis or language (§ 5). However, the differences of theological elaboration mentioned in the *Joint Declaration* (§ 40) can also be interpreted as differences of substance. The point is whether they are church-dividing or not and whether the differences are such that the condemnations of the sixteenth century apply to these differences today. The "Catholic Response" seems to have "total consensus" as a goal since it speaks of "the major difficulties preventing an affirmation of total consensus" (§ 1), while the *Joint Declaration* more modestly speaks of a "consensus in basic truths" with which the differing explications in particular statements are compatible (§ 14). This consensus in basic truths does not preclude further work to deepen the consensus already reached.

The ambivalent nature of the "Catholic Response" raised doubt on the part of Lutherans as to whether Catholics and Lutherans understood the *Joint Declaration* in the same way and what a mutual signing of it might signify. Lutherans and Catholics alike responded to the response with disappointment, dismay, and disillusionment. Calls for clarification by the Catholics were immediate. On June 25, the same day the "Catholic Response" was released, Dr. Ishmael Noko, LWF General Secretary, addressed the issue of the authority of the LWF process saying, "The authority of the LWF to speak in such a matter is based on its ability, affirmed in its constitution, to represent the churches in such matters as the churches assign to it."[81] He also noted the lack of clarity as to whether the condemnations of the Reformation era no longer applied to Lutherans and expressed hope that clarifications might be reached so that "the full intention of the 'Joint Declaration' might be accomplished."[82]

Cardinal Ratzinger, President for the Congregation of the Doctrine of the Faith (CDF), and Cardinal Cassidy, President of the Congregation for Promoting Christian Unity (PCPCU), as well as Bishop Pierre Duprey, Secretary of the PCPCU, and Bishop Karl Lehmann, President of the German Bishops' Conference, tried to reassure Lutherans on several occasions that the Catholic Church had accepted the *Joint Declaration*. They pointed to the different values to be attributed to the "Declaration," which affirmed a fundamental consensus, and the "Clarifications," which indicated points requiring further dialogue. The latter were not far from the LWF resolution, which had stated that dialogue needed to continue with respect to certain questions.[83]

It became clear that an additional step clarifying that both Lutherans and Catholics understood the agreements in the *Joint Declaration* in the same way was needed before a signing could take place. The solution eventually adopted was the construction of a supplementary statement elucidating the common understanding of the *Joint Declaration* that did not go beyond the agreements in the document, but which enabled a joint signing to proceed. Such a document posed particular difficulties for the Lutheran process since it was not feasible to send a new theological text to the LWF member churches for approval, as that would raise questions as to how this new text related to their earlier responses. Thus an additional text could only be affirmed if it were clear that it did not go beyond the *Joint Declaration*.[84] Dr. Noko proposed a very short formal joint endorsement of the *Joint Declaration*, later known as "Official Common Statement," to which would be attached an explanatory theological text, later known as the "Annex." The "Annex" was composed in the form of a compilation of biblical texts and quotations from confessional documents so that it would not need additional ratification by Lutheran member churches. In the midst of this and in spite of these mutual efforts, 243 Protestant theologians in Germany signed a statement expressing reservations as to whether a consensus was achieved.[85]

The Vatican approved the "Official Common Statement" and the "Annex" in May 1999, and Cardinal Cassidy wrote to Dr. Noko that he was authorized to sign the "Official Common Statement" together with the *Joint Declaration*. Dr. Noko announced, "Now it can be declared without reservation that the doctrinal condemnations which were set forth mutually by the Lutheran and Catholic sides at the time of the Reformation, do not apply to the teaching on justification by the two parties expressed in the *Joint Declaration*."[86] The *Joint Declaration on the Doctrine of Justification* was signed by representatives of the LWF and the Catholic Church on October 31, 1999, in Augsburg, Germany.[87]

Achievement of the JDDJ

The significance of the JDDJ is that for the first time since the Reformation schism, those Lutherans belonging to the Lutheran World Federation and Roman Catholics have a shared teaching on the doctrine of justification. Even though Lutherans and Roman Catholics have differing and sometimes divergent theological commitments with respect to justification and grace, this common teaching frames remaining differences on the doctrine of justification and robs them of their church-dividing potential while allowing for a diversity of emphasis and expression. All future joint dialogue takes this common teaching as both the point of departure and presupposition as Lutherans and Catholics continue to journey toward full communion.

Lutherans and Catholics had harbored deep suspicions of one another's doctrine of justification for five hundred years. When the Council of Trent defined justification as "not only remission of sins but also sanctification and the renewal of the inner person through voluntary reception of grace and gifts," it did not distinguish between justification (remission of sins) and God's transformation of the sinner (sanctification and the renewal of the inner person), a distinction strongly held by Lutherans.[88] This conflation of justification and sanctification does not clarify for Lutherans that "reception into God's grace or favor is the *foundation* of the Christian struggle for renewal, not its anxiously sought and uncertain *goal*."[89] Without this clarification, Lutherans fear that "our good works render us *more and more acceptable to God*, and are thus the real ground of our reception into eternal life."[90] This is nothing more than works-righteousness assisted by grace.

On the other hand, Catholics fear that Lutherans *separate* justification and sanctification in such a way that forgiveness and acceptance by God bear only a secondary and external relationship to any transformation of the sinner. Furthermore, Catholics fear that the Lutheran assurance of faith is an autonomous inwardness, a subjective belief abstractly held about oneself that becomes true simply because *I* believe it to be true. Thus chapter 9 of the Trent's decree titled "Against the vain confidence of the heretics" reflects this subjective interpretation when it admonishes, "It must not be said that anyone's sins are or have been forgiven simply because he has a proud assurance and certainty that they have been forgiven, and relies solely on that."[91]

If the truth be told, bad catechesis on the part of both Catholics and Lutherans has at times perpetuated these extreme and erroneous interpretations. Catholics need to recall to themselves and to their Protestant dialogue partner that Trent clearly taught that the first grace of justification is never merited and that merit only applies to an increase in justification and sanctification, what might be better expressed today as an ever deeper appropriation of a transformative relation to the Holy Spirit.[92] Lutherans need to remind themselves and their Catholic partners that justification by faith alone and assurance of salvation are embedded in embodied participation in the corporate life of the church and the means of grace through Word and Sacrament.[93]

The genius of the "Common Understanding" of the *Joint Declaration* lies in the trinitarian framework of the agreement on justification, which situates justification within the relationships of Father, Son, and Spirit and their attributed works. By situating justification within a trinitarian framework with Christ at the center, the *Joint Declaration* is able to distinguish justification and sanctification without separating them. When we enter into a relationship with Christ, by that fact, we are also related to the Father and to the Spirit. The work of the Father, forgiveness of sin and granting of righteousness and favor, is distinct but not separate from the work of the Spirit, transformation and inner renewal, just as the person of the Father is distinct but not separate from the person of the Spirit. Thus, as David Yeago expresses it, "Remission of sins" can be distinguished from "sanctification and the renewal of the inner person" as "the inseparable patrological and pneumatological concomitants of a christologically-focused faith."[94] Consequently, Catholics can affirm that justification is the *ground*, not the *goal* of sanctification, and Lutheran confidence in the Father's favor is inseparable from renewed life as the work of the Spirit. The "Common Understanding" in part 3 of the *Joint Declaration* thus provides the theological framework for Catholics to distinguish justification and sanctification and for Lutherans to connect them.[95]

The trinitarian framing of the consensus statement also provides the perspective and context for the resolution of remaining differences in the doctrine of justification enumerated in part 4. For example, section 4.1 on human powerlessness and sin in relation to justification is addressed in the first sentences of section 15 stating, "Justification is the work of the triune God. The Father sent his Son into the world to save sinners" and "the foundation and presupposition of justification is the incarnation, death, and resurrection of Christ." The preceding exposition demonstrates how both Catholics and Lutherans can affirm justification as both forgiveness of sin and making righteous (4.2, § 22). The primary content of the gospel message is precisely the Father sending the Son into the world to save sinners (§ 15). This grounds the primacy of Gospel in section 4.5, Law and Gospel. Obligation to the law follows from the Holy Spirit, "equipping and calling us to good works." The statement "By grace alone, in faith in Christ's saving work and not because of any merit on our part, we are accepted by God and receive the Holy Spirit, who renews our hearts while equipping and calling us to good works," directly correlates with 4.7, § 37 on the good works of the justified, in addition to addressing the question of transformational renewal in 4.2, § 22. Merit here cannot mean that we earn God's favor by our good works. Dialogue has shown that the Lutheran concept of faith is one that is "active in love" and includes hope (4.3, § 25).

Together we confess that we are justified "by grace alone, in faith in Christ's saving work" (§ 15). Some Lutherans may point out that this formula falls short of the traditional Lutheran "by faith alone" (§ 26). Here the question is what is added to faith or to what is the "alone" to be contrasted. As already seen, for Lutherans, faith has traditionally included love and hope. We have also seen that the context of faith is corporate ecclesial life where the gospel is preached in order that faith may respond. Baptism and Eucharist are sacraments of faith. A profession of faith is part of the liturgy of each, and faith, either personal or proxy in the case of baptism, is required for their graced reception. We've also seen that merit is not required for the first grace of justification. The "alone" in "by faith alone" appears to be a holdover from Reformation era polemics within a framework of supposed contrastive theologies. At best, it requires considerable nuancing and interpretation today.

One of the sticking points throughout the journey to the JDDJ was the issue of the justified as sinner (4.4). The final resolution is that in the JDDJ, Lutherans describe concupiscence as sin that does not "rule" the justified (§ 29). Thus, Lutherans in essence call concupiscence sin analogously. This means that although it is inconsistent with the will of God, it is not of the same order as sin, which definitively separates the Christian from God by bringing damnation and death "because in the daily return to baptism the person who has been born anew by baptism and the Holy Spirit has this sin forgiven" (§ 29).

Finally, Lutherans and Catholics agree on the objective trust-worthiness of Christ's promise of salvation and the subjective insecurity of looking at one's own weakness when assessing the assurance of salvation (4.6). The different emphases here between Lutherans and Catholics reflect the experiential perspective of the former, considering the relationship between a person and God to be one of direct address of promise and response in faith, and the sapiential interpretation of the latter, objectively taking into account the possibility of serious sin.

The consensus articulated in the *Joint Declaration* is "an indispensable criterion which constantly orients all the teaching and practice of our churches to Christ" (§ 18). As the Strasbourg Commentary explains, "This means that no teaching or practice of the church is to contradict the doctrine of justification as presented in the JD. Were such a contradiction to occur, then such a teaching or practice would be shown to be illegitimate.[96] The challenge of reception for both churches in preaching, teaching, and catechesis is to, first of all, make this consensus known, and then to ensure that all church activities are shaped by this joint agreement while banishing old stereotypes from our speech and instructional materials. Going forward in dialogue, subsequent bilateral conversations will take this consensus as a premise and seek to deepen its reception and to build on it.

Part II

A PRIMER OF
CONVERGENCE AND
DIFFERENCE

Chapter Three

Scripture, Interpretation, Tradition

One of the remarkable shifts in Roman Catholic/Lutheran relations that took place in the twentieth century involved a reevaluation of how to read historical documents. If, as was indicated in chapter 1, Renaissance humanism and its insistence on returning *ad fontes* (to the sources) shaped the contours of the struggle between Wittenberg and Rome, then the twentieth-century revolution in historical methods, begun already a century earlier, allowed an opening in ecumenical discussions not only to agree on important parts of the sixteenth century's historical record but also, perhaps even more importantly, to seek convergence on the biblical texts and hermeneutics that had been most hotly contested for four centuries or more.

ROMAN CATHOLIC AND LUTHERAN REEVALUATIONS OF MARTIN LUTHER AND THE REFORMATION

Chapter 1 ended with reference to Heinrich Denifle and Hartmann Grisar and their negative assessments of Luther constructed using some of the latest sources and scientific techniques. Roman Catholic interest in Luther, however, did not end there. In fact, the German church historian Josef Lortz (1887–1975) is widely credited with having ushered in a new era in Roman Catholic Luther research with his two-volume work, first published in 1949, *The Reformation in Germany*.[1] Lortz proposed that especially the early Luther was by and large Catholic in his perspective and rightly reacted against the semi-Pelagian (Luther's own word) Nominalist theology in which he had been trained. At the same time, in a theory sometimes labeled the "Lortz hypothesis," he argued that Luther would not have broken with the church had he known and been trained more thoroughly in the theology of Thomas Aquinas. This approach both bespoke a new openness to assessing the reformer's thought positively and indicated a willingness to criticize the late-medieval church out of which the Reformation arose. As the first director of the Institute for European History in Mainz, Lortz taught his successor in Mainz, Peter Manns, and Erwin Iserloh, both of whom continued careful research into Luther's theology and its late-medieval context.[2] The very subtitle of Manns's book, "Father in the Faith," indicates a remarkable sea change in Roman Catholic interpretation of Luther and the Reformation. English-speaking Roman Catholic historians carried on this same interest and blended Lortz's single-minded interest in historical texts with an ecumenical outlook determined to overcome the shibboleths of interpretations of Luther from the past.[3]

At the same time, shifts were taking place in Lutheran studies of the Reformation and Martin Luther as well. For one thing, the Dutch Reformation scholar, Heiko Augustinus Oberman, who taught at Harvard, Tübingen, and Arizona, produced a detailed analysis of Gabriel Biel's theology. He also trained a host of scholars determined to read the Reformation in the light of late-medieval thought.[4] Among German scholars, the early twentieth-century consensus that dated Luther's theological "breakthrough" to early in his career (before 1515) broke down to be replaced, first, by those arguing that Luther's theology left its late-medieval moorings in 1518 and, now, by a more complicated view of his theological development from 1509–1520.[5]

Both of these movements mirrored and, to some extent, supported changes among Roman Catholics. They did not bring to an end the more heroic depictions of Luther's life, but they did allow scholars to situate Luther more squarely within his late-medieval milieu and to view his work not as an invariable break with Rome and return to the pure teaching of Scripture but as development and struggle within the church over the fundamental issues of salvation and authority. This broader perspective on both sides allowed for a new assessment of the origins and intent of Luther's theology, especially as it developed between 1513 and 1520.[6]

THE HISTORICAL- AND LITERARY-CRITICAL METHODS OF BIBLICAL INTERPRETATION AND THEIR IMPACT UPON LUTHERAN/ ROMAN CATHOLIC DIALOGUE

At the same time that Luther and the Reformation were being evaluated outside of the immediate polemical debates arising from the sixteenth century (Tridentine Roman Catholicism and Orthodox, Confessional Lutheranism), a revolution was taking place among biblical interpreters that allowed for new approaches to the very scriptural passages over which so much ink had been spilt in the sixteenth century and beyond. This convergence in biblical method came about for the two communions following two very different paths.

Lutheranism: From Enlightened Skepticism and Liberalism to Biblical Theology

Because Lutherans do not look to a single magisterium by which to be guided and challenged, the movement among Lutherans from sixteenth-century interpretation of the Bible to the present may seem more arbitrary or serendipitous. Whatever their specific exegetical methods Lutherans have applied to the text over the centuries, however, certain hermeneutical principles, hardwired into the Lutheran Church's confessions and history, still played a role—sometimes an ancillary one and sometimes a central one. This suggests the dialogical nature of this development, as Lutherans continued to deepen their understanding of Scripture

71

while remaining (in their eyes at least) faithful to their confessions and to Martin Luther's own Scriptural insights.

When it comes to biblical interpretation, Lutheran exegetes always enjoyed a certain freedom regarding the interpretation of specific verses of the Bible. Already in a very early dispute between the (later antinomian) theologian John Agricola and Philip Melanchthon in 1527, when Agricola accused Melanchthon of interpreting a text in Galatians differently from Luther and, hence misinterpreting it, both Luther and Melanchthon responded with a sophisticated form of "So what?"[7] Indeed, this open approach to the interpretation of Scripture was hardly new, since the patristic and medieval commentaries on Scripture were filled with many and various interpretations for the literal meaning of individual passages—to say nothing of spiritual (or, allegorical) interpretations.[8] Moreover, it was not at all uncommon for interpreters to debate the meaning of a text, often calling upon past interpreters to support their views.

Yet this open-minded approach hardly meant anything goes. Indeed, many of the intra-Lutheran debates of the sixteenth century *did* revolve around the interpretation of specific texts of Scripture. Even here, however, theologians did not claim to rest their arguments on a single passage from the Bible.[9] What happened over time was the solidifying of a specifically Lutheran tradition for biblical interpretation, where many passages were interpreted over against Roman Catholic or Reformed theological positions.[10] From the beginning, however, the single-minded interest in the literal meaning of texts was accompanied by two sources for orthodox Lutheran hermeneutics: the distinction between law and gospel and an Aristotelian understanding of rhetoric and logic.[11]

The distinction between law (that shows sin, condemns, terrifies, and puts to death the old creature) and gospel (that reveals the savior, forgives, comforts, and brings to life the new creature of faith) arose from the notion that in Scripture, God's word works on its hearers to make them believers. Often in later Lutheran sermons and commentaries, this distinction shows up in comments about the terror or comfort that a particular text contains.[12]

At the same time, Lutherans also always understood that the biblical text itself was a literary text. Thus, they used the best tools for reading texts that they possessed. During the Reformation, this meant especially pressing the rhetorical and dialectical work of Cicero, Aristotle, and others into service. While all admitted that the philosophers could not understand, let alone believe, the message of the gospel, Lutheran exegetes—like their contemporary Reformed and Roman Catholic opponents—depended upon the basic work in grammar, rhetoric, and logic to understand what the biblical authors were trying to say.[13]

As Renaissance humanists, with their call to return *ad fontes* (to the original sources), Lutherans also insisted upon giving priority to the Greek and Hebrew texts of Scripture. Indeed, at the University of Wittenberg, the study of Greek and Hebrew coincided with the earliest stages of the Reformation. Thus, we discover that Luther's very earliest lectures on the Psalms (from 1513–15) and on the Pauline corpus (from 1515–18) used the work of Hebraists like Johannes Reuchlin, who had commented on the penitential psalms in Hebrew, and Greek scholars like Erasmus, whose first edition of the Greek New Testament appeared in 1516. When in 1518 the young but already renowned Greek scholar Philip Melanchthon was called to Wittenberg as professor of Greek, he immediately started lecturing on the Greek text of the New Testament. The German translation of the Bible published in Wittenberg, while not the first German version ever printed, was the first translated from the Hebrew and Greek originals.

A further contribution to early Lutheran understanding of Scripture was on the issue of authority—often abbreviated as the Lutheran claim of *sola Scriptura*, Scripture alone as authority in theology. The phrase itself, however, only came into widespread use later in the history of Lutheranism and first in the nineteenth century was it employed, along with *sola gratia* (grace alone) and *sola fide* (faith alone) as a slogan for Lutheran theology. Luther himself rarely used the term, and Philip Melanchthon seems never to have used it.[14] Moreover, when Luther used the term, it was never linked to an overall theory of its authority or inspiration but rather over against his opponents use of later papal or conciliar decrees to prop up what he viewed as "human laws."

Both Luther and Melanchthon insisted that, in addition to the priority of scriptural authority as—Melanchthon's words—the *primum et verum* (first and true [authority]), the creeds, the "fathers" of the early church, and the experience of faith were also essential authorities.[15] Later Lutheran thinkers sometimes distinguished between the Scripture as the *norma normans* (the norm norming [all other authorities]) and these other authorities as *norma normata* (norms normed [by Scripture]). It is unfortunate that even in ecumenical dialogues, some Lutherans have allowed the term *sola Scriptura* to define completely the far more complex relation to authority held by the reformers or their successors.[16] Scripture is self-interpreting, perspicuous, and efficacious, to be sure, but it is simply the written Word of God to be understood alongside the divine Logos and the proclaimed Word of God (oral and visible).

In the periods often designated as Lutheran Orthodoxy (1560–75) and Lutheran Pietism (1675–1750), the positions of Lutheran theologians, while resting upon their forebears in the faith, tended to mirror those of their Reformed cousins. Here, often using Aristotelian categories, theologians could insist upon Scriptural inerrancy and authority over against what they viewed as similar claims for the papacy made by their Roman opponents.[17] Commitment to careful study of languages and texts was never neglected, but Scripture's authority came to be seen as independent of Lutheran understanding of justification by faith (described in the nineteenth century as the formal and material principles of the Reformation). Although the heightened importance of experience in Lutheran Pietism left open another avenue to comprehending authority, by the eighteenth century, theologians of Orthodoxy and Pietism found themselves confronted with a new enemy, enlightened rationalism, and tended to emphasize biblical inspiration even more strongly.

The revolution in thought of the eighteenth century, usually designated as "the Enlightenment," brought with it tremendous pressure on Lutheran interpretations of the Bible. In what Hans Frei has designated the precritical world of Martin Luther and his followers, the historicity and natural science of texts were accepted almost without question.[18] During the Enlightenment, however, all of these cherished ideas came into question. At the same time, new modes of literary analysis opened new ways of viewing the Bible, especially the gospels, Genesis, and the Psalms. What is sometimes forgotten, however, is that this shift in interpretive methods was already implied in some of the earlier work of the reformers. For example, Philip Melanchthon had been the first Christian exegete to analyze Paul's letters as actual letters, employing the rules of rhetoric to organize and analyze the texts.[19] His student, Georg Major, noted that Philippians reads more like a friendly letter, jumping from topic to topic, than a well-worked out theological argument as one found in Romans.[20] Luther had notoriously questioned the apostolic authorship of James.[21] Thus, when in the early twentieth century, the Lutheran theologian and exegete Hermann Gunkel argued that the Psalms contained different genres of poetry, he could do so squarely within the Lutheran or even the broader Protestant tradition. Moreover, finding various sources in the biblical literature or even questioning the authorship of certain biblical writings was not unheard of.

What changed for Lutherans of this time was that these literary or historical theories also meant direct or indirect criticism of Christianity itself and of cherished Lutheran teachings about the centrality of faith in Christ for salvation. The very uniqueness of the Christian message was in danger of being subsumed under the Enlightenment's push for a worldwide religiosity shorn of its particularity. What might be termed a secularized version of the Vincentian Canon developed among "Enlightened" Christians who claimed that only beliefs accepted *semper, ubique, ab omnibus hominibus* (always, everywhere, and by all human beings, not just Christians) could be true.

Despite this pressure, Lutheran interpretation of Scripture did not disappear. Instead, the nineteenth century was marked, especially in Germany, by struggles between rationalists on the one side and a variety of Lutheran groups on the other, including those intent on invigorating Lutheran piety, others struggling to revitalize Lutheran orthodoxy, and still others developing a theological Liberalism. Movements in Denmark, led especially by Nikolai Grundtvig, sought to use baptism and the Apostles' Creed to return the church to its biblical and confessional roots. The piety of Word and Sacraments, central to Grundtvig's thinking, recovered a central Lutheran definition of the church.[22]

In Germany, the University of Erlangen became an especially important center for revitalizing Lutheran orthodoxy. Old Latin texts of sixteenth- and seventeenth-century theologians were excerpted and published in German and, later, English. The writings of the reformers, especially Luther, were now available in a critical Erlangen edition. With this orthodoxy (shorn of its Aristotelian roots) and in reaction to rationalism, came renewed interest by some in the inspiration of Scripture and its inerrancy and infallibility. But equally important was the continued use of Hebrew and Greek texts of Scripture and their interpretation within a Lutheran hermeneutic of law and gospel.

Liberalism (a theological movement in Germany in the late nineteenth century), represented by such thinkers as Albrecht Ritschl and Adolf von Harnack, also sought to answer rationalism's rejection of Christian theology, in part by using its methods.[23] The developing historical methods of biblical interpretation, far from undermining the Christian message, actually showed how Christianity itself was the culmination of religious thinking in Israel and later Judaism as it interacted with the dominant Greek culture. Then, too, questioning the authorship of certain Pauline texts, especially the Pastoral Epistles, could be placed within the developing early Catholicism and reflected historical issues and struggles also found in the apostolic fathers. Already the work of Ferdinand Christian Baur (1792–1860) at the University of Tübingen had paved the way for an approach to Scripture using the latest scientific tools and yet finally dismissive of the skepticism of Rationalism. He argued, following a kind of Hegelian dialectic, that second-century Christianity was a synthesis of Jewish and Gentile (Pauline) Christianity. Part of his historical and literary investigation led to a sharp reduction in the genuine Pauline letters to four (Romans, 1 and 2 Corinthians, and Galatians). Nevertheless, unlike his contemporary, David Friedrich Strauss (1808–74), whose *The Life of Jesus* radically stripped Jesus' life of the miraculous and mythical, Baur's work showed far more respect for the Christian tradition.

In the United States, Lutheran churches and their approaches to the Bible tended to be influenced far more by the deep piety of the German and Scandinavian immigrants and by the rehabilitation of Lutheran Orthodoxy undertaken by the Erlangen school. On the matter of Scriptural inspiration, nineteenth-century American Lutherans tended to be more conservative than their German or Scandinavian counterparts, especially in the groups that came to comprise the Wisconsin Evangelical Lutheran Synod and the Lutheran Church—Missouri Synod but also in other predominantly Midwestern churches. Under the influence of the struggles over

Scriptural inspiration being fought among American Presbyterians, Baptists, and Congregationalists, several American Lutheran churches added references in their constitutions to the inerrancy and infallibility of the Bible.

The twentieth-century movement toward a less restrictive view of biblical inspiration that nonetheless preserved a strong view of biblical authority emerged differently among different churches within the Lutheran communion.[24] On the Continent, for example, the dialectical theology movement and the strong influence of the Reformed theologian Karl Barth tipped the scales in favor of a more positive view of biblical authority as written Word of God always paired with the proclaimed Word. In the United States, first the United Lutheran Church in America (forerunner to the Lutheran Church in America [LCA] founded in 1962) allowed for the use of higher criticism in its seminaries already in the 1920s. The American Lutheran Church (TALC, founded in 1960), while having language about the inerrancy and infallibility of the Bible in its constitution, very quickly also began to teach and use critical methods for Scriptural interpretation, in large measure because its president, Fred Schiotz, arranged for professors of theology to tour the country explaining that the new method did not finally undermine scriptural authority. A similar movement in the Lutheran Church—Missouri Synod also took place in the 1960s but led instead in 1973 to the ouster of many faculty members from its seminary in St. Louis. The congregations, pastors, and teachers who left or were forced out of the Missouri Synod eventually formed the Association of Evangelical Lutheran Churches, which combined with the LCA and the ALC in 1987 to form the Evangelical Lutheran Church in America (ELCA). In its constitution, this church no longer had inerrant language, insisted upon a threefold definition of the Word of God (as Christ, proclaimed Word, and written Word), and referred to the Scripture as the authority and norm for faith and life.

Roman Catholicism: From Defense against Rationalism to Faithful Historical Criticism

The movement within Roman Catholicism toward acceptance of historical and literary methods of biblical interpretation may most easily be traced through a series of papal and conciliar pronouncements. On the one hand, these documents opened the way to a new understanding of Trent's championing of the Latin Vulgate and, on the other hand, they allowed for an acceptance of modern biblical interpretative methods without succumbing to rationalism.

The journey began with the encyclical of Leo XIII, *Providentissimus Deus*, from November 18, 1893. While still insisting on the use of the Vulgate publicly, it stated,

> At the same time, the other versions that Christian antiquity has approved should not be neglected, more especially the more ancient manuscripts. For although the meaning of the Hebrew and Greek is substantially [*ad summam rei*] rendered by the Vulgate, nevertheless wherever there may be ambiguity or want of clearness, the "examination of older tongues," to quote St. Augustine, will be useful and advantageous.[25]

Not only did this decree encourage the use of the original texts of Scripture, but it also reinterpreted Trent's decrees on the basis of the patristic tradition. Of course, in 1893, with Vatican I Council still ringing in the ears of the church's leaders, it was also necessary for this encyclical (DH 3281) to reiterate that council's insistence on the central role of the church and the "unanimous agreement of the Fathers" in interpretation. Yet it went on to insist (DH 3282) that "a wide field is still left open to the private student, in which his hermeneutical skill may display itself with signal effect and to the advantage of the Church," especially with texts not yet definitively interpreted or in setting forth already defined texts more clearly.

The encyclical also discussed a series of authorities—the analogy of faith, Catholic teaching, and the holy Fathers—and yet again opened the door to continuing research in the Scriptures (DH 3284). "But [the exegete] must not on that account consider that it is forbidden, when just cause exists, to push inquiry and exposition beyond [what the Fathers have done]." The reason is apparent in the next paragraph (DH 3285). "The authority of other Catholic interpreters is not so great; but the study of

Scripture has always continued to advance in the Church" both to explain difficulties and to refute assailants. Although in 1893 these assailants would surely have included Lutherans, in the light of the decree on ecumenism in *Lumen Gentium*, the "refutation of assailants" would come to mean those who accused the Roman Catholic Church of impeding unity between it and its separated brothers and sisters.

The upshot of this encyclical becomes clear when it opens the door to critical interpretation while still dismissing "'higher criticism,' that pretends to judge of the origin, integrity, and authority of each Book from internal indications alone."[26] It is the "alone" that expresses the worry of rationalism but, in the remaining sections, encourages Catholic interpreters to appreciate that the natural sciences and Scripture are not in conflict (par. 3287, p. 657): "There can never, indeed, be any real discrepancy between the theologian and the physicist." Here again the encyclical relies on Augustine (*De Genesi ad Litteram* II, 9, § 20) to emphasize that the Holy Spirit's inspiration of Scripture was not to reveal the secrets of nature but of salvation and, furthermore, restricted itself to the ways of speaking that the people of the time understood. Here Thomas Aquinas, who faced a similar problem in appropriating philosophy in a Christian manner, provided a way of distinguishing matters of faith from open questions of philosophy. This allows the encyclical in its final sections to insist upon the divine inspiration and inerrancy of Scripture while still pointing out that the inspired instruments of the Holy Spirit were mortals who could err, even when the Holy Spirit could not.

This encyclical did not prevent continued tension among Roman Catholic exegetes over the appropriate methods and conclusions that could be derived from Scripture. A second significant step came with the encyclical of September 30, 1943, *Divino Afflante Spiritu*, from Pope Pius XII. In the first place, this encyclical distinguished even more clearly Trent's support of the Vulgate and critical interpretation of Scripture. "Hence this special authority or, as they [the Tridentine fathers] say, *authenticity* of the Vulgate was not affirmed by the council particularly for critical reasons, but rather because of its use in the Churches throughout so many centuries."[27] The Vulgate then carries a juridical, not critical, authority, and the Tridentine decree did not forbid translations "directly from the original texts themselves." This encyclical went further in approving critical study of Scripture by defining more closely the difference between spiritual and literal senses of Scripture. While expressly basing its own arguments on *Providentissimus Deus* and allowing the full use of "historical, archaeological, philological, and other auxiliary sciences," the encyclical insists that such interpretation "not only aid the professors of theology…but may also be of assistance to priests…and, finally, may help all the faithful to lead a life that is holy and worthy of a Christian."[28] It is again the final goal, when read in the light of *Lumen Gentium*, that would push biblical interpreters toward ecumenical interpretations of disputed texts.

What follows is a clarion call to critical interpretation of biblical texts. "Let the interpreter, then, with all care and without neglecting any light derived from recent research, endeavor to determine the peculiar character and circumstances of the sacred writer, the age in which he lived, the sources written or oral to which he had recourse, and the forms of expression he employed."[29] The encyclical goes on to note especially the vast differences between writers and writings of the ancient Near East and today. Citing a passage from Thomas Aquinas's own interpretation of the biblical text for support, Pope Pius reminds the reader that "in Scripture divine things are presented to us in the manner that is in common use among human beings."[30] And then, in its own words, the encyclical states in no uncertain terms (par. 3831), "There is no reason why the Catholic commentator, inspired by an active and ardent love of his subject and sincerely devoted to Holy Mother Church, should in any way be deterred from grappling again and again with these difficult [exegetical] problems."

These two encyclicals, then, along with the contributions of countless Roman Catholic biblical interpreters, who risked criticism from members of their own communion, finally led to a decree of the Second Vatican Council, *Dei Verbum* (November 18, 1965). As a replacement for the proposed *De fontibus revelationis*, which amounted to little more than (in Denziger's words) "a canonization of Roman Scholastic theology," *Dei Verbum* provided unequivocal support for the critical interpretation of Scripture in the service of the faith of the Church.

The dogmatic constitution begins by emphasizing God's work in bringing people to faith, citing the Synod of Orange: "To make this act of faith, the grace of God and the interior help of the Holy Spirit must precede and assist, moving the heart and turning it to God, opening the eyes of the mind and giving 'joy and ease to everyone in assenting to the truth and believing it.'"[31] It then defines the purpose of revelation: "Through divine revelation, God chose to show forth and communicate himself and the eternal decisions of his will regarding the salvation of human beings. That is to say, he chose to share with them those divine treasures that totally transcend the understanding of the human mind."[32]

While continuing to describe the handing on of divine revelation in terms of both the written Scripture and sacred Tradition— described (par. 4208) as "a mirror in which the pilgrim Church on earth looks at God"—*Dei Verbum* nevertheless states that "the apostolic preaching, which is expressed in a special way in the inspired books, was to be preserved by an unending succession [of preachers] until the end of time." It also explains Tradition in terms of "a growth in the understanding of the realities and the words that have been handed down," a growth that takes place through "contemplation and study." This growth moves toward "the fullness of divine truth." This explicit norming of Tradition by study and by truth itself will also play a significant role in ecumenical rapprochement. The specific Tradition of the church fathers is also specifically defined as "witness to the presence of this living tradition, whose wealth is poured into the practice and life of the believing and praying Church." The Tradition functions to understand more deeply the Scriptures themselves through the work of the Trinity in the Church.[33] In this connection of Scripture and Tradition, the Church's teaching authority also plays a central role. Yet *Dei Verbum* makes clear (par. 4214) that "this teaching office is not above the Word of God, but serves it, teaching only what has been handed on, listening to it devoutly, guarding it scrupulously, and explaining it faithfully in accord with a divine commission and with the help of the Holy Spirit."

Out of these two basic chapters ("Revelation Itself" and "Handing on Divine Revelation"), the remaining sections arise. First, chapter 3 ("Sacred Scripture, Its Inspiration and Divine Interpretation") reiterates many of the points made in the encyclicals of Leo XIII and Pius XII and refers directly to them for support. Thus, it concludes that "the interpreter must [*oportet*] investigate what meaning the sacred writer intended to express and actually expressed in particular circumstances by using contemporary literary forms in accordance with the situation of his own time and culture."[34] At the same time, it also insists upon a canonical framework for interpretation but—making a point not found in the preceding encyclicals—in a way that respects God's "marvelous 'condescension' of eternal wisdom...'that we may learn the gentle kindness of God...and how far he has gone in adapting his language with thoughtful concern for our weak human nature.'"[35]

After two chapters outlining the basics of the Old (chap. 4) and New (chap. 5) Testaments and thus paving the way for open, critical analysis, a final chapter (6) concentrated on "Sacred Scripture in the Life of the Church."[36] Translations from the original languages—even those "produced in cooperation with the separated brethren as well"—are encouraged, as is study of the church fathers of East and West. Biblical study, by which (par. 4231) "theology is most powerfully strengthened and constantly rejuvenated," is even labeled "the soul of sacred theology." Such study is urged not just upon scholars but all clergy and, indeed (par. 4232), "all the Christian faithful," whom the bishops must provide with suitable instruction and proper translations "with the necessary and really adequate explanations."[37]

The result of *Dei Verbum* and the papal encyclicals that preceded it has shown its influence, in the first place, in the subsequent statements of Pope Paul VI. For example, in the "Instruction of the Pontifical Biblical Commission (*Sancta Mater Ecclesia*) on April 21, 1964, while still warning against rationalism, seems far more concerned to emphasize the historical nature of the biblical documents, concluding, "Unless the exegete pays attention to all these things that pertain to the origin and composition of the Gospels and makes proper use of all the laudable achievements of recent research, he will not fulfill his task of probing into what the sacred writers intended and what they really said."[38]

Another result of *Dei Verbum* may be seen in the widely respected *Jerome Biblical Commentary* of 1968.[39] Dedicated to Pope Pius XII and his promotion of biblical studies and graced with a quote from *Dei Verbum*, it begins with a preface by Augustin Cardinal Bea, SJ, a member of the Pontifical Biblical Commission and president of the Secretariat for Promoting Christian Unity.

There he makes explicit the crucial link between the renewal of biblical studies and ecumenism.

> Thus, by putting the reader himself in contact with the Written Word of God, *The Jerome Biblical Commentary* makes a real contribution toward realizing the goal firmly insisted upon in the constitution on Divine Revelation of Vatican II (#22): "It is necessary that the faithful have full access to Sacred Scripture." Nor can there be any doubt that this work will also be a fruitful contribution to the great cause of ecumenism; for as the conciliar decree on Ecumenism (#21) has said: "In the dialogue [with our non-Catholic brethren] Sacred Scripture makes an excellent tool in the powerful hand of God for the attainment of that unity which the Savior offers to all men."[40]

It is no accident that among the editors of this volume was Joseph Fitzmyer, SJ, who working alongside his Lutheran colleague on the US Lutheran-Roman Catholic Dialogue, John Reumann, found new convergences in the interpretation of St. Paul in general and his doctrine of justification by faith in particular.

The *Joint Declaration on the Doctrine of Justification* well expresses the contribution of biblical interpretation in Lutheran–Roman Catholic conversations. "The Lutheran churches and the Roman Catholic Church have together listened to the good news proclaimed in Holy Scripture. This common listening, together with the theological conversations of recent years, has led to a shared understanding of justification." This joint listening, unobstructed by the barriers and condemnations of the past and yet consonant (for both parties) with their traditions and confessions, forms the heart of the convergence on the doctrine of justification.

"The Righteousness of God" and Ecumenical Convergence

The examples of convergence in and conversation about the meaning of biblical passages between Roman Catholics and Lutherans are countless. Narrowing the field to the New Testament's, especially Paul's, exposition of justification by faith provides a helpful case study for this work and highlights the efforts of two exegetes, Joseph Fitzmyer and John Reumann, in this discussion, especially as it developed in the US Lutheran-Roman Catholic Dialogue, an important early step toward JDDJ.

The US dialogue's report, *Justification by Faith*, includes in its background papers Joseph Fitzmyer's article, "Justification by Faith and 'Righteousness' in the New Testament." He points out that "the common statement on 'Justification by Faith' presented in this volume would undoubtedly never have seen the light of day were it not for the modern Catholic biblical movement and its advocacy of a mode of biblical interpretation that had been dear to the hearts of many Lutheran interpreters for decades."[41] He also alludes to the background paper of John Reumann and the responses by Fitzmyer and Quinn, published separately as *"Righteousness" in the New Testament: "Justification" in the United States Lutheran—Roman Catholic Dialogue.*[42]

This book demonstrates precisely how modern biblical exegesis has served ecumenical dialogue and ecclesial rapprochement. Reumann's book begins with an overview of the Old Testament background, pointing to the central role that *zedek* played for Old Testament writers. Especially using the work of Henning Graf Reventlow, Reumann notes how this author eschews individualistic, introspective, and covenantal understandings of the term—this alone is a step forward in shedding certain Pietist and Reformed views of justification that stood in the way of an ecumenical understanding.[43] Whatever its weaknesses, Reventlow shows that the roots of New Testament understanding of the term lie in the Old Testament itself.

In the same section, Reumann also deals with Jesus' use of the term. Here he argues, on the basis of work by Eberhard Jüngel, that both Jesus and Paul insist on giving an eschatological nuance to the word (and the related term, *kingdom of God*), although Jesus is looking forward and Paul looks to Christ, especially faith in Jesus Christ, so that justification is "a theological interpretation of the faith-event."[44]

In order to set aside the objection that concentration on justification is a peculiarly Pauline way of reading the Gospel of the New Testament, Reumann devotes a chapter to teasing out portions of the pre-Pauline faith that nevertheless also use the concept. This proposal, supported by Roman Catholic exegetes, provides an important step forward in ecumenical conversation about justification. "Justification/righteousness terminology first appears in primitive Christianity not in the original work of some one theologian like Paul but as part of the common apostolic faith."[45]

In the section of the work dedicated to Paul, Reumann distinguishes between the accepted Pauline literature (letters written to churches in Rome, Galatia, Corinth, Philippi, and Thessalonica) and deutero-Pauline material (Colossians, Ephesians, and the Pastorals). By this time, both Roman Catholic and Lutheran scholars accepted this division, although Reumann allows room for those who assume that all were written by Paul. As in the previous section, Reumann had to refute the notion that Paul first uses the language of justification after encountering "Judaizers," because this would make the Lutheran position aberrant by "perpetuating the importance" of a minor part of Paul's theology.[46] Paul shared his understanding of justification with his Jewish–Christian opponents, Reumann claims. They differed only on the question of the doctrine's implications for Gentile Christians. He also rejects the notion of progression in Paul's thought (from the early correspondence with Philippi and Corinth to the Epistle to the Romans). "His eschatology emphasizes the decisive thing that God has done in Christ (which Paul can variously describe with regard to the cross and resurrection), and it regularly looks forward to a consummation to come....It is in this consistent theological stance of his...that righteousness/justification plays such a major role."[47]

After brief discussion of other Pauline correspondence, Reumann then focuses on three letters (Philippians, Galatians, and Romans). The complexities of the argumentation need not detain us here, but one important section involves the translation of the verb *dikaioo* as either "pronounced righteous" (and, thus, supporting a Lutheran reading) or "made righteous." Here Reumann and Fitzmyer come into direct conversation. In the latter's commentary on Galatians in *The Jerusalem Bible*, Fitzmyer argued that "it may mean no more than 'is pronounced upright,' if understood by its LXX usage; but Pauline usage seems to demand more, 'is made upright,' implying a new, ontological principle of activity for the new creature."[48] Reumann responds (with the Lutheran exegete

Hans Dieter Betz) by splitting the difference, "being justified" but in a declarative sense.[49] He also describes Paul's handwritten conclusion to Galatians, where the law and Christ's cross are placed in opposition, in this way: "What Lutherans seek to defend by the gospel of justification by grace through faith is here articulated in other terms."[50]

Skipping over the discussion of Philippians, it is especially Romans that merits attention. Reumann argues, "'The righteousness of God is revealed through faith for faith' [Rom 1:16–17] is the gospel and theme of Romans."[51] The problem, however, is in how Paul is defining this righteousness *of God*. Although Paul focuses on this term in Romans 3:21–31, his use of traditional phrases and brevity of expression still makes interpretation difficult. Using the arguments of Ernst Käsemann, Reumann argues that "the forensic declaration also means, because the power of God is involved, 'to be made righteous'…, but this 'righteousness of God' is, in the time before the judgment 'the righteousness of faith,' which, as obedience, has a 'no longer…not yet' character."[52] This excludes an interpretation of righteousness in terms of *habitus* but (citing Käsemann) "a right relation of the creature to the Creator" and "eschatologically transformed existence."[53]

A final section of the chapter titled, "The Pauline School," looks at alternatives to justification/righteousness as Paul's chief theme, using suggestions listed by Fitzmyer in *The Jerome Bible Commentary*. Reumann argues that despite their attractiveness, "the soundness of the Reformation choice in this perspective and the soundness of our contention that while righteousness/justification is by no means the only way to express Paul's message, the case for regarding it as the central one remains a persuasive one."[54] Reumann even rejected the proposal of the Lutheran professor and, later, Swedish bishop, Krister Stendahl, who wanted to replace justification with "salvation history," a particularly popular theme among Reformed biblical commentators. Reumann notes that salvation history arises from Paul's understanding of justification and *not* the other way around.[55]

After a substantial examination of other parts of the New Testament witness, Reumann then offers his reflections. First, he dismisses the notion that Lutherans operate with a "canon within the canon," showing that it was not true for the Lutheran confessional documents or even, rightly understood, for Luther. Instead, Lutherans have interpreted Scripture from its "middle." Moreover, Reumann cites *The Jerome Biblical Commentary* to the effect that "in practice the Church does not accept the whole NT as equally normative."[56] He then summarizes the "Lutheran claim": "Assuming that the word of God, in particular the gospel of God, stands supreme over the church (and Scripture, too), and that the apostolic gospel is preeminently witnessed to in the NT...we are confronted repeatedly, at least for each age or generation, with the task of stating as clearly as possible what this gospel/word of God is according to the NT."[57] Lutherans have been accustomed to seeing the center of that gospel in justification. This has meant that "they have been too quick at times to read justification-terms into other biblical writings and have used it in a heavy-handed way as a standard. But their experience has been that justification *sola fide propter Christum* [by faith alone on account of Christ] has served well in keeping God's work in Christ uppermost."[58]

> The conclusion of this paper is that the prevalence of righteousness/justification thought, even and especially when viewed under the impact of modern biblical scholarship, is even more impressive than the sixteenth-century confessors probably assumed, and certainly more varied than most Lutherans have realized. Appropriate to each document where such terms occur, and as the prime expression of "gospel" in the NT's first major theologian, Paul..., it has a sound claim for centrality in Scripture. To this extent it functions as *Mitte* [center] and Norm, directly in some parts of the NT and indirectly in others.[59]

Lutherans, Reumann concludes, like the hedgehog mentioned by the Greek poet Archilochus, know "one big thing," namely, justification by grace through faith on account of Christ.

Perhaps the most remarkable part of the book comes in Fitzmyer's response. Instead of picking a fight with a Lutheran opponent (as might have happened in the past), Fitzmyer's ecumenical methodology comes to the fore, as throughout his essay, he points to areas of convergence. Citing the Malta Report, he agrees

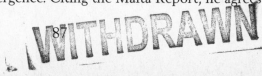

that "the gospel stands as norm and rule over the church, Ministry and ministries, bishops, councils, pope, and all the life of God's people."[60] Then, Fitzmyer agrees that (citing from the Lutheran [!] Formula of Concord) "justification/salvation 'rests solely on "the entire Christ" in his obedience, not on our love or virtues; it means forgiveness of sins, and also repentance, with love and good works following.'"[61] He even concedes that, properly understood, justification is equivalent to "*regeneratio, vivificatio,* even reconciliation, salvation, forgiveness of sins" in that "all these aspects of the relationship between God and human beings come ultimately from God himself (who is the sole origin of that relationship) through the work of Christ and his Spirit/grace."[62]

When he turns to the biblical arguments, he agrees largely with Reumann's summary of the Old Testament and of Jesus' own statements. He also, with some reservations, admits that justification "as an effect of the Christ-event" may be found in pre-Pauline material.[63] Turning to Galatians, Fitzmyer finds himself in agreement with most of what Reumann proposes but asks for more information about the tension between declared/made righteous in translating *dikaioun*. His question helped to shape the dialogue's subsequent conversation. "Is God's word, spoken in a verdict of acquittal, efficacious or not, i.e., does it terminate or not in a real change in the human beings so addressed? Or…is the 'power'…of the righteous God effective in his declaration?"[64] He also addresses the problem in Pauline interpretation of the relation between faith and love.

With Romans, the agreements are even more striking. Reumann, in a departure from the standard Lutheran interpretation, suggested that in Romans 1:17, the phrase "righteousness of God" is a subjective genitive (i.e., an attribute of God), and Fitzmyer agrees, while insisting that such a quality "must be understood as the dynamic power in God effecting through Christ's cross the justification of human beings."[65] Although Fitzmyer is skeptical about a cosmic side to Paul's understanding of justification, he insists that it is thoroughly corporate and thus not reducible to individualism. Although the jury is still out on the "I" in Romans 7, both Reumann and Fitzmyer agree that (despite Augustine, Thomas Aquinas, and Luther) it should not be construed as referring to the Christian's existence (and thus does not prove the Lutheran *simul iustus et peccator* [at the same time righteous and sinner]).[66]

Perhaps the most interesting contribution Fitzmyer makes comes in his reaction to Reumann's analysis of "Some Alternative Central Themes in Paul." Here Fitzmyer agrees that justification is the central theme in Romans, Galatians, and parts of Philippians and that it is an "inalienable constituent of Paul's theology."[67] He only takes issue with the centrality of "Christ" in Paul's theology—concepts borrowed from the early Christian tradition, to be sure, but nevertheless central for Paul as well. For him, the effects of the Christ-event would give pride of place to justification but include many other categories as well. (In this regard, he also rejects E. P. Sanders's claims to find the center of Paul's theology in "eschatological participation in Christ.")

Fitzmyer also agrees with Reumann's assessment of James as an attempt at a later corrective of early Christianity—not directly of Paul but of a caricature of Pauline teaching: "Not only have I nothing basic to criticize in [Reumann's] treatment of this epistle, but I was pleasantly surprised to find that he as a modern Lutheran NT interpreter would come so close to my own Roman Catholic understanding of it."[68] If this represented an important convergence, then so did Fitzmyer's analysis of Reumann's comments on canon and authority. Here, the clarity of *Dei Verbum* and its freeing effect for Roman Catholic interpretation would seem to have allowed for a renewed appreciation of the centrality of the gospel or Word of God in Scripture. Fitzmyer takes some exception to labeling justification as "the exemplary expression of the gospel" and prefers instead to call it "an exemplary expression of the Pauline gospel."[69] And he, like his collocutor Jerome D. Quinn, insists that the question of merit and reward needs separate studies.[70]

This somewhat detailed analysis of a single exchange between two well-known exegetes proves how convergence in biblical method assisted in the movement toward rapprochement on the doctrine of justification between the Lutheran churches and the Roman Catholic Church. When the collocutors agree that "our entire hope of justification and salvation rests on Christ Jesus and on the gospel whereby the good news of God's merciful action in Christ is made known: we do not place our ultimate trust in anything other than God's promise and saving work in Christ,"[71] one can hear echoes of the exegetical convergence underneath it, brought out explicitly in the first part of chapter 3, "The Biblical Data."[72]

The fruits of this early work also had an impact on later studies and, finally, on the tone and organization of the JDDJ. It begins with a section titled, "Biblical Message of Justification" and professing, "Our common way of listening to the word of God in Scripture has led to such new insights."[73] The variety of treatments of justification (§ 9) and Paul's perspective (§§ 10–11) manage to blend the insistence on the declarative understanding of justification with God's (effective) power. It goes further than Fitzmyer in declaring that justification *is* the forgiveness of sins (§ 11). Section 12 offers a particularly succinct version of this exegetical convergence:

> The justified live by faith that comes from the Word of Christ (Rom 10:17) and is active through love (Gal 5:6), the fruit of the Spirit (Gal 5:16–21). But since the justified are assailed from within and without by powers and desires (Rom 8:35–39; Gal 5:15–21) and fall into sin (1 Jn 1:8, 10), they must constantly hear God's promises anew, confess their sins (1 Jn 1:9), participate in Christ's body and blood, and be exhorted to live righteously in accord with the will of God.[74]

"The Common Understanding of Justification" also continues to echo this exegetical convergence. It insists that God accepts us "by grace alone, in faith in Christ's saving work and not because of any merit....Through Christ alone are we justified, when we receive this salvation in faith. Faith is itself God's gift through the Holy Spirit, who works through Word and Sacrament." Finally, it states, "We also share the conviction that the message of justification directs us in a special way toward the heart of the New Testament witness to God's saving action in Christ: it tells us that because we are sinners our new life is solely due to the forgiving and renewing mercy that God imparts as a gift and we receive in faith, and never [!] can merit in any way."[75] The presence of what sixteenth-century Lutherans called *particulae exclusivae* [exclusive phrases]—"grace *alone*," "Christ *alone*" and "*never* can merit"—are the results of this careful listening to God's word.[76]

UNDERSTANDING "TRADITION"

The ecumenical question of the Lutheran and Catholic position on Tradition was succinctly posed by the US statement, *Scripture and Tradition: Lutherans and Catholics in Dialogue IX*: "In the wake of Vatican II the question between Lutherans and Catholics amounts to this: Is the permanent interconnection between Scripture, tradition, and magisterium that is envisaged in Catholic thought compatible with the historic Lutheran principle that Scripture alone provides the norm by which tradition and magisterium are to be judged?"[77]

Two particular branches of the critical approach to Scripture, combined with ongoing analysis of fifteenth-century historiography, impacted Roman Catholic and Lutheran discussions of tradition. Form criticism, championed by Lutheran interpreters such as Rudolf Bultmann and Martin Dibelius, assumed the priority of the oral tradition. Then, too, source criticism, used by a wide variety of exegetes, assumed that especially the New Testament books were far more the product of later redaction than the *ipsissima verba* of either Jesus or the apostles. Suddenly, at least for the earliest church, Lutherans could no longer simply pit "tradition" over against "Scripture." At the same time, a simplistic understanding of apostolic authorization of doctrine could no longer explain either the earliest church's "authority" in passing on the words and deeds of Jesus or the "authority" of the anonymous biblical writers who shaped the final documents.

Strides were being made in understanding the nature of Tradition itself. On the ecumenical front, a highly regarded report from the Fourth World Conference on Faith and Order distinguished between traditions and Tradition. "By *the Tradition* is meant the Gospel itself, transmitted from generation to generation in and by the Church, Christ himself present in the life of the Church. By *tradition* is meant the traditionary process. The term *traditions* is used in two senses, to indicate both the diversity of forms of expression and also what we call confessional traditions."[78] This report influenced subsequent discussions at the Second Vatican Council and later ecumenical conversations between Lutherans and Roman Catholics.[79]

At the same time, careful work on the debate between conciliarists and curialists in the fifteenth century has emerged in which the limitations of papal infallibility were being clarified, since any papal decree had to respect the authority of the entire Tradition as a *sine qua non* for its own authority. Lutherans became aware that certain caricatures of the doctrine of papal infallibility, so prevalent for four hundred years, actually misconstrued the way this doctrine worked with Tradition to restrict papal authority. It is not without some irony that one of Luther's oft-repeated complaints (that teaching in the church for the past four hundred years had abandoned its authoritative sources) arose out of the same concern for restricting Christian doctrine to what the church (in his opinion) had traditionally taught.[80]

In the *Apology of the Augsburg Confession* of 1531, Philip Melanchthon objected to his opponents' distinction between particular and universal rites in the matter of church unity (discussed in article 7 of the Augsburg Confession). He wrote, "We do not quite understand what our opponents want. We are speaking about a true unity, that is, a spiritual unity, without which there can be no faith or righteousness in the heart before God. For this unity we say that it is not necessary to have similar human rites, whether universal or particular."[81] The question of rites or traditions, so important in sixteenth-century debates, does not gainsay the fact that Lutherans did not then and do not now deny the necessary presence in the church of traditions. Rather, the question today may find new orientation in accepting a variety of authorities within the church. To the unassailable authority of Scripture, Lutherans have always given authority to ancient creeds and past teachers as witnesses to the truth of God's Word in Scripture. This latter authority is, on the one hand, derived from Scripture—the creeds and teachers are, after all, *witnesses*, but on the other hand, it is a direct authority of the church's very experience and encounter with the Word of God in new and different times and places. Thus, the experience of the gospel and its comfort, which article 20 of the Augsburg Confession invokes as an authority, is precisely the kind of authority encountered in Tradition.[82]

Scripture and Tradition in Catholic Teaching

In order to maintain the purity of the gospel, the Council of Trent at its fourth session (1546), in its decree on the acceptance of the sacred books and apostolic traditions, endorsed as normatively traditional the Nicene-Constantinopolitan creed (with the *filioque*) and the Scriptures in the Latin Vulgate edition (based on the Septuagint, the Greek translation of the Jewish Scriptures), according to the interpretation held "by holy mother church, whose function is to pass judgment on the true meaning and interpretation of the sacred scriptures." The Council said that the gospel, first proclaimed by the lips of Jesus Christ, is "the source of the whole truth of salvation and rule of conduct (*fontem omnis et salutaris veritatis et morum disciplinae*)." It continued, saying, "This truth and rule are contained in written books and in unwritten traditions which were received by the apostles from the mouth of Christ himself, or else have come down to us, handed on as it were from the apostles themselves at the inspiration of the holy Spirit." The final point of the paragraph is that "the council accepts and venerates with a like feeling of piety and reverence all the books of the old and new Testament...as well the traditions concerning both faith and conduct, as either directly spoken by Christ or dictated by the holy Spirit, which have been preserved in unbroken sequence in the catholic church."[83] This text requires several points of interpretation and clarification.

Although at times the Catholic Church has been said to ascribe to a two-source theology of revelation, the text actually points to one source, namely Jesus Christ. The text speaks of the *source*, not sources, of the whole truth of salvation and rule of conduct. *Source* here means originating point, but its etymology is actually that of "wellspring," as in the source of a stream of water. From this one wellspring, or source, flow two streams, namely Scripture and Tradition. Both, as it were, flow from the mouth of Christ, the one source. ("This truth and rule are contained in written books and in unwritten traditions which were received by the apostles from the mouth of Christ himself.")

The metaphor system of the text centers on the evocative use both of "wellspring" and "source" and also of "mouth." It speaks of the gospel "proclaimed with his [Christ's] own lips," "this

93

truth and rule...received from the mouth of Christ himself," and of Scripture and traditions "spoken by Christ or dictated by the holy Spirit." The "wellspring" and "source" are equated with the "mouth" of Christ. Christ's mouth is the wellspring from which issues forth Scripture and Tradition. Such an evocative and poetic use of language is not usually associated with conciliar texts. The text of Trent supports a one-source theory of revelation, not a two-source theory. This one source is neither Scripture nor Tradition, but Christ himself.

Trent left open the disputed theological question of the sufficiency of Scripture, that is, whether or not all the truths of the Christian faith are in some way present in Scripture. It did this by avoiding saying that revelation was *partly* found in Scripture and *partly* in Tradition (*partim...partim*), which was one of the earlier redactions of the text. Instead, the text says, "This truth and rule are contained in written books *and* in unwritten traditions" (*et... et*). This meant that a Catholic could believe that every aspect of Catholic faith or practice has some relation to Scripture and is therefore not based exclusively in Tradition. Such a position is closer to the traditional view of Protestants.

In 1965, the Dogmatic Constitution on Divine Revelation (*Dei Verbum*), promulgated by the Second Vatican Council, expanded the teaching on Scripture and Tradition and taught that Christ himself is both the mediator and fullness of all revelation (§ 2). This recast the notion of revelation in personal terms, which also had an impact on the notion of faith. A personal commitment to Jesus Christ took precedence over intellectual assent to "eternal decrees of God's will." Both God's self-manifestation and the eternal decrees of God's will are mentioned in chapter 1 of *Dei Verbum* (§ 2), but Christ as the fullness of revelation is mentioned in the first section of that chapter and God's eternal decrees are mentioned in the final section of the chapter (§ 6). The pattern of revelation "unfolds through deeds and words bound together by an inner dynamism," God's works showing forth and confirming the doctrine, and the realities signified by the words proclaiming and throwing light on the meaning hidden in works (§ 2).

The council affirmed that apostolic teaching "is expressed in a special way in the inspired books" (§ 8). That which "has been handed down from the apostles includes everything that helps the people of God to live a holy life and to grow in faith" (§ 8). All that the church is and all that it believes, that is, Tradition in its broadest sense, is handed on to every generation "in its teaching, life, and worship" (§ 8). In other words, beliefs are not just notional disembodied ideas, but are embedded in the life and activities of the church. This Tradition is growing and dynamic, developing through contemplation, study, and preaching. Tradition is necessary for the transmission and interpretation of the Scriptures. The interpretation of Scripture is entrusted to the church's teaching function, which "is not above the word of God but stands at its service, teaching nothing but what is handed down" (§ 10). The ruling function of Scripture is expressed in article 21, which says, "All the church's preaching, no less than the whole Christian religion, ought to be nourished and ruled by holy scripture." The council concludes, "Tradition, scripture, and the church's teaching function are so connected and associated that one does not stand without the other, but all together, each in its own way, subject to the action of the one holy Spirit contribute effectively to the salvation of souls" (§ 10).

Dei Verbum confirms the one source of theology Scripture and Tradition saying, "Tradition and scripture together form a single sacred deposit of the word of God, entrusted to the church.... All that is proposed for belief, as being divinely revealed is drawn from the one deposit of faith" (§ 10). It picks up the language and imagery of Trent, where it describes the relationship between Scripture and Tradition:

> Hence sacred tradition and scripture are bound together in a close and reciprocal relationship. They both flow from the same divine wellspring, merge together to some extent, and are on course toward the same end. Scripture is the utterance of God as it is set down in writing under the guidance of God's Spirit; tradition preserves the word of God as it was entrusted to the apostles by Christ our lord and the holy Spirit, and transmits it to their successors, so that these in turn, enlightened by the Spirit of truth, may faithfully preserve, expound, and disseminate the word by their preaching. (§ 9)

95

None other than Joseph Ratzinger, in his commentary on *Dei Verbum*, noted that the text missed an opportunity to mention the possibility that at times a particular tradition may distort the Gospel, and that Scripture can and must be an element in the church that is critical of tradition.[84] If the church "is at one and the same time holy and always in need of purification" (*sancta simul et semper purificanda*, LG § 8), there must be a mechanism for ecclesial correction and a principle governing that correction. This is where the normative function of Scripture comes into play with respect to Tradition. Had this been included in the text, it would have brought a closer ecumenical consensus since Lutherans do not deny the interpretative function of Tradition, but give Scripture a critical function that makes possible an *Ecclesia semper reformanda* (church that always ought to be reformed).

One of the teachings of both Trent and *Dei Verbum* troubling to ecumenical partners is the statement that Scripture and Tradition are venerated with "a like feeling of piety and reverence" (*pari pietatis affectu ac reverentia*) according to Trent, and accepted and honored "with like devotion and reverence" according to Vatican II (*pari pietatis affectu ac reverentia*).

First, it must be noted that the council recognizes that not all traditions are equal. Some are apostolic; others are ecclesiastical. Trent referred to "traditions" in the plural and sought to defend the authority of long-standing traditions of faith and practice. Vatican II, on the other hand, distinguished between Tradition as a dynamic process under the guidance of the Holy Spirit of transmitting the original experience of encountering Jesus Christ and the content of Tradition.

William Henn has helpfully shown what is necessary for a correct interpretation of the phrase "a like feeling of piety and reverence."[85] *Dei Verbum* quotes Trent to show continuity with that council. It is important to note that *Dei Verbum* does give a certain preeminence to Scripture. *Dei Verbum* says, "Scripture is the utterance of God," while "tradition preserves the word of God" (DV § 9). The phrase "like feeling of piety and reverence" expresses the belief that Scripture and Tradition find their source in the same divine wellspring and both lead to the same goal, namely salvation. Finally, the phrase expresses the conviction that Scripture and Tradition cannot be separated. Nevertheless, the danger inherent to the expression is that it may obscure the fact that Jesus Christ is the fullness of revelation, that Scripture enjoys a certain preeminence over Tradition, and that apostolic tradition must be distinguished from ecclesiastical or merely human traditions.

Scripture and Tradition in Ecumenical Dialogues

The study document of the Lutheran-Roman Catholic Commission on Unity, *The Apostolicity of the Church* (2006), develops a differentiated consensus on the topic of Scripture and Tradition.[86] A differentiated consensus shows essential agreement while at the same time acknowledging differences in emphasis and perspective that do not negate the substantial agreement achieved.

The consensus statement of the text reads,

> Catholics and Lutherans agree, not only that Scripture developed historically from a process of tradition both in Israel and the apostolic church, but as well that Scripture is oriented toward a process of being interpreted in the context of ecclesial tradition. (§ 442)

When Catholics affirm that "tradition is indispensable in the interpretation of the word of God...they are connecting the gospel and Scripture with the Christian faith lived and transmitted in history, where transmission has given rise to valid expressions of faith" (§ 443). Examples cited include creeds, particularly that of Nicaea-Constantinople, and conciliar formulations of articles of faith. Catholics claim that these expressions of Tradition come from Scripture and are "among the principal means by which...the Holy Spirit has maintained the church in the truth of God's said word and believers have been led to grasp rightly the message of salvation present in Scripture" (§ 443). Catholics make the distinction that "scripture *is* the inspired word of God, while tradition is the living process which '*transmits* in its entirety the word of God entrusted to the apostles by Christ and the Holy Spirit' (DV § 9)" (§ 444). While this transmission does not result in new truth that supplements Scripture, it does "express and render certain the biblical content of faith" (§ 444).

Lutherans, in speaking of Scripture and Tradition, distinguish between "human traditions" and the creeds of the early church. "Human traditions" or "human ordinances in spiritual or ecclesiastical matters" are "practices of church life enacted by human beings without grounding in Scripture, but which people should observe because, and insofar as, they promote the good order of the church" (§ 445). They are not considered necessary for salvation and may not go against any commandment of God. If these conditions are met, "all enactments 'which are not contrary to the Holy Gospel' may be retained" (§ 445). Creeds, on the other hand, are considered to be "well grounded in scripture and have authority as accurate summaries of the gospel and as defenses against errors" (§ 446). When Lutherans identify these expressions of faith "traditions," "they are then seeing Scripture and tradition as belonging to each other" (§ 446). Lutheran confessional documents and the catechism contain expressions of faith and understandings of Scripture and have "an important role in communicating the apostolic gospel, which Scripture attests in a normative manner" so that the "the church's teaching prolongs the apostolic witness to the truth of God's revelation" (§ 446). Finally, Lutherans insist, and Catholics agree, "Scripture should not be absorbed into the tradition process, but should remain permanently superior as a critical norm" (§ 447).

The Lutheran-Roman Catholic Commission on Unity concluded, "Therefore regarding Scripture and Tradition Lutherans and Catholics are in such an extensive agreement that their different emphases do not of themselves require maintaining the present division of the churches. In this area, there is unity in reconciled diversity" (§ 448).

Chapter Four

Baptism and Eucharist

Both Lutherans and Catholics affirm the sacramentality of baptism and the Eucharist. For Lutherans, only these rites are properly sacraments, while for Catholics, they are the foundational sacraments of seven sacraments, which also include confirmation, penance, marriage, holy orders, and anointing of the sick. Lutherans, although they have practices corresponding to these sacraments, do not consider them to be sacraments because they do not have clear connection of a promise of grace attached to a visible sign, although Luther wavered on whether or not penance was a sacrament.[1]

Luther's concept of a sacrament involved three elements: (1) A sacrament is a sign instituted by God and connected with a promise of grace; (2) the sacrament only becomes efficacious through the individual's faith in the promise;[2] and (3) the effect of the sacrament is forgiveness of sin and reconciliation with God. The recipient's role in the sacramental encounter, then, is to receive the word of promise embodied in the sacramental sign with the response of faith. Faith does not make the sacrament valid, but it does make it efficacious.

For Lutherans, then, "a sacrament consists of two parts, the sign and the Word."[3] This follows closely Augustine's description of a sacrament: "The Word is added to the element, and a sacrament results."[4] The Word is God's promise of grace, which will immediately correlate with the Lutheran emphasis of receiving sacraments, that is, that word of promise, with faith.

Catholics describe sacraments as "perceptible signs (words and actions)," which "by the action of Christ and the power of the Holy Spirit...make present efficaciously the grace that they signify."[5] Rather than using the categories of word and element, Catholics traditionally followed the scholastic terminology, using the Aristotelian categories of *matter* and *form*. The matter—all that is physical and perceptible to the senses—is the sign of the sacrament, and the form—the interpretative and determinative words of the minister—is the principle that gives structure and definition, not the word of New Testament promise. Thus for baptism, the matter of the sacrament is the pouring of the water over the person to be baptized, and the form is the words "I baptize you in the name of the Father, the Son, and the Holy Spirit."

Catholics, who historically have had an underdeveloped theology of the Word, can profitably borrow from the Lutheran sacramental concept of Word and element. The danger for both Lutherans and Catholics would be to regard Word and Sacrament as two separate entities rather than an interrelated whole. The notion of a sacrament as a visible word received in faith is not in the consciousness of most Catholics.

After Vatican II, Karl Rahner was the theologian who incorporated a robust theology of the Word in his account of sacramentality and comes closest to Luther's concept of sacrament. He identified a sacrament as a "quite specific word-event within a theology of the word."[6] Rahner even says, "The word constitutes the basic essence of the sacrament and that by comparison with the word the 'matter,' the *elementum* has at basis the merely secondary function of providing an illustration of the significance of the word."[7] This Word is an event of grace and is a saving event made effective by the power of God.

Louis-Marie Chauvet, a contemporary Catholic liturgical theologian, in addressing what he calls the "false dichotomy between Word and Sacrament," speaks of the "word that deposits itself in the sacramental ritual as well as in the Bible" such that it is better to speak of "a liturgy of the Word under the mode of Scripture and of a liturgy of the Word under the mode of bread and wine."[8] For Chauvet, the baptismal formula is "the precipitate of the Christian Scriptures" since the baptismal formula, "In the name of the Father, and of the Son, and of the Holy Spirit" is like a "concentrate of all the Scriptures."[9] The baptismal formula functions as the symbol par excellence of Christian identity, and is inscribed in the body, which is to say, in the fabric of life.[10] Thus *word* is understood on three levels: the Christ-Word, the Scriptures, and the sacramental formula itself pronounced "in the person of Christ."

Chauvet's theology of the connection between Word and Sacrament extends beyond Luther's theology of the Word as promise and its reception in faith, but it perhaps bridges what is too often a dichotomy between Word and Sacrament and thus retrieves, in a contemporary key, Augustine's notion of a sacrament as a "visible word." Where the predominate Scholastic notion of faith tended to be intellectual assent to truths and Luther's notion of faith was fiduciary trust, Chauvet offers a third possibility, an embodied, enacted faith through participation in sacramental action wherein we enact that which we believe.

BAPTISM

Baptism has not been a church-dividing sacrament between Lutherans and Catholics; each recognizes the baptisms of the other. Luther had little quarrel with baptism as practiced in the Roman Catholic Church as evident in his comments in *The Babylonian Captivity of the Church*:

> Blessed be God and the Father of our Lord Jesus Christ, who according to the riches of his mercy [Eph. 1:3, 7] has preserved in his church this sacrament at least, untouched and untainted by the ordinances of men, and has made it free to all nations and classes of mankind, and has not permitted it to be oppressed by the filthy and godless monsters of greed and superstition.[11]

In 1966, the second US bilateral official ecumenical conversation of the Lutheran-Roman Catholic Dialogue sponsored by the USA National Committee of the Lutheran World Federation and the bishops' Commission for Ecumenical Affairs issued a joint statement written by Bishop T. Austin Murphy and Paul C. Empie saying, "We were reasonably certain that the teachings of our respective traditions regarding baptism are in substantial agreement, and this opinion has been confirmed at this meeting."[12] This "substantial agreement" does not mean, however, that there are not differences of emphasis or theology between the two communions.

Both Catholics and Lutherans consider baptism necessary for salvation, to forgive sins, and to be the foundation of Christian life. In his Large Catechism, Luther emphasized the importance of baptism for daily life:

> Therefore let all Christians regard their Baptism as the daily garment that they are to wear all the time. Every day they should be found in faith and with its fruits, suppressing the old creature and growing up in the new. If we want to be Christians, we must practice the work that makes us Christians, and let those who fall away return to it. As Christ, the mercy seat, does not withdraw from us or forbid us to return to him even though we sin, so all his treasures and gifts remain. As we have once obtained forgiveness of sins in baptism, so forgiveness remains day by day as long as we live, that is, as long as we carry the old creature about our necks.[13]

Baptism calls us to a daily dying to sin and rising to new life. Thus it is a continuing call to repentance, faith, and obedience to Christ. As Luther's Large Catechism puts it, living in repentance is walking in baptism.[14] Catholics would agree with this insofar as the sacrament of penance returns a person to the state of grace initially effected by baptism. Even though the Council of Trent in canon 10 condemned the position "that by the sole remembrance and the faith of the baptism received, all sins committed after baptism are either remitted or made venial," this canon does not take into account the role of repentance in the return to baptismal justification. The Catholic and Lutheran positions are similar in the effect produced even though differences remain in how that effect is produced, Lutheran emphasizing the role of faith in the process of repentance and Catholics the objective role of the sacrament of penance within repentance, which of course also requires faith for fruitful reception. Where Lutherans say that we always have access to baptism,[15] Catholics say that we always have the possibility of returning to the condition created by baptism and its promises.

Efficacious Sign of Baptism

For both Lutherans and Catholics, the essential sacramental sign of baptism is water flowing over the head of the person to be baptized accompanied by the trinitarian formula, "I baptize you in the name of the Father, the Son, and the Holy Spirit.

The sacrament is called "baptism" after the central rite. "To baptize" means "to 'plunge' or 'immerse'; the 'plunge' into the water symbolizes the catechumen's burial into Christ's death, from which he rises up by resurrection with him, as 'a new creature.'"[16] It is also called "*the washing of regeneration and renewal by the Holy Spirit*,' for it signifies and actually brings about the birth of water and the Spirit without which no one 'can enter the kingdom of God.'"[17] Thus the two principal effects of baptism are purification from sins and new birth in the Holy Spirit.[18] We participate in Christ's dying and rising, symbolized by immersion in the baptismal waters from which the baptized arise by resurrection with Christ as "new creatures," and become members of the church. "For in the one Spirit we were all baptized into one body" (1 Cor 12:13).

Traditional Roman Catholic theology has distinguished between the objective efficaciousness of the sacraments and their fruitfulness. The Roman Catholic teaching that the sacraments act *ex opere operato* (literally: "by the very fact of the action's being performed") means that the sacraments act by virtue of the saving work of Christ, accomplished once for all.[19] Consequently, they do not act by virtue of either the power of the celebrant or his holiness, or the work of the recipient, but only by the power of God.[20] Efficaciousness means that the sacrament actually occurs, that is, is effected.

Fruitfulness means that the recipient receives the grace of the sacraments. This depends on the disposition of the one who receives them. Some sacraments ("sacraments of the living" such as Eucharist, confirmation, marriage, holy orders) require that a person be in a state of grace to receive them. Faith is a condition for all the sacraments. The grace of the sacrament is proper to each sacrament and makes the faithful partakers in the divine nature.[21] Sacramental grace, however, is not a "thing," but is best perceived as a relationship with God or the very presence of God indwelling the person, which we speak of as uncreated grace.

Luther objected to the Catholic understanding of sacramental efficacy *ex opere operato*.[22] Studies have shown that one source of this divergence may be because the Protestant side looks at the *reception* of the sacrament, while Catholics interpret the terms from the point of view of the *dispensation* of the sacrament.[23] Accordingly, Protestants viewed the teaching of *ex opere operato* as affirming an automatic salvific sacramental efficacy when the ritual was rightly performed. The teaching on *ex opere operato* was intended to stress that the divine offer of grace is independent of the worthiness of the one administering the sacrament and the one receiving it. Lutherans would agree that the sacraments' validity is independent of the worthiness of the one administering or receiving them, but would say that sacraments effect salvation only through faith. Thus, they would also affirm the objective validity of baptism apart from faith. For example, in a sermon on the Catechism, Luther states, "My faith does not make the baptism, but rather receives the baptism, no matter whether the person being baptized believes or not; for baptism is not dependent on my faith but upon God's Word."[24] Catholics interpreted the Protestant denial of the teaching on *ex opere operato* as a denial of sacramental efficacy in general, particularly when combined with a teaching of efficacy through faith. Both sides, however, taught that Christ is the primary actor in the sacraments. Catholic doctrine requires believing reception in order for the sacrament to be "for salvation."

Effects of Baptism

For both Lutherans and Catholics, the new birth of baptism incorporates us into Christ and his Body, the church, forms us into God's priestly people, and pardons all our sins.[25] The effect of baptism is thus christological, ecclesiological, and soteriological. The baptized become adopted heirs of God, partakers of the divine nature, members of Christ's body, and temples of the Holy Spirit. When Catholics say that the baptized receive sanctifying grace, this is understood to be the grace of justification.[26] Lutherans also say that God justifies those who receive baptism in faith.[27]

When it is said that baptism incorporates a person into the church, membership in the church is not to be understood in a juridical sense in the way that one might join an organization, but rather incorporation in the church, the ecclesial Body of Christ, is inseparable from participation in Christ. This theology rests on an interpretation of Paul's First Letter to the Corinthians, which closely associates the ecclesial community and the risen Christ.

In baptism, all sins are forgiven. Participation in Christ's dying and rising and the indwelling of the Holy Spirit reconcile us with God. Catholics say that after baptism, certain temporal consequences of sin remain such as suffering, illness, death, and concupiscence, the inclination to sin. Roman Catholics do not consider concupiscence to be sin since it does not engage a person's freedom and knowledge until that person chooses to sin.[28] Lutherans also say that concupiscence remains after baptism, but consider this to be sin insofar as it is contrary to God.[29] However, this is not a sin that is said to "rule" the Christian "for it is itself ruled by Christ with whom the justified are bound in faith."[30]

Baptism, Sacrament of Faith

Baptism is a sacrament of faith. Roman Catholicism emphasizes the need for a community of believers, for "it is only within the faith of the Church that each of the faithful can believe."[31] The church does not require a perfect and mature faith for baptism, but "a beginning that is called to develop."[32] The rite asks of a catechumen or godparent: "What do you ask of God's Church?" The response is "faith!"[33] The presupposition is that the church's faith precedes that of a catechumen who is invited to adhere to it.[34]

The mission to baptize is implied in the mission to evangelize. The Word of God and the faith, which is assent to this Word, is preparation for this sacrament. The Decree on the Ministry and Life of Priests from Vatican II makes this connection between the preaching of the Word and sacramental ministry:

> The People of God is formed into one in the first place by the Word of the living God....The preaching of the Word is required for the sacramental ministry itself,

since the sacraments are sacraments of faith, drawing
their origin and nourishment from the Word.[35]

The sacraments in the Roman Catholic Church presuppose faith
and also nourish, strengthen, and express it.[36] Since the restoration
of the catechumenate after Vatican II and with the promulgation
of the Rite of Christian Initiation for Adults, adult baptism is normative for Roman Catholic understanding of the sacrament even
though statistically more infants may be baptized than adults.
Adult baptism is normative because of the faith engaged and also
because the rite involves a conversion of life not experienced by
an infant. In the case of infant baptism, there is faith by proxy, the
faith of parents, godparents, and the Christian community.

The baptismal rite includes a threefold confession of faith
from the catechumen or the parents and godparents. The celebrant and the congregation then give their assent to the profession
of faith in these words or in some other way in which the community can express its faith:

> This is our faith. This is the faith of the Church. We are
> proud to profess it, in Christ Jesus our Lord.
>   All: Amen.

Thus, baptism contains an act of faith as a component of the rite.
However, the very act of baptism is itself an act of faith in Jesus
Christ in response to his command to "go therefore and make disciples of all nations, baptizing them in the name of the Father
and of the Son and of the Holy Spirit, and teaching them to obey
everything that I have commanded you" (Matt 28:19–20).

Luther's Large Catechism expresses the connection between
faith and sacrament, showing both the necessity of faith and the
necessity of baptism:

> Our know-it-alls [Zwinglians or Anabaptists], the new
> spirits, assert that faith alone saves and that works and
> external things contribute nothing to this end. We
> answer: It is true, nothing that is in us does it but faith,
> as we shall hear later on. But these leaders of the blind
> are unwilling to see that faith must have something to

believe—something to which it may cling and upon which it may stand. Thus faith clings to the water and believes it to be Baptism in which there is sheer salvation and life, not through the water, as we have sufficiently stated, but through its incorporation with God's Word and ordinance and the joining of his name to it. When I believe this, what else is it but believing in God as the one who has implanted his Word in this external ordinance and offered it to us so that we may grasp the treasure it contains?

Now, these people are so foolish as to separate faith from the object to which faith is attached and bound on the ground that the object is something external. Yes, it must be external so that it can be perceived and grasped by the senses and thus brought into the heart, just as the entire Gospel is an external, oral proclamation. In short, whatever God effects in us he does through such external ordinances....We have here the words, "he who believes and is baptized will be saved." To what do they refer but to Baptism, that is, the water comprehended in God's ordinance? Hence it follows that whoever rejects Baptism rejects God's Word, faith, and Christ, who directs and binds us to Baptism.[37]

This text shows that baptism includes a faith-filled response to God's Word.

From earliest times, Roman Catholics and Lutherans have baptized infants as well as adults. The introduction to the Catholic rite notes that the church has always understood the words "unless a man is reborn in water and the Holy Spirit, he cannot enter the kingdom of God" to mean that children should not be deprived of baptism.[38] Children "are baptized in the faith of the Church, a faith proclaimed for them by their parents and godparents, who represent both the local Church and the whole society of saints and believers."[39] Infant baptism requires a post-baptismal catechesis in the faith. Lutherans strongly defended the practice of infant baptism against the Anabaptists.[40]

An area for exploration in an ecumenical context is not the necessity of faith for the reception of baptism, but the relative emphasis on individual faith versus the faith of the church in our respective traditions. Roman Catholics consider all the sacraments as forms of liturgical prayer. Liturgical prayer is the public, official prayer of the church, not the prayer of a private individual. In the profession of faith within liturgical prayer, the "I" of "I believe" is not only the individual, but the whole church professing its belief.[41] Thus there is a complex dynamic between the faith brought to the sacrament by an individual and the faith of the community, which invites, supports, and sustains that faith.

Sacramental Character: Ecclesial Relationship and Deputation to Worship

According to Roman Catholic theology, baptism, along with the sacraments of confirmation and holy orders, confers a sacramental character.[42] Each of these sacraments can be received only once. Consequently, when the Roman Catholic Church recognizes the baptism of another faith communion, it does not rebaptize a person from that communion who seeks full communion with the Roman Catholic Church. Because of the sacramental character, the recipient shares in Christ's priesthood and is put into a relationship with Christ, the priest, and the church as a priestly community. Baptism makes the recipient a member of the church and deputes that person for public worship in the church. The doctrine of sacramental character, then, is about what is permanent in the sacrament of baptism even though baptismal grace can be lost through serious sin.

Since Lutherans would also say with Catholics that loss of salvation remains a possibility for a Christian and that baptism is never left behind, for both communions, there is something permanent in baptism and something that can be lost. Both communions would affirm that that which is permanent is on the side of God's activity in the sacrament, Lutherans describing this as promise and Catholics speaking of a definitive character of the sacrament. Both communions speak of the possibility of a subjective turning from baptism by the baptized. Finally, both speak of a return to baptismal grace, while Lutherans speak of this as a clinging to baptism through faith in God's promise (and count absolution as such a clinging) and Catholics hold that this occurs not through faith in baptism, but through recourse to the sacrament of penance and contrition. Perhaps this account shows unity as well as difference in Lutheran and Catholic accounts of the permanence of baptism and the return to baptismal grace.

EUCHARIST

Lutherans and Catholics have reached substantial agreement on the Eucharist. Since they agree that fellowship in eucharistic celebration is an essential sign of church unity, striving for altar fellowship is imperative for all who seek the unity of the church. The international document *Church and Justification* (1994) spells out how the Lord's Supper draws believers into communion with the Trinity and builds the church: "The celebration of the Lord's Supper draws believers into the presence of the triune God through thanksgiving (*eucharistia*) to the Father, remembrance (*anamnesis*) of Christ, and invocation (*epiclesis*) of the Holy Spirit."[43] Because the Eucharist is *koinonia* (communion, fellowship) with the crucified and risen Lord, it also creates and strengthens the *koinonia* of the faithful with one another. They agree that the Lord's Supper is "par excellence the visible and effectual expression of the congregation as a 'sharing in the body of Christ' (1 Cor 10:16ff)."[44]

While Lutherans and Catholics have agreed on the real presence of Christ in the Eucharist, the chief differences between them have been over the explanation of that presence as transubstantiation by Catholics and the sacrificial character of the Eucharist. There have also been additional differences regarding whether or not the cup should be given to the laity, whether the sacramental presence of Christ persists after the eucharistic service, and whether the eucharistic elements are proper objects of adoration after the eucharistic liturgy.[45]

The Presence of Christ in the Eucharist

Luther understood the sacrament of the Lord's Supper as a *testamentum*, the promise of someone who is about to die. Although he first understood Christ's promise (*testamentum*) as promising grace and forgiveness of sins, Luther also emphasized the trustworthiness of Christ's promise to be truly present in his Body and Blood and affirmed the plain meaning of Christ's words, "This is my body" (cf. *Apology* X.4). Thus Luther did not differ from Catholics on the truth of Christ's bodily presence in the sacrament, but he did distance himself from the Swiss reformer, Huldrych Zwingli, who held a doctrine of the spiritual presence of Christ in the Eucharist. While both emphasized the importance of faith of the communicant, Luther refused to make faith the cause or condition of Christ's eucharistic presence. He firmly held that faith does not make Christ present, but Christ gives himself, his body and blood, to communicants, whether or not they believe this.

Luther's theology of the real presence drew an analogy between the Chalcedonian doctrine of the two natures of Christ and the relationship of the body and blood of Christ to the bread and wine. Just as Christ is completely human and completely divine in his person (hypostatic union), so the Eucharist is completely the body and blood of Christ and completely bread and wine. Luther thus objected to the Catholic teaching of transubstantiation, that the substance of bread and wine are changed into the substance of the body and blood of Christ, based on what he considered the false and unnecessary miracle of the annihilation of the substance of the bread and wine. For Luther, Christ's body and blood are present "under" the species of bread and wine. This is somewhat analogous to the exchange of properties (*communicatio idomatum*) between the divine and human natures of Christ. This creates a sacramental union between bread and Christ's body and the wine and Christ's blood, analogous to but distinct from the union of the two natures in Christ: "This union of Christ's Body and Blood with the bread and wine, however, is not a personal union, as is the case with the two natures in Christ. Rather...it is a *sacramentalis unio* (that is, a sacramental union)."[46] Luther compared this new type of union formed by an exchange of properties to the union of iron and fire in a fiery iron.

Luther's theology of real presence leads to one of the remaining differences between Catholics and Lutherans—whether or not bread is present after the words of institution, Lutherans affirming this and Catholics saying that the presence of Christ's body and blood replaces the substance of bread and wine, leaving only the "accidents," that is, the appearances of bread and wine. *Substance* and *accidents* when used to refer to sacramental realities are metaphysical categories, that is, philosophical categories, not physical categories. Thus it would be incorrect to assert that Christ is physically present in the sacrament. One says, rather, that he is substantially present. Likewise, when Roman Catholics say that the "accidents" of bread and wine remain after the consecration, even though a physical analysis may reveal them to be bread and wine, Catholic teaching is that the metaphysical substance has been changed.

At times, one finds the term *consubstantiation* used to describe Luther's doctrine of the presence of both bread and the body of Christ in the Eucharist, but this is not Luther's term since he rejected the use of philosophical categories to describe the Eucharist. He did not use *consubstantiation* any more than he used *transubstantiation* to describe what happens in the Eucharist since neither term occurs in Scripture.

The bottom line is that Lutherans and Catholics agree on the real presence of Christ in the Eucharist. The Augsburg Confession of 1530 states, "Concerning the Lord's Supper they teach that the body and blood of Christ are truly present and are distributed to those who eat the Lord's Supper."[47] Lutherans do not try to explain this other than through Jesus' words of institution given in Scripture. Catholic doctrine requires belief in the real presence, that is, the conversion of bread and wine to the body and blood of Christ, but does not require a particular explanation of how this occurs. The Council of Trent said that the Catholic Church "properly and appropriately" and "most aptly" calls this conversion transubstantiation, but it is the conversion not the explanation of transubstantiation that requires belief.[48] Canon 2, directed against the Lutheran position, condemns the position that bread and wine remains conjointly with the body and blood of our Lord Jesus Christ in the sacrament. The teaching of Trent enables one to distinguish between the reality of the sign, on the one hand, and the reality of the transformation, on the other hand, and to connect both to the concept of sacrament as event. Even though Trent's teaching does not answer all questions about the presence of Christ, it was the starting point for an understanding of the mystery of the real presence of Christ in the Eucharist.

Lutheran teaching on the true and substantial presence of Christ in the Eucharist as expressed in article X of the Augsburg Confession was accepted in the Roman Catholic Confutation of the Augsburg Confession: "The words of the tenth article contain nothing that would give cause for offense. They confess that the Body and Blood of Christ are truly and substantially present in the Sacrament after the words of consecration." The Confutation does, however, criticize the Lutherans for not explicitly affirming the doctrine of concomitance, the teaching of the Roman Catholic Church that both the body and blood of Christ are present in each of the consecrated elements of bread and wine: "If only they believe that the entire Christ is present under each form, so that the Blood of Christ is no less present under the form of bread by concomitance than it is under the form of the wine, and the reverse" (Roman Confutation—To Article X). The doctrine of concomitance had developed along with the doctrine of transubstantiation and led to the practice of "communion under one kind," a practice widespread in the twelfth century that was decreed by the Council of Constance in 1415 and reaffirmed by the Council of Trent in 1545. The Reformers objected to this practice of withholding the cup from the laity, while denying the concomitance could be true.

The Doctrine of the Real Presence in Ecumenical Dialogue

Statements of ecumenical dialogues generally reflect a broad consensus on the issue of eucharistic real presence. The Lutheran-Roman Catholic Joint Commission in the report *The Eucharist* (1978) asserted, "In the Sacrament of the Lord's Supper Jesus Christ true God and true man, is present wholly and entirely, in his Body and Blood, under the signs of bread and wine." It further specified this agreement by recognizing "in common a rejection of a spatial or natural manner of presence, and a rejection of an understanding of the sacrament as only commemorative or figurative" (§ 16).

What seems to have made these convergences possible is first, an enriched understanding of the category of sacramentality as a modality of presence distinctly different from a physical-historical presence, on the one hand, and a spiritual non-substantial presence, on the other hand. The former does not sufficiently take into account the fact that the *risen* Christ is present in the Eucharist. The latter does not sufficiently account for a real presence of Christ in the Eucharist. Second, a renewed appreciation of epiclesis emphasizes the action of the Holy Spirit through whose power the body and blood of Christ are made present in the Eucharistic elements. The work of the Holy Spirit removes any automatic or mechanical notion of sacramental efficacy by transforming the bread and wine into the body and blood of Christ and also effecting our union with Christ.[49] An area not explored by the dialogues, but which could be fruitful in the future, would be the development of a theology of the presence of Christ as the first fruits of the new creation. This theology would synthesize the work of the Holy Spirit with a Christology of Christ's resurrection and emphasize not only the incarnational aspects of the real presence as a substantial "enfleshment," as it were, of the eucharistic elements, but would also emphasize the fact that it is the *risen* Christ who is present in the Eucharist. Here the Eucharist not only looks to the past in its *anamnesis*, but also forward in anticipation as the pledge of eschatological fulfillment in Christ.

The Eucharist as Sacrifice

Luther was convinced that one of the most substantial differences between his teaching and that of the Catholic Church was the question of the sacrificial character of the Mass. From very early on, Luther emphasized the Eucharist as a sacrifice of praise and tried to eliminate every trace of the Mass as a propitiatory sacrifice of the church. Luther considered that the notion of Eucharist sacrifice violated what he saw as the essential character of the Mass, which was first of all God's own service, a *beneficium* received rather than a *sacrificium* offered.[50] Last but not least, Luther found the logical conclusion of the theology of eucharistic sacrifice was that the Eucharist is a bloodless repetition of the Lord's sacrifice and thus a repudiation of the once-for-all sacrifice of Christ.[51]

Luther insisted that in the Lord's Supper, Christ gives himself to those who receive him, and that, as a gift, Christ could only be received properly in faith and not offered. Luther thought that

113

understanding the Eucharist as sacrifice would mean that it is a good work that we perform and offer to God. This would transform what was a most precious gift into a good work. In the course of the Reformation, the order of the Mass was changed so that it was no longer celebrated as a sacrifice. Nor could it be understood as a good work. Nevertheless, Luther considered the Mass to be a sacrifice of thanksgiving and praise insofar as in giving thanks, a person acknowledges that he or she is in need of the gift and that his or her situation will only change by receiving the gift. Thus true receiving in faith contains an active dimension not to be underestimated.

The Council of Trent reaffirmed the traditional teaching of the Eucharist as the sacrifice of both Christ and the church. The Council stated that Christ has given the church a visible sacrifice "by which the bloody sacrifice which he was once for all to accomplish on the cross would be represented, its memory perpetuated until the end of the world, and its salutary power applied for the forgiveness of the sins which we daily commit."[52] The two main points of the teaching are (1) the sacrifice of Christ, which he offered as gift of his entire life, and (2) the Eucharist as sacrifice, which is offered by the priest in the person of Christ and on behalf of the church. The Mass makes present, commemorates, and applies to the living and the dead the merits of the sacrifice of Christ.

It was not fully grasped at the time that the sacrifice of the Mass precisely as sacrament makes present the unique sacrifice of Christ on the Cross without repeating that sacrifice (SC § 5). Today, a stronger connection between sacrifice and sacrament along with the retrieval of the liturgical notion of *anamnesis* in eucharistic doctrine and practice make it possible "to express together the faithful conviction of both the uniqueness and full sufficiency of the atoning event in Jesus Christ."[53] Therefore, canon 4 of the Council of Trent is essentially not applicable today to Lutheran eucharistic theology, and the sharp criticism of the Roman Mass in the Smalcald Articles and even the (Reformed) Heidelberg Catechism cannot be said to apply to the actual teaching of the Roman Church.[54]

Catholics understand memorial (*anamnesis*) and the invocation of the Spirit (*epiklesis*) in a strong sense. The church not only calls to mind the passion and resurrection of Christ Jesus in the Eucharist, but also "presents to the Father the offering of his Son which reconciles us with him."[55] The once-for-all sacrifice of the Son becomes sacramentally present, that is, in a certain way is made present and real.[56] This is not a repetition of the sacrifice of Christ, but a re-presentation of it by means of *anamnesis* through which the church joins itself to Christ's sacrifice in his self-offering to the Father to intercede for all of humanity.

Eucharistic Sacrifice in Ecumenical Dialogues

The Lutheran-Roman Catholic Dialogue proposed using the category of memorial as understood in the Passover celebration at the time of Christ, the making present of an event in the past, as the way to understand Christ's sacrifice and the Eucharist.[57] The agreement on the sacrificial character of the Eucharist follows from an agreement on the real presence of Christ, who "is present as the Crucified one who died for our sins and rose again for our justification, as the once-for-all sacrifice for the sins of the world. This sacrifice can be neither continued, nor repeated, nor replaced nor complemented; but rather it can and should become effective ever anew in the midst of the congregation."[58] Because Christ who is present is the sacrificed one, the sacrifice of the Eucharist is inseparable from his presence. Once again, the category of sacramentality provides the modality of this sacrifice, so that the once-for-all sacrifice is present within the modality of sacramentality, and therefore is not a repetition or continuation of Christ's sacrifice.

Historically, a major point of difference between Catholics and traditions issuing from the Reformation has been whether or not the church "offers" Christ in the eucharistic celebration. This problem recedes when the issue is no longer treated extrinsically as if the church were separate from Christ. When the category of participation is introduced, the members of the Body of Christ are united with him in such a way that they become participants in his self-offering and sacrifice to the Father.[59] The assembly does not offer Christ as if it were apart from Christ, but in union with Christ the assembly consents to be included in his self-offering.

115

The international Lutheran-Catholic Dialogue, *The Eucharist* (1978), addressed this:

> All those who celebrate the Eucharist in remembrance of Him are incorporated in Christ's life, passion, death and resurrection....So they give thanks "for all his mercies, entreat the benefits of his passion on behalf of the whole church, participate in these benefits and enter into the movement of his self-offering." In receiving in faith, they are taken as His body into the reconciling sacrifice which equips them for self-giving (Romans 12:1) and enables them "through Jesus Christ" to offer "spiritual sacrifices" (1 Peter 2:5) in service to the world. Thus is rehearsed in the Lord's Supper what is practiced in the whole Christian life. "With contrite hearts we offer ourselves as a living and holy sacrifice, a sacrifice which must be expressed in the whole of our daily lives." (§ 36)

This statement says that those who celebrate the Eucharist are taken up into the sacrifice of Christ. However, it does not yet say that the church "offers" Christ, which was the point of contention at the time of the Reformation. The statement, however, addresses this point where it says,

> As members of His body the believers are included in the offering of Christ. This happens in different ways: none of them is added externally to the offering of Christ, but each derives from him and points to him: The liturgical preparation of the Eucharist with the offering of bread and wine is part of the Eucharistic sacrifice. Above all, inner participation is necessary: awareness and confession of one's own powerlessness and total dependence on God's help, obedience to His commission, faith in His word and His promise. It is in the eucharistic presence of the offered and offering Lord that those who are redeemed by Him can, in the best sense, make an offering....It is this act of testifying to one's own powerlessness, of complete reliance on Christ and of offering and

116

presenting Him to the Father which is intended when the Catholic church dares to say that not only Christ offers Himself for man, but that the church also "offers" Him. The members of the body of Christ are united through Christ with God and with one another in such a way that they become participants in His worship, His self-offering, His sacrifice to the Father. Through this union between Christ and Christians the eucharistic assembly "offers Christ," consenting in the power of the Holy Spirit to be offered by Him to the Father. Apart from Christ, we have no gift, no worship, no sacrifice of our own to offer to God. All we can plead is Christ, the sacrificial lamb and victim, who the Father himself has given us." (§ 58)

This statement helped to answer Lutheran fears that the sacrificial offering of the Mass detracts from the sufficiency of Christ's sacrifice.

This line of reasoning also responds to the propitiatory nature of the Mass, for if Christ's sacrifice is expiatory, that is, if this sacrifice is efficacious for the forgiveness of sin, then the sacramental modality of that same sacrifice carries the same efficacy and is therefore propitiatory. Here again, the resolution of the difference is achieved by uniting the concepts of *sacrificium* (sacrifice) and *sacramentum* (sacrament). The offering of the gift occurs sacramentally.

The point of difference with Lutherans, however, is whether or not it is propitiatory for the dead as well as for the living. This was not addressed in the international statement, *The Eucharist*, although the issue was raised, but not answered, in the US document, *The Eucharist as Sacrifice*.[60] That document noted that the *Apology of the Augsburg Confession* does not forbid prayer for the dead (XXXIV, 94).[61] Round XI of the US Lutheran-Catholic Dialogue discussed prayer for the dead at length in *Hope of Eternal Life*, approaching the topic through a theology of the communion of saints. Citing the German Lutheran *Evangelische Erwachsenenkatechismus* (539), it explained prayer for the dead: "The communion of believers, the church, is not broken by death. As in life, so in death the Christian is dependent on the community. In prayer the congregation intercedes before God for the one who has fallen asleep. They ask for the forgiveness of his sin, acceptance by God, and eternal life" (§ 248). The dialogue notes, however, that the language of satisfaction remains problematic for Lutherans (§§ 256–58).

Reservation and Adoration of the Sacrament

Catholics believe that the presence of Christ in the sacrament extends beyond the eucharistic celebration as long as the species of bread and wine remain. Lutherans often take exception to Catholic practices associated with this belief, regarding them as inadmissibly separated from the eucharistic meal.[62] Shortly after the Second Vatican Council, the Sacred Congregation for Rites[63] issued the document *Eucharisticum Mysterium*, which articulated the principle that "the celebration of the Eucharist in the sacrifice of the Mass is the origin and consummation of the worship shown to the Eucharist outside Mass."[64] The primary reason for reserving the sacrament outside of Mass is to make the sacrament available to those unable to participate in the Mass, especially the sick and the aged. Eucharistic reservation led to the practice of eucharistic adoration, a secondary reason for reservation of the sacrament outside of Mass.[65] On account of belief in the real presence of Christ in the sacrament, the faithful show the sacrament the worship due to God. *Eucharisticum Mysterium* comments, "Nor is it to be adored any less because it was instituted by Christ to be eaten."[66]

Lutherans consider that a number of eucharistic practices violate the proper "use" of the sacrament. This principle, that "nothing has the character of a sacrament apart from the use [*usus*] instituted by Christ or the divinely instituted action [*actio*]" (Formula of Concord, Solid Declaration, VII.85), governed the Lutheran rejection of reserving the sacrament in tabernacles or using it in monstrances for adoration. This did not mean, however, that Lutherans necessarily thought that the presence of Christ ceased to exist after the service. According to the proper "use" of the sacrament, leftover consecrated eucharistic elements were to be consumed so that there were no remaining unconsumed eucharistic elements following communion. Luther had instructed the

Lutheran pastor Simon Wolferinus not to mix leftover consecrated eucharistic elements with consecrated ones. Luther told him to "do what we do here [i.e., in Wittenberg], namely, to eat and drink the remains of the Sacrament with the communicants so that it is not necessary to raise the scandalous and dangerous questions about when the action of the Sacrament ends."[67] The teaching was that sacramental union remained until the last communicant had received and the elements had been entirely consumed:

> Therefore, we shall define the time of the sacramental action in this way: that it starts with the beginning of the Lord's Prayer and lasts until all have communicated, have emptied the chalice, have consumed the hosts, until the people have been dismissed and [the priest] has left the altar.[68]

Given the shared belief of the presence of Christ in the Eucharist, Catholic sensibilities are offended by the casual way in which some Lutherans treat the elements remaining after communion. The International Lutheran-Roman Catholic Commission on Unity proposed that Lutherans adopt the best means of showing respect to the elements that have served for the celebration of the Eucharist, "which is to consume them subsequently, without precluding their use for communion of the sick."[69]

Luther and the other Protestant Reformers, in not continuing the practice of the reservation of the Eucharist, also abandoned the various devotional practices associated with the worship of the Eucharist. The Formula of Concord, Solid Declaration is quite strong in its condemnations concerning any use of the sacrament apart from the meal itself. As for eucharistic adoration, Lutherans are asked to consider that "adoration of the reserved sacrament not only has been very much a part of Catholic life and a meaningful form of devotion to Catholics for many centuries, but that also for them as long as Christ remains sacramentally present, worship, reverence and adoration are appropriate."[70] On the other hand, Catholics need to remember that the original intention in preserving the sacrament was to distribute Eucharist to the sick and those not present and to take care that their eucharistic devotions do not contradict the common conviction of the meal character of the Eucharist.[71]

Growing Convergence through Liturgical Renewal

Lutherans have wished to see a better use of proclamation within each celebration of the Eucharist and the administration of Holy Communion under both species.[72] The liturgical renewal mandated by the Second Vatican Council (1962–65) promoted Catholic liturgical practices that foster a growing convergence with Lutheran practices. For example, a wider use of the vernacular, the language of the people, was permitted (SC § 36, 54). A more ample, varied, and suitable selection of readings from Sacred Scripture were restored (SC § 35). The primary source for sermons was Scripture, and the liturgy and the ministers were instructed to carry out the ministry of preaching "properly and with the greatest care" (SC §§ 35, 52). Provision was made for extending communion under both kinds to the laity (SC § 55). Worship in the language of the people, attention to Scripture-based preaching, and extending the cup to the laity bridged Lutheran and Catholic eucharistic practice.

While the focus of ecumenical dialogues has largely been the doctrine of the Eucharist, the liturgy itself is an important ecumenical resource for ascertaining ecumenical convergence on the Eucharist. Lutherans have no typical edition of a normative liturgical book such as the Roman Catholic Sacramentary, so the diversity of worship forms among Lutheran congregations may be greater than what *Evangelical Lutheran Worship,* the 2006 worship book adopted by the Evangelical Lutheran Church in America, or any other Lutheran book of worship may indicate. Nevertheless, Maxwell Johnson, Lutheran liturgist, reports that Lutheran liturgical renewal has been largely the recovery of Luther's *Formula Missae,* rather than the *Deutsche Messe,* for the pattern of worship, "the recovery of the classic Lutheran confessional norm of the centrality of the Eucharist for Sunday and festival worship (moving from quarterly to monthly to every-Sunday celebrations," and thirdly, the recovery of a full eucharistic prayer.[73] Nevertheless, the use of the institution narrative alone following the Sanctus remains an option in the United States and Germany.[74]

All four of the Eucharistic Prayers in the ELCA *Lutheran Book of Worship* (1978) and eleven in *Evangelical Lutheran Worship* (2006) follow the model of the Strodach-Reed anaphora, a classic anaphora structure with parallels to the Jewish table prayer, which dates from the 1930s for use in India and was included in the 1958 *Service Book and Hymnal*.[75] Roman Catholic liturgical scholar Louis Bouyer said of this prayer,

> It would be hard to be more ecumenical! But all of these elements, chosen with great discernment, have been molded into a composition that is as moderate as it is natural. In its brief simplicity this prayer has a concise fullness that we are not accustomed to seeing except in Christian antiquity. Here…its eschatological orientation gives it a very primitive sound. Once again, this liturgy must be judged Catholic and orthodox to the extent that the traditional formulas it uses, with hardly an echo of the polemics of the Reformation, are in fact taken in their full and primary sense by the Church that uses them.[76]

In spite of this great ecumenical liturgical convergence, Johnson's study of eucharistic liturgies shows how this was weakened in *Evangelical Lutheran Worship* when the Latin phrase *offerimus tibi panen et calicem* ("we offer to you this bread and cup") was translated in *Lutheran Book of Worship* as "we *lift* this bread and cup before you," but was rendered as "we *take* this bread and cup" in *Evangelical Lutheran Worship*, effectively reversing the direction of the liturgical action.[77] Johnson concludes,

> Lutherans, especially in the United States, have been reticent to embrace either specific "offering" language or explicit consecratory epicleses of the Holy Spirit in Eucharistic praying. Indeed, the recovery of Eucharistic praying in modern Lutheranism has not been without great theological controversy,[78] and the texts of the Eucharistic prayers included in Lutheran worship books

are often the result of painstaking compromise and nuance.[79]

Roman Catholic eucharistic prayers also refer to a "sacrifice of praise."[80] However, the Eucharistic Prayer also includes the church's offering of Christ. For example, Eucharistic Prayer III says after the memorial acclamation, "We offer you in thanksgiving this holy and living sacrifice. Look with favor on your Church's offering, and see the Victim whose death has reconciled us to yourself." Eucharistic Prayer II says, "We offer you, Father, this life-giving bread, this saving cup."

If the church believes as it prays according to the principle of *lex orandi, lex credendi* (the law of praying is the law of believing),[81] then it would be important that eucharistic prayers incorporate a strong *epiklesis* and not shy away from what is offered in the Eucharist. The notion of offering or sacrifice is undoubtedly the topic requiring further dialogue and then catechesis. Actually, a theology of offering Christ in the Eucharist avoids the Lutheran fear of works-righteousness, for one does not offer oneself and one's own accomplishments or merits, but only oneself insofar as one participates in Christ's self-offering.[82]

Toward Eucharistic Sharing

The ultimate goal of ecumenical dialogue is full visible unity, one important aspect of which is unity at the table of the Lord. While the Eucharist is both a sign of unity and a means to grow in unity, Catholics have stressed the former, saying that ecclesial disunity precludes unity at the table. Lutheran members of the Lutheran World Federation more typically admit all the baptized to the table as they continue to grow in unity with their ecumenical partners.[83]

Catholics do admit Lutherans to the Eucharist in some exceptional cases outlined in the *Directory for the Application of Principles and Norms on Ecumenism*.[84] The conditions are "that the person be unable to have recourse for the sacrament desired to a minister of his or her own Church or ecclesial Community, ask for the sacrament of his or her own initiative, manifest Catholic faith in this sacrament and be properly disposed."[85] A Catholic, however, finding herself in these circumstances, may ask for the sacrament only "from a minister in whose Church these sacraments are valid or from one who is known to be validly ordained according to the Catholic teaching on ordination."[86] An asymmetrical relationship exists here that can only be resolved through the Catholic recognition of Lutheran ministry.

The problem of recognition of ministry shows that more than the substantial agreement shown in this overview concerning what Lutherans and Catholics believe about the Eucharist is required for eucharistic sharing. More than agreement of what each believes to be true about their own eucharistic celebrations is required. First, the question of how much ecclesial unity is necessary for eucharistic sharing must be addressed. Then Catholics must be able to affirm that Christ is substantially present in the Lutheran Lord's Supper. This affirmation has usually been tied to a recognition of Lutheran ministry, arguably the major roadblock to mutual eucharistic sharing between Lutherans and Catholics.

Future work toward this may build on the US Lutheran-Catholic Dialogue's observation that the judgment on the authenticity of Lutheran ministry need not be of an all-or-nothing nature.[87] The dialogue pointed to developments in *Unitatis Redintegratio*, the Decree on Ecumenism from the Second Vatican Council, which affirmed:

> Our separated brothers and sisters also celebrate many sacred actions of the Christian religion. These most certainly can truly engender a life of grace in ways that vary according to the condition of each church or community, and must be held capable of giving access to that communion in which is salvation. (UR 3)

The dialogue found that the category of validity, as traditionally determined, might be too restrictive to evaluate the eucharistic presence within churches in a relationship of imperfect communion with the Catholic Church. The dialogue cited a letter that Joseph Cardinal Ratzinger, at that time prefect of the Congregation of the Faith, wrote in 1993 to Bavarian Lutheran bishop Johannes Hanselmann:

I count among the most important results of the ecumenical dialogues the insight that the issue of the eucharist cannot be narrowed to the problem of 'validity.' Even a theology oriented to the concept of succession, such as that which holds in the Catholic and in the Orthodox Church, need not in any way deny the salvation-granting presence of the Lord [*Heilschaffende Gegenwart des Herrn*] in a Lutheran [*evangelische*] Lord's Supper.[88]

The dialogue concluded from this comment and from the text from the Decree on Ecumenism,

> If the actions of Lutheran pastors can be described by Catholics as "sacred actions" that "can truly engender a life of grace," if communities served by such ministers give "access to that communion in which is salvation," and if at a eucharist at which a Lutheran pastor presides is to be found "the salvation-granting presence of the Lord," then Lutheran churches cannot be said simply to lack the ministry given to the church by Christ and the Spirit. In acknowledging the imperfect koinonia between our communities and the access to grace through the ministries of these communities, we also acknowledge a real although imperfect koinonia between our ministries. (§ 107)

More ecumenical work remains to be done on both ministry and apostolicity for eucharistic sharing to become a reality between Lutherans and Catholics. Nevertheless, substantial agreement has been reached on eucharistic doctrine.

Chapter Five

Ministry

The subject of ministry is usually treated as a subsection of the broader category "church" with which it is closely intertwined. Ministry has been one of the most important and yet most contentious and intractable topics in ecumenical dialogue despite substantial convergences. The essential issues for ecumenical dialogue include the relationship of ordained ministry to the universal priesthood of the baptized, the character of the ministry, the ordering of the ministry, the effects of ordination, and the apostolicity of ministry and its relationship to the apostolicity of the church. In recent times, the additional divisive issue of who can be ordained has added another stumbling block to the mutual recognition of ministry between Lutherans and Catholics.

Historical studies show that the ministerial office as it exists among Lutherans today resulted from steps taken in an emergency situation when the Reformers considered themselves to be faced with a decision between fidelity to the gospel, or continued episcopal ordinations at the price of conscience. No bishop in communion with Rome would ordain a minister with Reformation sympathies. Thus, as early as 1972, in the Malta Report, the Catholic members requested that the appropriate authorities in the Roman Catholic Church "consider whether the ecumenical urgency flowing from Christ's will for unity does not demand that the Roman Catholic Church examine seriously the question of the recognition of the Lutheran ministerial office."[1]

From the Lutheran side, the recognition of Catholic ministry by Lutherans has never been in question, for Lutherans have always accepted the churchly character of the Roman Catholic communion. For Lutherans, the church, as the assembly of believers, exists wherever the gospel is purely preached and the sacraments rightly administered. Vatican II's stronger emphasis on ministry to the Word of God by the ordained has largely removed the reasons for the Reformers' criticism of Catholic ministry.[2]

SUBSTANTIAL CONVERGENCES

Ecumenical dialogues over the past fifty years have uncovered substantial convergence in the convictions that Lutherans and Catholics share about ministry, particularly regarding the basis and function of the ministry as well as the manner of its transmission.[3] For example, in a recent study, both Catholics and Lutherans affirm that the ministry is of divine institution, that it is necessary for the being of the church, that it is for a lifetime of service, and that it is not to be repeated.[4] Both traditions ordain through the laying on of hands and invocation of the Holy Spirit by another ordained person. They agree that all ministry is subordinated to Christ, who in the Holy Spirit acts in the preaching of the Word and in the administration of the sacraments. Since this ministry is instituted by Christ, its authority is never simply a delegation "from below."[5] The office of ministry exercises authority over against the community, as well as being within the community, but never "above" or "outside" the community.[6]

For both Lutherans and Catholics, the primary responsibility of the ordained minister is to proclaim the gospel in Word and Sacrament. The ordained minister assembles and builds up the Christian community through this proclamation by celebrating the sacraments and by presiding over the liturgical, missionary, and diaconal life of the community. Both Lutherans and Catholics understand the authority of ministry not to be the individual possession of the minister, but rather "an authority with the commission to serve in the community and for the community."[7]

ORDAINED MINISTRY AND THE PRIESTHOOD OF THE BAPTIZED

Lutherans and Catholics agree that "all the baptized who believe in Christ share in the priesthood of Christ."[8] Moreover, the priesthood of the baptized, sometimes called the "common priesthood" and the special, ordained ministry do not compete with one another.[9] Both office holders and the universal priesthood are essential to the church as is evident in Luther's assertion, "Where you see such offices or office holders, there you may know for a certainty that the holy Christian people must be there. For the Church cannot exist without such bishops, pastors, preachers and priests. And again, they cannot exist without the church; they must be together."[10] Later in his career, Luther numbered the ministerial office among the marks of the church.[11]

The notion of the priesthood of the community is much older than the concept of ordained ministerial priesthood. In the Letter to the Hebrews, only Christ is called a priest. An identification of the church as a priestly community dates to such New Testament texts as 1 Peter 2:9 and Revelation 5:10, while the term *priest* (Latin: *sacerdos*; Greek: *hieros*) has been used to designate the bishop only since the beginning of the third century. The term *priest* was applied to presbyters much later when their role expanded from being an advisory council for the bishop to include leadership of smaller communities where they presided at the Eucharist. Its use to designate church ministers is related to their liturgical role in the Eucharist, considered as a sacrifice. Lutherans generally avoid the nomenclature of priesthood and instead refer to their ordained ministers as *minister, presbyter*, or *pastor* because of Luther's rejection of the sacrificial character of the Mass as well as his insistence that there is but one class of Christians. Because of the scriptural uses of the term and the manner in which an ordained priest represents the priesthood of Christ and serves the priesthood of the community, where the concept of *priest* is used, it applies first to Christ, then to the community, and finally to an ordained minister.

Catholics express the difference between the common and the hierarchical priesthood by saying that they differ "essentially and not only in degree" from one another (*Lumen Gentium* § 10). This means that the two cannot be seen as two points on a continuum with the ordained priest being more intensively a priest or a "higher" priest than a baptized person. Such a view would consider the two priesthoods as two degrees of priesthood. The assertion of a difference in essence also means that this ministry is not derived from the congregation, that this ministry is not simply an enhancement of the common priesthood, and that the ordained minister is not a Christian to a greater degree.[12] The fact that the two priesthoods differ essentially means they are two different kinds of participation in the priesthood of Christ even though they are interrelated. Both priesthoods, common and ordained, are rooted in the priesthood of Christ, but differently.

For Catholics, the threefold priestly ministry of preaching the Word, guiding the faithful, and celebrating divine worship come together most visibly in eucharistic worship. There, the priest proclaims the Word of God to the assembly and, acting both in the person of Christ and in the person of the church, unites the prayers and self-offering of the people with the sacramental offering of Christ to the Father. This is not a repetition of the once-for-all sacrifice of Christ, but a sacramental representation of that once-for-all sacrifice of Christ through the liturgical category of *anamnesis*, a liturgical remembering, which makes present under sacramental sign the past historical event that is recalled. This is illustrated in the prayer over the offerings for the feast day commemorating the Baptism of the Lord:

> Accept, O Lord, the offerings
> we have brought to honor the revealing of your
>   beloved Son,
> so that the oblation of your faithful
> may be transformed into the sacrifice of him
> who willed in his compassion
> to wash away the sins of the world
> Who lives and reigns for ever and ever.[13]

The primary relationship lies between the church and the Eucharist before one considers the relationship between the priest and the Eucharist.[14] The priest's role in representing Christ is defined in relation to the broader priesthood of the entire church. Although the ordained priest presides at the Eucharist, the entire liturgical assembly, which includes the priest, is the subject of the liturgical action. The ordained priesthood enables the common priesthood to exercise its priesthood. The instruction, *Eucharisticum Mysterium*, clearly teaches that the priesthood of the faithful also participates in actively offering the sacrifice and by actively entering into communion:

> The priest alone, insofar as he acts in the person of Christ, consecrates the bread and wine. Nevertheless, the active part of the faithful in the Eucharist consists in: giving thanks to God as they are mindful of the Lord's passion, death, and resurrection; offering the spotless victim not only through the hands of the priest but also together with him; and, through the reception of the body of the Lord, entering into the communion with God and with each other that participation is meant to lead to.[15]

The ordained priest both engages the priesthood of the faithful and represents the priesthood of Christ to that priesthood.[16] The priestly act of Christ is twofold: the sanctification of humankind in a descending (katabatic) act through the sacraments and the worship offered to God by the church in an ascending (anabatic) act of worship. The priestly community, brought into being through baptism, becomes the body of Christ and joins itself to Christ the Priest in his return to his Father in his self-offering.[17]

Some may fear that making the assembly the subject of the liturgical action makes the priest a delegate of the assembly, thereby obliterating the distinction in essence between the priesthood of the baptized and the ordained priesthood. Here it is necessary to distinguish between delegation and authorization. Delegation would consist in arranging for a member of a congregation to preside at the congregation's assembly without empowering that person with a presbyteral relationship to the assembly. This constricts liturgical presidency to discrete liturgical actions rather than relating it to a larger pastoral role. Authorization to ministry, however, always occurs in the context of prayer to the Holy Spirit accompanied by the laying on of hands. In the Catholic

Church, authorization to ministry also links the present assembly to other assemblies in the recognition that no particular church can be a church apart from communion with other particular churches or apart from the apostolic church with which it is in continuity and communion. Finally, a priest can never been seen as a delegate of the assembly if we envision the priest and assembly with a head-body relationship. The priest in speaking the Eucharistic Prayer in the name of the people (*in persona ecclesiae*) speaks as the head of that community, *in persona Christi capitis*.

Like Catholics, Lutherans believe that in baptism, persons are initiated into the priesthood of Christ and thus into the mission of the whole church. This priesthood is a true *sacerdotium* of the baptized. Luther restricted the language of priesthood to Christ and, by extension, to all the baptized, saying, "A sacerdotal priest is not what a presbyter or minister is: The former is born; the latter is made."[18] All the baptized are called to participate in and share responsibility for worship (*leitourgia*), witness (*martyria*), and service (*diaconia*).[19] However, only the ordained exercises the public office of ministry. For Luther, ordination makes ministers *presbyteroi*, not *sacerdotes*.[20]

Luther first presented his view of the universal priesthood of all the baptized in his *Treatise on the New Testament* (1520) in a polemic against the Roman view of the division of Christians into two categories, a temporal estate and a spiritual estate. He asserted,

> It is pure invention that pope, bishop, priests, and monks are called the spiritual estate while princes, lords, artisans, and farmers are called the temporal estate. This is indeed a piece of deceit and hypocrisy. Yet no one need be intimidated by it, and for this reason: all Christians are truly of the spiritual estate, and there is no difference among them except that of office.[21]

For Luther, there was one category of Christians and thus one priesthood, the universal priesthood, through which (by faith) Christ is offered to God: "Thus it becomes clear that it is not the priest alone who offers the sacrifice of the mass; it is this faith which each one has for himself. This is the true priestly office, through which Christ is offered as a sacrifice to God, an office which the priest, with the outward ceremonies of the mass, simply represents. Each and all are, therefore, equally spiritual priests before God."[22]

Statements like this lead Catholics sometimes to assume that Lutheran ministry is a delegation to exercise the ministry of the universal priesthood. However, this view does not take into account the asymmetry between the Catholic distinction between the common and ministerial priesthoods, on the one hand, and the Lutheran distinction between the universal priesthood and office, on the other hand. In other words, Luther does not consider the ministerial office to be a priesthood distinct from the universal priesthood, but he does see it, insofar as it is an office, as something that is not either contained in or derived from the universal priesthood. Catholics consider both the common priesthood and the ministerial priesthoods to be priesthoods, but ones that differ in essence and not in degree. Thus the asymmetry of the discussion is between a ministerial priesthood, which is also an office in Catholic parlance, and a Lutheran office, which is not a priesthood.

Lutherans also hold that baptism of itself does not confer an office of ordained ministry. As Luther stated, "No individual may arrogate to himself, unless it is the common property of all, unless he is called."[23] The Augsburg Confession echoes this, stating that no one should teach publicly in the church or administer the sacraments without a proper public call.[24] This call is properly part of a process of authorization and a requirement for ordination and never simply a delegation to act on behalf of a congregation. In addition to baptism, ordination requires a proper call, prayer to the Holy Spirit, and the laying on of hands. For Luther, all the baptized are priests, but not all are given the office of ministry—let alone authorized by baptism to arrogate this office to themselves. This is reflected in Luther's language for he used the term *sacerdos/sacerdotes* (priest) for the universal priesthood of the baptized, reserving the term *minister/ministri* (minister, servant) for the ordained pastor.[25]

This point is reinforced when one understands that the authorization to exercise the authority of the public office of ministry does not mean that the authority of the office is derived from such authorization. The source of the authority of office is the office itself and "the word of God that created the office and for which Christ established the office."[26] The fact that Luther required that ordinations be performed at Wittenberg (usually presided over by pastor and general superintendent of Saxony, Johannes Bugenhagen) rather than in the congregation issuing the call is further evidence that a call and ordination are not synonymous. Ordination has legitimacy as an office that serves in the larger church and not only in a particular congregation.

This office is public, meaning that it is perceived *coram ecclesia* (in the presence of the church) and *in nomine ecclesiae* (in the name of the church) and is related to a specific congregation.[27] It is entrusted with the task of public proclamation of the gospel, a task not given simply to individual Christians, as well as with the administration of sacraments, care of souls, and leadership of the congregation. In the office, the pastor acts as an apostle and a prophet of Jesus Christ and speaks in his name as well as in the name of the church.[28]

While the Catholic analysis of ordained priesthood given above explained the language of *priest* with reference to the liturgical action of offering sacrifice, it is instructive to note that Luther's analysis of the liturgical action emphasized not the consecration, and especially not the notion of sacrifice, but rather the distribution in order to call attention to the original intent of the Lord's Supper, namely to be a meal shared in common.[29] Such a shift transforms ministerial identity from *priest* to *servant*. Ministerial identity in this instance follows the perspective and emphasis within a particular analysis of the liturgical action. However, just because there is a different perspective and emphasis does not mean that the conclusions are incompatible. Catholics would also affirm the servant identity of priests. It remains to be seen whether resolution of ecumenical difference regarding eucharistic sacrifice enables Lutherans to accept the designation of *priest* as one possible designation for ordained ministers even if they themselves choose not to use it. The rejection of the term by most Lutherans results in part from Luther's polemic against the Roman hierarchy and the medieval notion of a hierarchy of estates. The rejection is also the result of their reading of Scripture, where the word is only used in the New Testament for Christ and the community of believers, and *presbyteros* (along with *episcopos*) is a designation for an office in the church.

To date, the ecumenical work on the Eucharist has not been correlated to this question of ministerial identity because this work has been more concerned with questions of apostolicity and validity. In doing this work, it would be a mistake to try to impose the Catholic ministerial debate about function versus ontology onto Lutheran theology since those categories are foreign to the Lutheran confessional writings. Finally, additional theological work needs to be done regarding the distinction between the laity and clergy, not in terms of office, but in terms of two "orders" of Christians. *Lumen Gentium* refers to the people of God as the *Christifideles*, a category of all the baptized inclusive of laity and clergy, which could be a point of departure for such a study (§§ 12, 31, 33, 37, 40–42, 43, 65, 69).

ORDINATION AND ITS EFFECTS

Both Lutherans and Catholics hold that entry into the apostolic and God-given ministry is by ordination and that no one ordains himself or herself or can claim this office as his or her right. God calls a person to ordination and that person is designated in and through the church. In both communions, ordination is for a lifetime of service and is not to be repeated.[30] Both Lutherans and Catholics ordain through prayer to the Holy Spirit and the laying on of hands by another ordained person. Both consider the office a ministry of proclamation and the administration of the sacraments.[31]

While Catholics consider ordination to be a sacrament, Lutherans do not. It can be noted, however, that Melanchthon considers the possibility in the *Apology of the Augsburg Confession*, saying, "But if ordination is understood with reference to the ministry of the Word, we have no objection to calling ordination a sacrament."[32] Catholics require that a bishop administer ordination, and while not all Lutherans have that requirement, many do. Lutherans do not consider the office to be a sacrificial ministry, while Catholics do.[33] However, since substantial progress has been made regarding the Lutheran rejection of the sacrificial character of the ministry through the liturgical category of *anamnesis*, it may be time to determine whether this is any longer a church-dividing issue. The study, *The Condemnations of the Reformation Era: Do They Still Divide?* raises the question "whether the wide degree of agreement about essential components of the act of ordination does not justify recognition of the sacramentality of the ordination carried out in the Protestant church, provided that an understanding can be reached about the observance of the apostolic succession in this act."[34]

WHO CAN BE ORDAINED?

The ordination of women is a divisive ministerial issue that has arisen in recent decades between Lutherans and Catholics. Most Lutheran member churches of the Lutheran World Federation hold themselves free under the gospel to ordain women. Those that do ordain women consider the practice to be a necessary witness to the gospel at this time in history. Many member churches also elect them to episcopal ministry, a practice consistent with the conviction that there is but one office of ministry. Lutherans see in this practice "a renewed understanding of the biblical witness" that reflects "the nature of the church as a sign of our reconciliation and unity in Christ through baptism across the divides of ethnicity, social status and gender."[35]

The Catholic Church does not consider itself to be authorized to ordain women based on the tradition of Jesus only calling men to be his apostles (*Ordinatio Sacerdotalis* 4). Even though this issue presently impedes a mutual recognition of ministries between Catholics and Lutherans, it by no means halts all ecumenical discussion on ministry. The Roman Catholic-Lutheran Joint Commission states in its document *The Ministry in the Church* that the Catholic Church "is able to strive for a consensus on the nature and significance of the ministry without the different conceptions of the persons to be ordained fundamentally endangering such a consensus and its practical consequences for the growing unity of the church."[36]

Since Catholics consider ordained women ministers to be proper ministers within the Lutheran communion, even a partial mutual recognition of ministry with Lutherans would involve the recognition of these women ministers to be in a partial or imperfect ministerial relationship within a Catholic *presbyterium* or college of bishops. Given the Catholic Church's stance on the topic, the only solution at present appears to be to explore whether a differentiated practice within the two communions would be possible, perhaps analogous to the differentiated practice of married clergy in Eastern rite churches. However, the Catholic Church regards the requirement of celibacy to be a disciplinary rather than a doctrinal issue, which gives that practice a different character from the teaching on the ordination of women according to the *"Responsum ad Propositum Dubium"* issued by the Congregation of the Doctrine of the Faith on October 28, 1995. The congregation claimed infallibility for this teaching, prohibiting the ordination of women according to the universal ordinary magisterium.[37] At this time, it is difficult to find a way forward for the full mutual recognition of ministers required for the full, visible communion that is the goal of our ecumenical work. This issue should not be allowed to eclipse the ecumenical agreement achieved on nature and purpose of ordained ministry and the relationship of that ministry to the universal priesthood of the baptized.

THE ORDERING OF THE MINISTRY

Both Lutherans and Catholics consider that there is one ministerial office, and both accept that *episcopé* is rightly exercised in the church. For most Lutherans, such oversight is exercised by bishops. Where there are bishops, they exercise *episcopé* over presbyters/pastors.

For Catholics, the one sacrament of order is exercised by three ministries or major orders: bishops, priests (presbyters), and deacons.[38] Even though this structure of ministry evolved during the apostolic age or later, Catholics understand this basic threefold structure to be irreversible and as belonging to the fullness of the nature of the church.[39]

Before Vatican II, the status of the episcopacy as an order remained a disputed question in the Western church. Some theologians followed the opinion of Jerome that there was no essential difference between a bishop and a presbyter, the only difference being one of jurisdiction. The reference point for the analysis was the Eucharist, which a bishop could not consecrate any more intensively than a simple priest. The conclusion was that there was no sacramental distinction between the two.[40] One of the problems of this position was that jurisdiction and governance risked being cut off from their sacramental moorings, while leadership of worship became divorced from leadership within the Christian community. The presbyter risked being reduced to a man empowered for cult. Vatican II taught that episcopal consecration constitutes the fullness of sacramental ordination to office (*Lumen Gentium* § 21). Consequently, the episcopate is "the basic form of ministry and the point of departure for the theological interpretation of church ministry."[41] Since this is a relatively new teaching and one that may potentially distance Catholics even more from Lutherans, it is important to examine the implications of this teaching in some detail and to suggest how it may be received ecumenically.

Two criteria sometimes used to distinguish the episcopacy from the presbyterate, configuration to Christ and sacramental power, are ultimately inadequate to distinguish the uniqueness and essence of the episcopacy. According to the first view, both a presbyter and a bishop are vicars of Christ who act *in persona Christi*, in the place of the person of Christ.[42] Vatican II expresses this perspective when it says, "Through that sacrament priests by the anointing of the Holy Spirit are signed with a special character and so are configured to Christ the priest in such a way that they are able to act in the person of Christ the head" (*Presbyterorum Ordinis* § 2). The difference between the configuration of the baptized to Christ and that of the ordained priest or bishop is that the latter is configured to the headship of Christ in relation to his body, the church, while the former are configured to Christ as members of the Body of Christ. This configuration is significant for a theology of ministry since it is Christ who acts in the sacraments through the mediation of the priest.

This perspective distinguishes an ordained person from the baptized, but it does not adequately distinguish a bishop from a presbyter. Moreover, here the sacrament of order becomes a sacrament essentially *for* the church rather than a sacrament *of* the church. Since all sacraments are efficacious signs, in addition to ordained ministry signifying Christ in their relationship to the community, Catholics also look for an ecclesial referent of the sign, that is, some ecclesial relationship of the bishop to the church that will distinguish a bishop from a presbyter.

A second attempt locates the distinction between presbyters and bishops in the powers proper to each, since a bishop can ordain and confirm while a priest cannot. This argument does not take into account the history of sacramental theology, which shows that bishops were the original ministers of baptism, Eucharist, confirmation, penance, and holy orders. Historical research shows that some abbots were given jurisdiction to ordain their monks in the medieval period.[43] Even today, bishops delegate confirmation to a parish pastor in certain circumstances, especially during the Easter Vigil. According to Karl Rahner, "No truly definable borderline can be clearly and convincingly drawn between priest and bishop which is *absolute* as regards the power of order."[44]

A better solution is found in the representative role of the bishop in signifying the church. The sacrament of order signifies a reality beyond itself. This is not only Christ the head, but also the church. In particular, a bishop represents his particular church within the communion of churches by his membership in the communion of bishops, the episcopal college, which is the successor of the apostolic college (*Lumen Gentium* §§ 23, 9). The personal and communal apostolic succession of bishops manifests and serves the apostolic tradition of the church. A bishop is charged with maintaining communion with the apostolic past, communion within his church, and communion with all the other particular churches, including the church and Bishop of Rome. Thus there is a parallelism between the communion of churches and the communion of bishops in the episcopal college.[45]

Here the distinction between a bishop and a presbyter becomes evident. A presbyter does not represent a particular church—defined in Catholicism both eucharistically and ministerially as a community of the altar under the sacred ministry of the bishop (*Lumen Gentium* § 26).[46] Nor is he a member of the episcopal college. When the sacramentality of episcopal ordination is viewed through the lens of communion ecclesiology, the distance between Catholic and Lutheran theologies of the episcopacy does not appear to be as great, for Lutherans accept the episcopal charge of witnessing and serving the communion of churches.

Much of the theology of priesthood was given earlier, so here it can simply be reiterated that for Catholics, priests are "sharers in a special way in Christ's priesthood and, by carrying out sacred functions, act as ministers of him who through his Spirit continually exercises his priesthood role for our benefit in the liturgy" (*Presbyterorum Ordinis* § 5).[47] While both bishops and presbyters are priests, diaconal ordination is not an ordination to the ministerial priesthood (*Lumen Gentium* § 29).

For Catholics, the third order within the one sacrament of holy orders is the diaconate. Ordained to assist bishops and presbyters in the ministry of Word, the liturgy, and charity, the service of deacons has varied in terms of its relative permanence, emphasis, and specific tasks. While ordination to a transitional diaconate has been a long-standing practice, Pope Paul VI restored the permanent diaconate after a lapse of a millennium by establishing canonical norms for the permanent diaconate and opening it to married men. His apostolic letter *Sacrum Diaconatus Ordinem* (June 18, 1967), promulgated a revision of the rite of ordination in 1968, and he established norms for the diaconate in 1972. Deacons currently are able to preach and preside at the liturgies of baptism, matrimony, and Christian burial, in addition to engaging in ministries of charity.

The Lutheran tradition has one order of ordained ministers, usually called *pastors* in English, but "*Pfarrer*" in German.[48] The pastor who has received this ministry possesses the fullness of that which ordination confers.[49] Lutherans do not reject the division of the one office into different ministries as they have developed in the church. In contemporary practice, some Lutheran churches have "one threefold ministry," while others do not.[50] While questions of church order remain intensely discussed, there is no expectation of a single proper form given the varied experiences of the church between the Reformation and now.[51]

Historically, Luther never challenged the office of bishop, largely because of the biblical evidence for the office, and did not object to episcopal oversight on the condition that it conformed to the gospel. He even tried to maintain an episcopal leadership of the church in vacated sees, but this did not finally succeed.[52] The

Augsburg Confession affirms the desire of the Lutheran reformers to preserve, if possible, the episcopal polity inherited from the past.[53] Here it can be observed that some non-German Lutheran churches, most notably the Nordic churches, did preserve their episcopacies.[54] In lands comprising the Holy Roman Empire, however, the role of *episkopé* was not abandoned but taken over by superintendents (the Latin equivalent of the Greek *episkopos*).

According to the Augsburg Confession, power of the bishops "is the power of God's mandate to preach the gospel, to forgive and retain sins, and to administer the sacraments."[55] By divine right, bishops have jurisdiction "to forgive sins, to reject teaching that opposes the gospel, and to exclude from the communion of the church the ungodly whose ungodliness is known."[56] Insofar as bishops teach according to the gospel, churches are bound by divine right to be obedient to them, but insofar as they teach or establish anything contrary to the gospel, "churches have a command from God that prohibits obedience."[57] Other powers accrue to bishops by human right such as administering justice for the sake of maintaining public peace or deciding marriage cases or tithes. They may establish ordinances for the good order of the church, but may not establish anything contrary to the gospel to burden consciences.

At the time of the Reformation, because of the Catholic bishops' unwillingness to participate in the reform, Lutheran reformers in Germany adopted a number of alternative measures, including organizing ministries of oversight for their territorial churches. These had had various titles, including *superintendent* and *bishop*, but all were considered to be episcopal in terms of responsibilities.[58] Moreover, the Evangelical prince assumed a certain responsibility for many of the bishop's juridical duties. Luther called these "emergency bishops" (*Notbischöfe*) and considered them to be a temporary measure. After 1918 and the end of the church-state system where the princes had exercised a quasi-episcopal role, the German Lutheran churches reintroduced the title *bishop*. Meanwhile, the Nordic Lutheran churches had generally preserved the pre-Reformation episcopal order as well as the title.[59] In the United States, the predecessor bodies of the ELCA introduced the title *bishop* in the second half of the twentieth century.[60] Since the presence or absence of the episcopacy does not affect the mutual recognition of ministry with other traditions for Lutherans, the Lutheran position is that episcopal succession represents an ecclesial good, but not a necessary one for the recognition of authentic ministry.[61]

One additional historical note shows that Lutherans were much closer to Catholic understandings about bishops than their descendants have come to imagine. Part of it has to do with the word *superintendentes* translated generally as "superintendent," a term still used in some German Lutheran churches and picked up by the Methodists. When Lutherans used that term in the sixteenth century, they were drawing on a remark made by St. Augustine, who—noticing that *episcopus* was a loan word into Latin—translates it into Latin in one of his sermons on the Psalms as *superintendents*.[62] Since the word *bishop* designated not simply an ecclesiastical office, but also a princely dominion—the only bishops Luther knew were "prince-bishops"—the Lutherans could not use the term (especially after 1555) and thus, to designate the people with oversight in the church, they called these people superintendents—borrowing the word from Latin into German and, eventually, English. Thus it can be posited that even German Lutherans never practiced presbyteral ordination but rather ordination by superintendents, that is, by ecclesiastical (and not princely) bishops.[63] When Luther consecrated a prince, Georg von Anhalt, to be the actual bishop of Merseburg, he only did it because the bishop of Brandenburg had recently died and the archbishop of Cologne was too far away. In any case, originally a Lutheran understanding of the office of oversight, *episkopé* was far closer to current Roman Catholic practice than anyone fifty years ago could have imagined.

The ordination of deacons is an open matter for Lutherans globally. They also differ among themselves in understanding how "the ministries of deacons, pastors, and ministers of *episkopé* may relate to each other with reference to the one ministry of the church."[64] Some Lutheran churches are moving toward recognizing a threefold ministry, while others do not find it to be an appropriate model. In some places, deacons are lay ministers, while in others they are an integral part of the ordained ministry.[65]

MINISTRY AND APOSTOLICITY

One of the impediments to the recognition of Lutheran ministry by Catholics has been the issue of apostolicity. At the time of the Reformation, when no Catholic bishops joined the reformers in Germany, Lutherans, appealing to Jerome's position on the essential equality between bishops and priests, practiced what appear now to be presbyteral ordinations, although they were never ordinations without *episkopé*. From the Catholic point of view, these pastors, because not ordained by a bishop in apostolic succession, were themselves no longer in apostolic succession.

In recent ecumenical conversations, both Catholics and Lutherans affirm, "The church is apostolic on the basis of the apostolic gospel and in its faithfulness to it. This gospel is continually prior to the church."[66] They further agree about the contribution of ordained ministry to apostolicity, saying, "The ordained ministry belongs to the essential elements which, through the power of the Holy Spirit, contribute to the church being and remaining apostolic."[67] These two statements affirm that apostolicity is first an attribute of the church, something broader and more extensive than apostolic ministry, but that apostolic ministry is an essential component of that broader characteristic of the church. Ordained ministry in apostolic succession is a sign of the apostolicity of the church and is charged with maintaining the church in its apostolicity so that it continues to profess the faith and to manifest the characteristics of the church of the apostles. Episcopal ordination is also a sign of the catholicity of the church because the ordaining bishops signify their and their churches' acceptance of the new bishop. Ordination within apostolic succession, however, is neither a guarantee of the personal faithfulness of the ordinand nor a guarantee that a church will remain faithful to every aspect of apostolic faith, life, and witness, as church schisms have sadly demonstrated.

For Catholics, the succession of the laying on of hands is a sign of "a connection with Christ, of continuity of gospel proclamation effected by the Spirit, and of the unity of the church over time."[68] Yet, essentially, apostolic succession is more than a succession of ministers. *Lumen Gentium* teaches that there is also a communal dimension of apostolic succession insofar as the college of bishops succeeds the college or permanent group of the apostles (§ 20). Vatican II's Dogmatic Constitution on Revelation, *Dei Verbum*, also acknowledges a broader transmission of the apostolic tradition when it says, "The expression 'what has been handed down from the apostles' includes everything that helps the people of God to live a holy life and to grow in faith. In this way the church, in its teaching, life and worship, perpetuates and hands on to every generation all that it is and all that it believes" (§ 8). Thus the bearers of the apostolic tradition include individual bishops, the college of bishops, and the entire church's teaching, life, and worship.

The study document, *The Apostolicity of the Church*, notes that Luther himself rarely spoke of an "apostolic church," although the marks of the church as he identified them certainly reflect the reality of apostolicity, namely continuity in practicing baptism, the Lord's Supper, the office of the keys, the call to ministry, public gathering for worship in praise and confession of faith, and the bearing of the cross as Christ's disciples.[69] His Large and Small Catechisms contain expositions of the Apostles' Creed, baptism, the Lord's Supper, and (private) confession. Recitation of this creed or the Nicene Creed in which the church confesses itself to be apostolic is an integral part of Lutheran prayer at the Lord's Supper as well as in morning and evening prayer. Certainly, these are indicators of an intention to maintain the church in apostolicity.

While Lutherans point to multiple forms of apostolic continuity such as "the continuity of the people of God in the faith of the Gospel, continuity of the ordained ministry, and the continuity of place," all Lutheran churches understand themselves to have preserved the one apostolic ministry instituted by God.[70] In recent times, Lutherans have entered into ecumenical agreements with Anglicans, where the visible succession of bishops through ordination by a bishop in succession has not stood in the way of such agreements and has come to be called beneficial part (*bene esse*) of church life.

The first of these is the *Porvoo Common Statement* of 1992, signed by Lutheran and Anglican churches of the Nordic countries.[71] Since apostolicity is embodied in a number of church structures, worship, and activities, entering into an apostolic succession of ministry is not perceived as establishing the apostolicity of Lutheran churches, but rather as an embrace of a historic sign of apostolicity to strengthen further the unity and communion of churches and to witness to apostolicity. Furthermore, the use of the sign of apostolic succession does not constitute a mutual acknowledgment of either churches or ministry, since such acknowledgment precedes the use of the sign. This is significant since in some Catholic discussions, the apostolicity of a minister is seen to be integral to the full apostolicity of a church.[72] The Porvoo Statement explains, "Resumption of the use of the sign does not imply an adverse judgment on the ministries of those churches which did not previously make use of the sign. It is rather a means of making more visible the unity and continuity of the Church at all times and in all places."[73]

The Porvoo agreement committed the participating churches to a number of initiatives including, but not limited to, welcoming one another's members to sacramental and pastoral ministration, to mutually recognizing and exchanging one another's episcopally ordained ministers, to inviting "one another's bishops normally to participate in the laying on of hands at the ordination of bishops as a sign of the unity and continuity of the Church," and to establishing appropriate forms of collegial and conciliar consultation.[74]

In a similar vein, The Episcopal Church, USA, and the Evangelical Lutheran Church in America entered into a relationship of full communion with the adoption of the document *Called to Common Mission* in 1999. One part of this agreement commits the ELCA to share an episcopal succession that is both Evangelical and historic by regularly including "one or more bishops of the other church to participate in the laying-on-of-hands at the ordinations/installations of their own bishops as a sign, though not a guarantee, of the unity and apostolic continuity of the whole church."[75]

Lutheran structures do not include a worldwide college of bishops. Lutherans have, however, developed "various synodical and collegial structures, which include the participation of both lay and ordained persons, and in which the episcopal ministry has a clearly defined role."[76] In this asymmetry lie possibilities for mutual enrichment, for the Catholic Church would benefit from a more robust practice of synodality including participation of the laity, while Lutherans may benefit from exploring the inter-relationship of bishops and regional expressions of the church within an ecclesiology of communion. Since the episcopal office is exercised "not only in personal contact with the congregation (personal dimension), in which it is essentially rooted (communal dimension), but also requires communion with the other bishops (collegial dimension),"[77] the development of a theology of the collegial relationship of Lutheran bishops would seem to be advantageous. Since the predecessor bodies of the ELCA restored the title of bishop in the 1970s, practical experiences of the episcopacy, expressed more in church constitutions than in theological or historical documents, are nevertheless gradually contributing to a theology of the episcopacy.

The irony of these relationships with respect to the Catholic Church is that the Catholic Church has not officially recognized Anglican ministry since Leo XIII declared the nullity of Anglican orders in 1896 in his encyclical, *Apostolicae Curae*.[78] Thus the Catholic Church does not presently recognize the succession that the Lutherans are adopting with the Anglicans.[79] The historical presupposition has been that the Catholic Church does not consider Lutheran orders to be valid, but the Catholic Church has never officially declared their nullity as was done for Anglican orders. Nevertheless, most Lutheran bishops have not been consecrated in an apostolic succession recognized by Catholics, and they are not in a relationship of full communion with the Bishop of Rome. However, the adoption of episcopal structures and the strengthening of communion between Anglicans and Lutherans with their mutual recognition of ministry and mutual participation in episcopal ordinations are of great ecumenical significance to Catholics, for they put into place a theology and practice of the episcopacy that bring closer the day when Catholic, Lutheran, and Anglican ministries may be reconciled. It may be time to reexamine the historical reasons for the decree of Leo XIII to see if they are still applicable to dialogue partners today given changes in the ordination rites and ecumenical convergences in eucharistic theology and in theologies of ministry.

According to Catholic doctrine, the sacramental sign of ordination is not fully present in Lutheran ministers because those who ordain do not act in communion with the Catholic episcopal college. The Second Vatican Council consequently speaks of a *defectus sacramenti ordinis*, which is usually translated as "lack of the sacrament of order (*Unitatis Redintegratio* 22)."[80] The US Lutheran-Catholic document *The Church as Koinonia of Salvation* recommends that *defectus* be translated as "defect" or "deficiency" since, as Walter Cardinal Kasper has stated, "On material grounds, and not merely on the basis of the word usage of the Council, it becomes clear that *defectus ordinis* does not signify a complete absence, but rather a deficiency in the full form of the office."[81] The dialogue maintains that such a translation would be consistent with a real, but imperfect, recognition of ministries and provide the basis for first steps toward a reconciliation of ministries. This means that the reality of ordination cannot be evaluated on the basis of either "all" (complete mutual recognition) or "nothing" (absence of the reality of ordination). Such a translation would be in line with a comment in a letter from then Joseph Cardinal Ratzinger to the German bishop Johannes Hanselmann in 1993, suggesting the need to move beyond categories of validity in assessing ministry.[82]

WORLDWIDE MINISTRY

Lutherans and Catholics agree that ministry is differentiated to serve local and regional realizations of the church. Thus pastors/presbyters serve congregations and parishes, while bishops and superintendents serve regional expressions of the church such as synods and dioceses. Furthermore, Lutherans and Catholics agree "that the worldwide expression of ecclesial life is a communion of churches, embodying the apostolicity and catholicity of the church."[83] They also agree "that all ministry, to the degree that it serves the koinonia of salvation, also serves the unity of the worldwide church."[84]

At the worldwide level, Catholics speak of the universal church as a communion of particular churches under the leadership of the Bishop of Rome, the pope, who as teacher and shepherd (pastor) of the whole church (*Lumen Gentium* § 22) exercises the Petrine ministry to serve the unity and communion of the church (§ 18). The Lutheran World Federation also identifies itself as a communion of churches, but does not identify itself as a church. Nor does it conceive of its president as a pastor.

The ministry of oversight of the whole church remains one of the major differences between Catholics and Lutherans. *Church and Justification* recommends that this topic be dealt with "in the context of ecclesial *koinonia* in general, but also in the particular context of the Roman Catholic understanding of the relationship between the episcopal college and the papal office."[85] Within an ecclesiology of communion, which envisions each expression of the church—local, regional, worldwide—to be in communion with each other and with two of these three expressions having a pastor both to serve that expression of the church and to oversee its communion with other expressions, it is logical to inquire into the advantages and role of a ministry for the worldwide expression of the church.

Catholics point to the beginning of their teaching on the papacy in the biblical witness concerning the special position of Peter. The concrete shape of this office may vary greatly in accordance with changing historical conditions.[86] The second millennium shows significant differences when compared with the first one thousand years, the former corresponding to a more centralized papacy necessary at that time to fend off secular political powers. The Second Vatican Council placed the primacy in a new interpretive framework within a comprehensive ecclesiology, with recovery of the local realizations of communion and highlighting the bonds of communion in the *collegium* of all bishops, within which the pope has his role.[87] The primacy of jurisdiction must be understood as ministerial service to the community and as bond of the unity of the church. This service of unity is, above all, a service of unity in faith. The office of the primacy also includes the task of caring for legitimate diversity among local churches.[88]

Lutheran rejection of the papacy focuses on the concrete historical papacy as it confronted them at the time of the Reformation. Lutherans disagreed with papal claims regarding the biblical warrant for the papacy, its origin from Christ, and the extent of its supervisory authority and power.[89] The Reformation also rejected papally sanctioned practices, such as indulgences and ecclesiastical laws, which seemed to show that the pope did not subordinate himself to God's Word in Scripture. It saw the pope as arrogating to himself what Christ gave to all the apostles, thereby contradicting the equality of bishops evident in early history. Lastly, it considered the pope's worldly power to be alien to Christian ministry and to Christ's spiritual reign and kingdom.

In recent times, the necessity of acting within a worldwide realization of the church is becoming more evident with Lutheran participation in the World Council of Churches and with growing instances where the Lutheran World Federation finds itself speaking on behalf of its member churches. Three instances of this include the statement against apartheid by the 1984 LWF Assembly, the ratification of the consensus for the *Joint Declaration on the Doctrine of Justification* in 1999, and the act of repentance toward the Mennonite World Conference in 2010.

These and other experiences give rise to considerations of the universal dimensions of church unity and ways to institutionalize this.[90] Lutherans have in recent times also emphasized the communion of churches, holding that no local church should exist in isolation. Thus the Lutheran legacy is open to a rightly exercised primacy.[91] While Lutherans do not accept the Catholic belief that the papacy is divinely instituted, ecumenical conversations suggest that the Petrine office of the Bishop of Rome need not be excluded by Lutherans as a visible sign of the unity of the church as a whole "insofar as [this office] is subordinated to the primacy of the gospel by theological reinterpretation and practical restructuring."[92] The task of this ministry would be "to care for the maintaining of the universal church in the apostolic truth and for the world-wide full communion of churches, and to encourage local and regional churches in faith and ministry (cf. Lk 22:32)."[93]

Catholics are open to this reform of the office of the papacy. Although they hold that the papacy is part of God's will for the church, Catholics acknowledge that while the juridical expressions employed in Vatican I's dogmatic declaration of papal primacy were perhaps fitting for the nineteenth century within their historical context, they may require reformulation today in ways that underscore the evangelical and spiritual core of papal primacy.[94] John Paul II, in his encyclical *Ut Unum Sint*, invited church leaders to a fraternal dialogue with him on this subject (§ 96). He acknowledged the desire of Christian communities "to find a way of exercising the primacy which, while in no way renouncing what is essential to its mission, is nonetheless open to a new situation," and asked all the pastors and theologians of the churches to seek together "the forms in which this ministry may accomplish a service of love recognized by all concerned" (§ 95). Although John Paul II recognized that changes needed to be made in the exercise of the papacy so that it would no longer be an obstacle to ecumenical unity, to date, these changes have not occurred. Thus it may be premature to ask Lutherans to accept the ministry of the Bishop of Rome. It is not too soon, however, to engage in the dialogue of the form that such a ministry might take and to take steps on the way to full visible communion that remove barriers to unity.

While it remains to be seen how these reforms will be accomplished and what form they will take, Catholics can point to a new context in which the highest pastoral authority must function to be more consonant with our era. The doctrine of episcopal collegiality as developed by the Second Vatican Council provides a new interpretive framework for the exercise of papal primacy. The Council emphasized the bonds of communion in the college of bishops within which the pope has a special role. Today, his preferred title is "Bishop of Rome," showing that he is within the college, not outside of it or above it, and that his role in the church is inseparable from the historical role that the Church of Rome exercised in adjudicating disputes in the early church. The primacy of jurisdiction, defined by Vatican I, must be understood today as a ministerial service to the community and as a bond of unity in faith. Within an ecclesiology of communion, a task of primacy includes caring for legitimate diversity among the local church in communion with one another.

While a significant amount of work remains to be done both to reach a consensus on a theology of ministry and to reconcile ministerial practices, an overview of ecumenical dialogue of the past fifty years shows significant convergence. Today the historical exigencies and polemics of the sixteenth century are seen in a clearer light. Both Lutherans and Catholics draw closer to each other as they benefit from historical, biblical, and liturgical study that puts past divisions into new perspectives. Both have developed their understanding of liturgy and ministry since the sixteenth century, and these developments potentially blunt or render inapplicable some of the past condemnations.

Chapter Six

Church

Since the church in history is always embedded in time and place, the roots of the different understandings of the church by Lutherans and Catholics understandably lie in the particular historical circumstances of the Reformation and its aftermath. This history shaped the territorial boundaries of the Lutheran Church, its engagement with secular power, convictions about the holiness or sinfulness within the church and its membership, its visibility, its relationship to Word and Sacrament, its ministry, and its teaching structures and convictions about authority. As those original historical circumstances have changed and understandings of the theology and functioning of the church have developed in both traditions, the edge of disagreements has been blunted so that many remaining differences are seen to be ones of emphasis or complementarity rather than as church-dividing.

Luther originally intended not to create a Lutheran church, but to call the church of his time to reform according to his understanding of Scripture and Tradition when he posted his *Ninety-Five Theses* examining the sale of indulgences on October 31, 1517. Because, in his opinion, the bishops responsible for oversight had neglected their office to provide oversight of the correct preaching of the gospel, Luther later appealed to the princes to allow for the reform of the churches in their territories. The role of the prince, originally envisioned as an emergency measure, became the norm in Lutheran territories, thus contributing to a form of church governance in Germany shared by secular officials and clergy. Outside of central and northern Europe, where there was no such relationship to the state, Lutheran churches also organized around national linguistic or territorial boundaries.

The 1555 Peace of Augsburg officially recognized Lutheran churches within the Holy Roman Empire, defined as those churches adhering to the Augsburg Confession. Lutheran churches are united and identified by common confessional documents collected in *The Book of Concord* (1580), which contains the Apostles', Nicene, and Athanasian creeds and seven Reformation texts.[1] Thus Lutheran churches comprise a confessional communion identified by the acceptance of some or all of these confessions.

Both Lutheran and Catholic theologies of the church during the Reformation and post-Reformation periods are marked by Reformation polemics. The Finnish ecumenist Risto Saarinen argues that Lutheran ecclesiology developed more as a result of interaction with other traditions and by the influence of broader theological currents in Protestantism than through the intellectual achievements of prominent Lutheran theologians.[2] When one moves beyond these Reformation polemics, Saarinen notes, "Any theologically valid ecclesiology should become an ecclesiology of the one, holy, apostolic and catholic church." Hence Saarinen does not see a narrowly confessional, that is, "Lutheran" ecclesiology as something advocated by academic Lutheran theologians and ecumenically minded church leaders.[3] This reflects the origins and self-identity of Lutheranism as a reform movement within the catholic church.

Reflecting the polemics of the Reformation, the Lutheran confessions present an ecclesiology contrasted with what was perceived to be the errors of both Roman Catholicism and the radical Reformers. Similarly responding to the polemics of the time, the theological writing of Robert Bellarmine (1542–1621), the great Jesuit theologian of the Catholic Reformation, refutes certain ecclesiological themes in Lutheran theology, such as the notion of a hidden church, through his emphasis on the institutional church as a society visible through the profession of faith, communion of the sacraments, and governance by legitimate pastors.[4] Likewise, Roman Catholics did not significantly pursue a theology of the priesthood of the baptized until the twentieth century, in part because such a theology figured so prominently in Protestant theology.

Given the Reformation roots of Lutheran confessional ecclesiology, it is consequently not surprising that traditionally this has been one of the more divisive topics between Catholics and Lutherans. Nevertheless, significant ecumenical progress has been made with respect to agreement on the trinitarian and christological origins of the church, the relationship of the church to the Word of God, the church as both a recipient and instrument of salvation, and the church as a communion of saints. Some remaining differences on these topics represent differing emphases. For other differences, such as ecclesial identity through theologies of Word and Sacrament, theological developments since the Reformation have brought the two traditions closer together. In yet other instances, Lutherans and Catholics have maintained different aspects of a common inherited tradition. For example, although Lutherans and Roman Catholics identify the local church differently, they have both kept aspects of the local church as it was known in the Patristic period. Perhaps the sharpest differences in the ecclesiologies of the two traditions are found at the worldwide level, with Catholics having a robust theology of the universal church, the ministry of the Bishop of Rome, and a well-developed teaching office (magisterium) functioning for the whole church. Lutherans and Catholics also differ in the role played by laypeople in the church's teaching function as well in the binding character of that teaching. Lutherans traditionally grant greater autonomy to territorial churches, do not self-define as a church at the worldwide level, and thus would not, for example, consider the presidency of the Lutheran World Federation to be a pastoral office.

Five ecumenical documents deal primarily with ecclesiology: the document of the international Lutheran-Catholic Joint Commission, *The Gospel and the Church* (1972);[5] a second document of that same commission, *Church and Justification* (1994); the German Catholic-Lutheran Dialogue statement, *Communio Sanctorum: The Church as the Communion of Saints* (2000); the US Lutheran-Catholic Dialogue statement, *The Church as Koinonia of Salvation: Its Structures and Ministries* (2005); and the study document of the Lutheran-Roman Catholic Commission on Unity, *The Apostolicity of the Church* (2006).[6] Other ecumenical documents dealing primarily with ministry certainly touch on ecclesiology since ministry and the church are so closely related.

THE TRINITARIAN ORIGINS OF THE CHURCH

Lutherans and Catholics are united in their conviction that the church originates in the life of the triune God such that it is named the new people of God, the Body of Christ, and the temple of the Spirit. It originates in the saving work of God in Jesus Christ and is founded on the totality of the Christ-event beginning with the election of the people of God of the Old Testament and developing through Jesus' proclamation of the reign of God, his gathering of disciples, his institution of the Lord's Supper, his death on the cross and resurrection, and the outpouring of the Spirit on Pentecost.[7] The church is not identical with the kingdom of God, but reaches forward to an eschatological future when the kingdom of God will be manifest in its fullness. The church is "God's eschatological community of salvation" since justification by faith is the path of entrance into the church.[8] The present communion of the church is an "anticipatory reality," a real partaking "of the *koinonia* of the Father, Son, and Holy Spirit," but this is done as a pilgrim church in a provisional and fragmentary way in anticipation and expectation of its final destination and eschatological consummation.[9]

The origin of the church in the triune God and the presence of Christ with his church constitute the foundation of any claim for the holiness of the church.[10] Both Lutherans and Catholics share the confession of the creeds of the early church that the church is holy. The church knows that this holiness is indestructible from Christ's promise that he is present "to the end of the age" (Matt 28:20) and that "the gates of Hades will not prevail against it" (Matt 16:18). Even though the church is assured that it will persevere in the truth necessary for salvation (sometimes termed the church's "indefectibility") in its visible and temporal reality, the church is a pilgrim on the way to its final perfection, engaged in a struggle against sin, and in need of daily repentance. *Lumen Gentium*, echoing the Lutheran assertion *simul iustus et peccator*, states that the church "containing sinners in its own bosom, is at one and the same time holy and always in need of purification [*sancta simul et semper purificanda*]" (*Lumen Gentium* § 8). The *Malta Report* thus asserts, "The abiding in the truth should not be understood in a static way but as a dynamic event which takes place with the aid of the Holy Spirit in ceaseless battle against error and sin in the church as well as in the world."[11] Likewise, *Church and Justification* states,

> It is not in dispute between us that the church is "holy" and "sinful" at the same time, and that the imperative calling to holiness is always a concomitant of the indicative that holiness has been bestowed (cf. 1 Thess 4:3f, 7; 2 Cor 7:1). Thus the church is in constant need of repentance and the forgiveness of sins, and of cleansing and renewal. Vatican II stated this repeatedly, even if it does not use the term "sinful" of the church.[12]

Nevertheless, differences between Lutherans and Catholics emerge regarding the necessary limits of the need for renewal, how sinfulness may be applied to the church, and the possibilities of error. Lutherans have found Catholics to objectivize holiness and freedom from error in specific ecclesial offices and decisions to such a degree that they appear to be exempt from critical questioning and immune from the human capacity for human error and sinfulness.[13] From the Catholic perspective, Christ's promise to the church that it will abide in the truth provides the basis for the church's conviction that the truth can be articulated in propositional expressions of the gospel that are inerrant and infallible. Furthermore, the Catholic Church believes there to be established ecclesial offices willed by God's providence and that some saints named by canonization can be addressed as the perfected of God.[14] The commission concluded that despite these differences regarding the holiness of the church, there existed "a broad consensus within which remaining differences are neither abolished nor denied."[15]

CREATURA VERBI/CREATURA SACRAMENTORUM

Article 7 of the Augsburg Confession states the nature of the church for Lutherans: "The church is the assembly of the saints in which the gospel is taught purely and the sacraments are administered rightly." The church is the assembly gathered by the proclamation of the gospel. Thus, Lutherans traditionally refer to it as a "creature of the Word" (*creatura verbi*). The Reformation emphasized that the church "lives on the basis of the proclamation of the gospel," stressing perpetual dependence on the gospel and subordination to it.[16] The Lutheran-Catholic dialogue in the *Malta Report* (1972) echoes CA VII when it states that the church "has the gospel as its superordinate criterion" and that "its gospel ministry is to be carried out through the sacraments, and, indeed, through its total life."[17] In the *Malta Report*, both Catholics and Lutherans affirm together that the church "as *creatura et ministra verbi*...stands under the gospel and has the gospel as its superordinate criterion."[18]

Even though Catholics also affirm this Lutheran account of the church, they more commonly speak of the Christian community emerging from the sacraments, especially baptism and the Eucharist. Lutherans, who, following Augustine, consider baptism and the Lord's Supper to be visible and audible words of gospel proclamation, do not disagree. Sacraments, as visible words, serve a function of proclamation and, from that proclamation, serve a function of gathering the church.

In the post-Reformation period, a polemical wedge was often driven between Word and Sacrament, with Lutheran churches emphasizing Word and the Catholics emphasizing sacraments. This, however, is a false dichotomy if understood absolutely, for Lutherans unambiguously identify the church by Word *and* Sacrament even while linking the latter to the former, and the Council of Trent (1545–63), a response to the Protestant Reformation, attempted to improve clergy education and provide for more adequate preaching.[19] Nevertheless, as the actual practice of the churches developed after the Reformation, it would be fair to say that the Lutheran tradition clearly emphasized preaching and the Catholics, the sacraments. On the Catholic side, the Second Vatican Council (1962–65) addressed this imbalance by urging that the administration of every sacrament include Scripture readings and a word of explanation with pastoral application by the sacramental minister (SC §§ 24, 35). This Liturgy of the Word *precisely as liturgy* forms part of the ritual action of the sacrament. Furthermore, the Council's teaching that preaching is the first responsibility of priests and bishops supports this emphasis on the Word. The homily within the sacramental rituals forms an intrinsic part of the Liturgy of the Word.

The Catholic theologian Karl Rahner proposed that a theology of the Word in the church as the eschatological presence of God could be a fresh common point of departure for both the Catholic and Protestant traditions.[20] Although at the time of his writing there had been very little developed theology of the Word in Catholic theology, he believed that this could be "the basis for a theology of the sacraments in which the sacrament figures as the supreme human and ecclesiastical stage of the word in all its dimensions."[21] Rahner suggested that the dichotomy between Word and Sacrament could be overcome by understanding the sacrament as a "word-event within a theology of the word."[22] The sacraments are embodied proclamations. Baptism and the Eucharist proclaim the death and resurrection of the Lord. In this proclamation, the saving event is itself made present in sacramental sign, and the grace of that event is extended in a personal way to the recipient of the sacraments.

In addition to the liturgical connection between Word and Sacrament, both emphases—Word and Sacrament—have a christological center, for the subject of the preaching is the Gospel, which is to say Jesus Christ. The same is true of the sacraments of baptism and Eucharist. Baptism is immersion into Christ's dying and rising, and the Eucharist makes present the crucified and risen Christ. To say that the sacraments constitute the church is to say that Jesus Christ constitutes the church. Similarly, since the Word of God is none other than Jesus Christ, the principle of the church being constituted by the proclamation of the Word also underscores the christological center of the church.

Since theologies of Word and Sacrament both elicit faith, they also share a common role with respect to justification by faith. The traditions of the Reformation emphasize the role of the Word in eliciting faith, which serves as an identifier of the church. The Second Vatican Council emphasized the dynamic role of the sacraments in the process of maturing in faith: "Sacraments not only presuppose faith, but by words and object they also nourish, strengthen, and express it. That is why they are called 'sacraments of faith.' They do indeed impart grace, but in addition, the very act of celebrating them disposes the faithful most effectively to receive this grace in a fruitful manner, to worship God rightly, and to practice charity" (SC § 59). A coming-to-faith, inseparable from reception of the Word, is an essential moment within all sacramental acts.

The Norwegian theologian Ola Tjørhom summarizes the characteristics of a sacramentally grounded ecclesiology for Lutherans.[23] He finds the core of sacramental theology to be the conviction that the risen Christ is truly present in his church. The sacramental sign of the church refers not to itself, but to our salvation in Christ. The church is an instrument of this salvation and a "sign and expression of the mystery of faith as this mystery is revealed in the church.[24] The relationship between church *being* a sacrament and *having* sacraments is a mutual one. The key manifestation of the church's sacramentality is the administration and celebration of sacraments, whatever the number of them. The church is a sacrament in and for the world by being a sign of the fulfillment of the kingdom of God, including a redeemed creation and a reunited humankind.[25]

The different emphases on Word and Sacrament were made less acute by developments among present-day Lutherans that included more frequent celebration of the Lord's Supper on Sundays. As evidenced in the *Apology of the Augsburg Confession*, Lutheran congregations celebrated the Lord's Supper every Sunday and on festivals.[26] Nevertheless, for historical reasons largely due (in at least the early American context) to the scarcity of pastors and a reluctance among some Pietists to celebrate the Supper too often, the practice developed in many places of having communion only once a month or even once a quarter. The ELCA and its predecessor bodies have been fighting against this trend. In 1997, the Fifth Biennial Churchwide Assembly of the ELCA, the highest governing body of the church, adopted the document, *The Use of the Means of Grace: A Statement on the Practice of Word and Sacrament.*[27] The document sets the standards by which the use of the sacraments should be followed. It encourages the weekly celebration of the Lord's Supper even though not every service need be a Eucharist.[28] Similar increases are found in other churches of the Lutheran World Federation.

The historical disparity in the eucharistic practices between Catholics and Lutherans no doubt contributed to the perceived ecclesial differences, Lutherans considering the church to be a *creatura verbi*, and Catholics considering the church to be constituted by the sacraments. Now that the ecclesial practices are more aligned, so is the ecclesiology. These differences are now seen not to be church-dividing, but tendencies to different emphases since both are christocentric and both elicit faith.

THE CHURCH AND SALVATION

Lutherans assert that the doctrine of justification is the *articulus stantis et cadentis ecclesiae* ("the article by which the church stands and falls"), since without justification in Christ by grace through faith, there would simply be no new people of God and thus no church.[29] In this sense, justification is theologically prior to ecclesiology. Nevertheless, a person comes to faith in Christ through grace only by hearing the Word, only through the proclamation of the gospel, and through the means of grace such as the sacraments administered within the church. A complex dynamic exists between the faith of an individual and the faith of the community, which invites, supports, and sustains that faith. A person does not simply come to faith and then seek a faith community as if faith is prior to or independent of the church. In some sense, the faith of the church precedes individual faith. Roman Catholics, for example, emphasize the need for a community of believers, for "it is only within the faith of the Church that each of the faithful can believe."[30] Lutherans state in Article V of the Augsburg Confession, "So that we may obtain this faith [that is a prerequisite of justification], the ministry of teaching the gospel and administering the sacraments was instituted." In both traditions, a ministry of proclamation within a faith community prepares for faith by proclamation of the Word and then receives those who believe into the community of the faithful.

This interrelationship between justifying faith and the church becomes clearer when the church is considered the place of salvation. Lutherans and Catholics affirm that the church is the recipient and mediator of salvation.[31] The church shares in salvation, shares salvation with others through its mission and evangeliza-tion, and is a community shaped by salvation.[32] The grounds for this are, first, the church's origin as a communion founded in the life of the triune God and, second, its task of mission to mediate the salvation it has received. Thus it is both the place of God's sav-ing activity and God's instrument of salvation.[33] As Ola Tjøsrhom observes, "Jesus Christ is the chief link between justification and the Church, salvation and ecclesiology. He is the one who justifies, and the church is his body. When the church is seen as Christ's body, a role in the process of justification must be attributed to it."[34] It is the place where we participate in Christ's sacrificial self-offering in the power of the Holy Spirit through the mediation of Word and Sacrament, especially in the Eucharist.

THE HIDDEN AND VISIBLE CHURCH[35]

Nevertheless, within the commonalities between Lutheran and Catholics lies a difference in emphasis. Lutherans stress the church as the recipient of salvation, while Catholics emphasize the church as a mediator of salvation.[36] The emphasis on the church as media-tor is one reason Catholics describe the nature of the church and its universal mission as a kind of "sacrament" (*veluti sacramentum*), that is, a sign and instrument of "intimate union with God and of the unity of all humanity" (*Lumen Gentium* § 1).[37] Three different arti-cles in *Lumen Gentium* identify the church as a sort of sacrament, each with a slightly different nuance: sacrament of communion with God and of the unity of the entire human race, sacrament of saving unity, and sacrament of salvation (§§ 1, 9, 48). In addition, at three instances, the church is identified as a sign in the Constitution on the Sacred Liturgy.[38] Such a description of the church clarifies the inner connection between an outward, visible structure and the hid-den, spiritual reality it signifies, since sacraments are outward signs of invisible grace, what Paul VI described as "visible realities imbued with the hidden presence of God." This description is also helpful in avoiding too close an identification between the church and Christ since in the concept of sacrament, there is both unity and differ-ence: unity between the sign of the sacrament and what is signified, difference, because what is signified is not absolutely identical with the sign that makes it present. Historical presence and sacramental presence are two different modalities. The German Catholic-Lutheran dialogue recognized this when it noted that the use of the term *sacrament* "serves to illustrate that the church, although it is the body of Christ, may not simply be identified with Christ, the "primal sacrament."[39]

The relationship between the invisible interior dimension of the church and its visible expression gives the church a quasi-sacramental structure since the outward, visible manifestation of the church reflects an inner spiritual component of the church. This complex relationship between outward sign and inward spiritual dimension, the one inseparable from the other, is one reason for the insistence on the visibility of the church, although it must be noted that at the time of the Reformation, the dominant view of the church was that of a society rather than a sacrament. The great theologian of the Catholic Reformation, Robert Bellarmine, SJ, defined the church institutionally: "The one true Church is the society of men bound together by profession of the same Christian faith, and by communion of the same sacraments, under the rule of legitimate pastors and in particular under the one vicar of Christ on earth, the Roman Pontiff....And it is as visible as the kingdom of France or the Republic of Venice."[40] The emphasis in this definition of the church is on observable characteristics and actions: profession of faith, communion of the sacraments, and the rule of pastors. This post-Reformation Catholic polemical reaction against Reformation ecclesiology focused on the church almost exclusively as a visible entity identified by creed, sacramental structure, and hierarchy. More spiritual conceptualizations of the church came later with the retrieval of the notion of the church as the Body of Christ in Pius XII's encyclical, *Mystici Corporis* (1943), and the application of the category of sacrament to the church by the Second Vatican Council. This history of Roman Catholic ecclesiology is significant for ecumenism because it represents a development that softens the polemics of the sixteenth century.

Although Lutherans agree that the church is a sign and an instrument, they do not generally apply the language of sacramentality to the church, but reserve it to refer to baptism and the Lord's Supper.[41] The World Council of Churches document *The Nature and Mission of the Church: A Stage on the Way to a Common Statement* says that the churches who identify the church as a sacrament do so because they understand the church to be an effective sign of communion of all human beings with each other and the triune God. Those churches that reject the concept do so because they consider that this does not sufficiently distinguish between the church and sacraments. They consider the sacraments to be "means of salvation by which Christ sustains the Church, and not actions by which the Church realizes or actualizes itself."[42] Some churches also reject a concept of the church as sacrament because they consider the church to be a communion that, while being holy, is still subject to sin. The WCC document also observes that "behind this lack of agreement lie varying views about the instrumentality of the Church with regard to salvation" even though "those who have become accustomed to call the church 'Sacrament' would still distinguish between the ways in which baptism and the Lord's Supper on the one hand, and the Church on the other, are signs and instruments of God's plan."[43]

The Augsburg Confession identifies the church as "properly speaking, the assembly of saints and those who truly believe."[44] The *Apology of the Augsburg Confession* responds to the Roman Confutation's critique: "The seventh article of the confession, in which it is affirmed that the church is the assembly of saints, cannot be admitted without prejudice to faith if by this definition the wicked and sinners are separated from the church."[45] The *Apology* makes the clarification that "we grant that in this life hypocrites and evil people are mingled with the church and are members of the church according to the external association of the church's signs—that is, the Word, confession of faith, and sacraments—especially if they have not been excommunicated."[46] It asserts that even though wicked people are associated with the true church according to the external rites, nevertheless, the church defined as the living Body of Christ is the assembly of the saints since those in whom Christ is not active are not members of Christ.[47] It rejects an understanding of the church as an external government consisting of both the good and the wicked. The true church "is a spiritual people...a true people of God, reborn through the Holy Spirit."[48] The people of God according to the gospel are only those who receive the promise of the Spirit. The ungodly are not in the church even though they intermingle with the church and hold offices in the church.

Thus, for the Lutheran Confessions, the true church is a hidden church in the sense that no one but God knows its members. As Luther said, "The church is a so deeply hidden thing that no one can see it or know it but can only grasp and believe it in baptism, the Lord's Supper, and the word."[49] There are not two churches, the visible congregation and the church of the saints. The church of the saints exists within the visible congregation. The hidden church of the justified exists within the mixed church comprised of both wheat and tares. Yet, paradoxically, for Luther, the mixed church is indeed "church" because the marks of the church are to be found there, namely the Word, the sacrament of baptism and that of the altar, holy communion, the office of the keys, the confessions of sins and absolution or announcement of forgiveness, ministry and public worship, and finally, holy possession of the sacred cross, which for Luther, functions as metonymy for suffering.[50] The connection between these two uses of "church" is that these marks or signs of the church elicit and support faith. Nevertheless, a tension exists in these two descriptors of the church as a community of saints and as an assembly.

The ecumenical document *Church and Justification* acknowledges the tension in the Lutheran description of the church as both an outward association recognizable by the marks of the church and an invisible association of the saints.[51] It describes the visibility or invisibility of the church from the perspective of faith since only the eyes of faith recognize an assembly as the people of God.[52] For Lutherans, there is an analogy between the hidden church and the hidden God on the cross. Both are unrecognizable by earthly standards; both must be discerned in what seems opposed to them in sinful structures and in suffering and death.

Catholics, too, share the difficulty of church membership "according to the heart" and membership "according to the body."[53] *Lumen Gentium* says,

> They are fully incorporated into the society of the church who, possessing the Spirit of Christ, accept its whole structure and all the means of salvation that have been

established within it, and within its visible framework are united with Christ, who governs it through the supreme pontiff and the bishops, by the bonds of profession of faith, the sacraments, ecclesiastical government and communion. That person is not saved, however, even though he might be incorporated into the church, who does not persevere in charity; he indeed remains in the church "bodily", but not "in his heart." (§ 14)

While this passage builds on Robert Bellarmine's definition of a church as a society with all its emphasis on the visibility of the church, simply being a member of the visible church does not guarantee salvation because full incorporation into the church requires charity.

Although Vatican II did not solve the problem of membership in the church presented by the incidence of membership "in the body" but not "in the heart," it provided a synthesis of the spiritual reality of the church and its visible social reality.[54] It did this not only through the category of sacramentality discussed earlier, but also by comparing it to the mystery of the Incarnate Word:

> Christ, the one mediator, set up his holy church here on earth as a visible structure, a community of faith, hope and love; and he sustains it unceasingly and through it he pours out grace and truth on everyone. This society, however, equipped with hierarchical structures, and the mystical body of Christ, a visible assembly and a spiritual community, an earthly church and a church enriched with heavenly gifts, must not be considered as two things, but as forming one complex reality comprising a human and a divine element. It is therefore by no mean analogy that is likened to the mystery of the incarnate Word. (*Lumen Gentium* § 8)

Furthermore, the council's teaching that the church "is at one and the same time holy and always in need of purification" shows that it does not simply identify the salvation-community with visible church structures and its sinful members. Nor does it separate them, even though it distinguishes between them.

The consensus statement between Lutherans and Catholics in *Church and Justification* addresses the relationship between the visible and hidden dimensions of the church where it reads,

> Catholics and Lutherans are in agreement that the saving activity of the triune God calls and sanctifies believers through audible and visible means of grace which are mediated in an audible and visible ecclesial community. They also agree that in this world the salvation-community of Christ is hidden, because as a spiritual work of God's it is unrecognizable by earthly standards, and because sin, which is also present in the church, makes ascertaining its membership uncertain.[55]

This consensus statement is possible because it speaks of the hiddenness of the "salvation-community" rather than the "church." The "salvation-community" is hidden because only God knows who are saved; because only the eye of faith can see Christ and the Spirit present in the community, because in the historical community, some without faith are not true members of Christ's body; and because the church remains under the sign of the cross engaged in spiritual struggle against sin until its final vindication in Christ at the end of time.

The church is not simply identified with the communion of saints but is a mixed community of saints and sinners this side of the eschaton and is a complex society with a visible structure. Lutherans say that the church this side of the eschaton exists *sub cruce*, under the cross, meaning that the Christian people as church "must endure every misfortune and persecution, all kinds of trials and evil from the devil, the world, and the flesh (as the Lord's Prayer indicates) by inward sadness, timidity, fear, outward poverty, contempt, illness, and weakness, in order to become like their head, Christ."[56] Conversations among ecumenical partners on this point must identify when the spiritual and therefore "invisible" dimension of the church, on the one hand, and the "visible" dimension of its embodiment as an assembly gathered around Word and Sacrament, on the other hand, are treated in a dialectical way and when these two aspects are treated synthetically. The dialectic potentially drives a wedge between the two expressions

of the church, while a synthetic approach develops two complementary aspects of the church. The eschatological church is in
our midst as a community of faith that exists and finds expression in and through the historical community. Yet that historical
community cannot simply be identified with the eschatological
church in terms of its fullness and perfection, although they are
not two churches.

Catholics express this reality by speaking of a pilgrim church.
The first chapter of *Lumen Gentium* introduces the image, saying,
"While we are still making our pilgrimage on earth and follow
in his footsteps in tribulation and persecution, we are associated
with his [Christ's] sufferings as a body with its head, sharing his
suffering that we may also share his glory (see Rm 8, 17)" (§ 7).[57]
Chapter 7 capitalizes on the image of a pilgrim church in speaking of the eschatological nature of the church, which "will reach
its completion only in the glory of heaven, when the time for the
restoration of all things will come." In the interim time, this eschatological completion is anticipated in such a way that "already on
earth the church is adorned with true though imperfect holiness."
The institutions and sacraments of the church belong to this age,
the time when the church "carries the figure of this world which
is passing" and where it "dwells among creatures who groan and
till now are in the pains of childbirth and await the revelation of
the children of God (see Rm 8, 19–22)" (§ 48). This is far from an
image of a triumphalisitic church and one that accords well with
a Lutheran theology of an eschatological church that exists in this
age *sub cruce*, that is, under the sign of the cross.

For Luther, revelation is hidden in its opposite (*abscondita
sub contraria specie*), that is, hidden in weakness and manifested in
what exists in our midst. Luther said, "If you want to meet Christ
don't stare at heaven; in the alleys, at your doorstep there you find
Christ."[58] In this sense, the cross of Christ is the decisive revelation
in which God becomes manifest. In this sense, the church is hidden to our sight, but is made manifest in the marks (Latin: *notae*)
of the church and the assembly of believers on earth even when it
is hidden under persecution and sin.[59]

WHERE IS THE CHURCH?

A fundamental question regarding the church is, "Where is the church?" Lutherans and Catholics agree that there is one holy, catholic, and apostolic church that is spread throughout the earth, transcends time, and pervades the whole of history. This one church is realized in local churches, which are in a relationship of *koinonia* with other local churches in regional expressions of the church in synods or dioceses and all together in a worldwide or universal church. Both Lutherans and Catholics hold that "there is a local body which is not merely a part of the church, but is wholly church, even if not the whole church and not in isolation from the rest of the church."[60] The local church is that expression of the church that has everything necessary to be a church. Lutherans and Catholics differ, however, in their understanding of what constitutes the local church, although both are faithful to the pattern of the early church in different ways. By the second and third centuries, the local church found expression in a community gathered around the bishop, who was surrounded by a council of presbyters and assisted by deacons. This was a face-to-face community defined by its participation in Word and Sacrament under the ministry of a bishop with the assistance of a variety of other ministers.

Lutherans understand the one holy church (*una sancta ecclesia*) to find outward visible expression in the local congregation, that is, where "people assemble around the gospel proclaimed in sermon and sacrament."[61] Thus Lutherans kept the pattern of the local church being a geographically local, face-to-face community gathered by Word and Sacrament, but did not exactly retain the early pattern of the bishop heading the local church. The Lutheran understanding of the local church described in *Church and Justification* does, however, include as essential to Lutheran understanding a reference to ministers who preach the Word and administer the sacraments since these cannot exist apart from the ministry:

> Assembled for worship the local congregation therefore is to be seen, according to the Lutheran view, as the visible church, *communio sanctorum*, in the full sense. Nothing is missing which makes a human assembly church: the preached word and the sacramental gifts through

which the faithful participate in Christ through the Holy Spirit, but also the minister who preaches the word and administers the sacraments in obedience to Christ and on his behalf, thus leading the congregation.[62]

The pastor of the congregation, as was seen in the last chapter, is understood as possessing the fullness of ministry.

Catholics understand the particular church, most often identical with the administrative division known as a diocese, to be the local church. Catholics define the local church as "a portion of the people of God whose pastoral care is entrusted to a bishop in cooperation with his priests. Thus, in conjunction with their pastor and gathered by him into one flock in the Holy Spirit through the gospel and the Eucharist, they constitute a particular church" (*Christus Dominus* § 11).[63] Consequently, the local church is defined in terms of Word, Sacrament, and the ministry of the bishop. In today's church, the particular church is most often not a face-to-face community since most Catholics attend a eucharistic liturgy celebrated by the bishop only rarely, if ever. Most Catholics experience the church most immediately in a local parish more than in a diocese, since the parish is the place where "individuals are instructed in the faith, baptized, confirmed, ordained, married and receive the Lord's Supper."[64]

Within the particular church, the bishop "functions as a connecting link of the church, both as the representative of the whole church in his church, and as the representative of his church in relation to all the others."[65] Catholics understand the bishop to be a member of the college of bishops by virtue of his episcopal ordination and communion with the Bishop of Rome. The communion of churches within the universal church parallels the communion of bishops within the episcopal college, each bishop representing his particular church within that communion.

The church's communion occurs at various levels: locally within the congregation, regionally, and worldwide. Lutheran congregations are in regional communion with other local churches in synods or juridically autonomous provincial or national churches. First efforts toward forming a worldwide Lutheran fellowship can be traced to the meetings of the Lutheran World Convention between 1923 and 1946. Globally, many Lutheran churches are members of the Lutheran World Federation (LWF), founded in 1947 as a "free association" of Lutheran churches, but now, as a result of a constitutional change in 1990, "a communion of member churches." In 2015, the LWF numbered 144 churches in the Lutheran tradition, representing over 72 million Christians in 79 countries.[66] The LWF conducts extensive relief work and represents the Lutheran churches in bilateral dialogues worldwide with other world Christian communions. It was the signatory of the *Joint Declarations on the Doctrine of Justification* with the Roman Catholic Church in 1999.

The LWF does not self-identify as a church and cannot be considered a Lutheran version of a "Vatican" or a "Canterbury" since it understands its member churches to be self-regulating entities. Nevertheless, in recent times beginning with the judgment on apartheid in South Africa, it has on occasion adopted the practice of making normative confessional judgments and in doing so has forcefully raised the issue about common decision making on behalf of Lutherans. As is explained in the chapter on the *Joint Declaration on the Doctrine of Justification*, the LWF also exercised a role on behalf of its member churches in the agreement and signing of the JDDJ with the Catholic Church. The Finnish Lutheran ecumenist Risto Saarinen sees this as evidence that "Lutherans in many ways today act as a communion, although the territorial churches still remain the final decision makers."[67] He concludes that "Lutheranism is no longer a 'free association' of churches, but a communion bound together by doctrinal consensus."[68] Lutheranism's reticence to call itself a worldwide church actually positions it ecumenically, for precisely as a communion can Lutherans seek communion with Rome. The alternative would be the situation where one worldwide church would be in direct conflict with another worldwide church. Since Lutherans have no worldwide body that considers itself to be a church, there is no ministry for worldwide Lutheranism. Pastors are ministers of congregations and bishops or superintendents exercise regional ministries.

The Catholic Church understands itself to be one church present concretely and historically in a plurality of particular churches: "The Catholic Church herself subsists in each particular church, which can be complete only through effective communion in faith, sacraments and unity with the whole body of

Christ."[69] The universal church is not the result of an addition or federation of particular churches, but is embodied in each particular church. These particular churches are "formed in the likeness of the universal church" and "in and from these particular churches there exists the one unique catholic church" (*Lumen Gentium* § 23). Each particular church manifests its universality in its communion with all other particular churches. The bishops in communion with the Bishop of Rome and with one another keep their churches in communion with their apostolic past, oversee the unity and communion within their particular church, and represent their churches in communion with other particular churches. A particular ministry exists for each level of ecclesiality. Priests are pastors of parishes, bishops are charged with the pastoral oversight of dioceses, and the Bishop of Rome, the pope, exercises the Petrine ministry for the unity of faith and communion of the universal church.

APOSTOLICITY OF THE CHURCH

The church is "apostolic" because it is "built up on the foundation of the apostles and prophets" (Eph 2:20) and proclaims the gospel as they did (1 Cor 1:17; Acts 9:15). The issue of apostolicity emerged early in the Lutheran-Catholic dialogues. In 1972, the statement "Gospel and the Church" gave this understanding of apostolicity: "The church is apostolic insofar as it stands on this foundation [the apostles] and abides in the apostolic faith. The church's ministry, doctrine, and order are apostolic insofar as they pass on and actualize the apostolic witness."[70] In other words, "The Church is apostolic because the gospel that she hears in faith and to which she gives witness is apostolic."[71]

Differing claims to the apostolicity of their traditions have been an obstacle to the full communion of Lutherans and Catholics. The issues of the apostolicity of the church and the recognition of ministry have historically gone hand in hand as mutually interrelated. A ministry of *episcopé* in apostolic succession has been associated in the Catholic mind with the recognition of another ecclesial community as "church."[72] Nevertheless, the apostolicity of the church is more encompassing than simply the apostolic succession of its ministers. Even though the apostolic preaching is preserved "by a continuous succession until the end of time," the Dogmatic Constitution on Revelation, *Dei Verbum*, states, "The expression 'what is handed down from the apostles' includes everything that helps the people of God to live a holy life and to grow in faith." The church transmits and perpetuates this "in its teaching, life and worship" (§ 8). This reflects the theology of Acts 2:42, in which the first community of believers "devoted themselves to the apostles' teaching and fellowship, to the breaking of bread and the prayers," arguably the constitutive elements of the church according to Luke.[73] The apostolic ministers of the church are charged with the preservation and transmission of the apostolicity of the church in sound doctrine, but this very apostolicity is also embedded in all the church's life, prayer, and teaching. As the Study Document of the Lutheran-Roman Catholic Commission on Unity, *The Apostolicity of the Church* (2006), puts it, there is a "*depositum fidei* [deposit of faith], but it [the apostolic legacy] also comprises a *depositum vitae* [deposit of life], inviting the community to imitate the apostolic life in its spiritual discipline and practices."[74]

The document observes that Lutherans are often understood to continue apostolic succession *only* through preaching and teaching of the gospel with ministry playing no essential role, while Catholics "are thought to hold that the unbroken line of rightful episcopal succession is *of itself* a guarantee of the apostolicity of the church."[75] It notes that both conceptions are misleading and shows that "Catholics and Lutherans are in greater agreement on ecclesial apostolicity than is ordinarily supposed."[76]

The aim of the Reformation was actually to preserve the apostolicity of the church by a new reception of the apostolic gospel and associated ecclesial practices along with a corresponding rejection of misconceptions of the gospel and deformations of ecclesial practice. It was essentially an effort to return to what was thought to be the true message of the gospel. The Reformers thought that the Catholic Church of their time had falsified the gospel by making God's favor dependent upon good works, by turning the Lord's Supper into a sacrifice to propitiate God, and by the papal hierarchy adding new articles of faith and imposing practices binding on consciences.[77] For Luther, the marks of the apostolic church by which the Holy Spirit creates faith and the church were "continuity in proclaiming the same message as the apostles, continuity in practicing baptism, the Lord's Supper, the office of the keys, the call to ministry, public gathering for worship in praise and confession of faith, and the bearing of the cross as Christ's disciples."[78] Thus the Lutheran position has been that the coherence of teaching with the gospel message rather than the rank or role of the person teaching legitimates teaching.[79] Even so, the person speaking this message in public must be authorized by a pastoral call. In spite of his critique of the church of his time, Luther recognized elements of apostolicity such as "the true Holy Scriptures, true baptism, the true sacrament, the true keys for the forgiveness of sins, the true office of proclamation, and the true catechism" in the Roman Catholic Church.[80]

As the Reformation sought to lift up the gospel as the center of ecclesial apostolicity, so too did the Council of Trent when it taught in 1546 that the gospel of Christ preached by the apostles is the "source of the whole truth of salvation and rule of conduct."[81] This gospel is the good news proclaimed by the lips of Jesus Christ and expressed in both Scripture and the unwritten traditions transmitted by the apostles to the church.[82] The Council of Trent did not develop a dogmatic theology of the church, but inaugurated a post-Reformation era of apologetic theology that sought to provide evidence for the legitimacy of its authority in teaching, of its hierarchical ministry in the apostolic succession of Pope and bishops, and of its sacramental system. As *The Apostolicity of the Church* observes, "Ecclesiology was dominated by the formal issue of *legitimacy*."[83] Such a focus precludes a more comprehensive ecclesiology, which was not developed at Trent.

Theological advances articulated in the documents of the Second Vatican Council paved the way for a *rapprochement* with Reformation concerns. The Dogmatic Constitution on Revelation, *Dei Verbum*, emphasizes the soteriological focus of revelation by identifying Christ as the fullness of revelation (DV 2), who through his death and resurrection expresses the gospel message of God's offer of salvation (DV 4). Thus Jesus himself is the gospel message. The Council identified preaching the gospel as the first and primary responsibility of the bishop, including the Bishop of Rome (*Lumen Gentium* § 25).[84] *The Apostolicity of the Church* identifies the apostolic succession of bishops and popes as a "*successio verbi* ('succession in the word'), to build up the church from its foundation of faith in Christ."[85]

As for the Catholic Church's ministry, Vatican II taught that the primacy of the Bishop of Rome is exercised within the episcopal college of which he is a member. The college as a body is the successor to the apostles as a group. The college of bishops as a whole, in union with the Bishop of Rome, is protected through the guidance of the Holy Spirit in faithfully transmitting the gospel message. An individual bishop in apostolic succession has no guarantee that he will not either lapse into error or break communion with the episcopal college.

To sum up, apostolic succession is today understood to involve a number of possible components: the succession of individual bishops, the succession of the college of bishops, and the succession of the whole church in the entirety of its teaching, life, and worship. In the past, an evaluation of apostolicity emphasized the succession of individual bishops, but today within an ecclesiology of communion, more attention has been turned to apostolicity in the life of the church.

Margaret O'Gara points to the importance of intention in an assessment of apostolicity.[86] For instance, she points to *The Porvoo Common Statement* (1992), affirmed by the British and Irish Anglican Churches and the Nordic and Baltic Lutheran churches, which views the appointment of Lutheran bishops to historic sees as evidence of their "intention to continue the life and ministry of the One, Holy, Catholic and Apostolic Church"[87] as well as "to continue to exercise the apostolic ministry of word and sacrament of the universal Church."[88] The notion of intention extends to the church as a whole. O'Gara notes that where previously the reconciliation of church communions followed the recognition of ministries, today within an ecclesiology of communion "the reverse is the order of preference" such that an assessment has to incorporate not only the intention of the ordained minister, but also that of the community.[89] Recognition of each other as churches leads to the mutual recognition of ministry.

The intention of the community is to be apostolic in its proclamation of the word, in its prayer, and in its witness. *The Porvoo Common Statement*, while asserting that the apostolic succession of the ministry is a focus for the church's continuity and faithfulness (PCS 40) and while affirming both that the ordination of a bishop in historic succession both signifies and reinforces the church's continuity in the apostolic faith (PCS 50) and that this succession in apostolic ministry represents a summons and commission to realize more fully the characteristics of the church of the apostles (PCS 51), nevertheless finds the primary manifestation of apostolic succession "in the apostolic tradition of the church as a whole" (PCS 39). As early as 1972, the Catholic-Lutheran joint statement, *The Gospel and the Church*, reflected this same view saying, "In the New Testament and the early fathers, the emphasis was obviously placed more on the substance of apostolicity, i.e., on succession in apostolic teaching. In this sense the entire church as the *ecclesia apostolica* stands in the apostolic succession."[90] The document *The Ministry in the Church* also refers to the apostolicity of the entire church, saying that while apostolic succession is "normally taken to mean the unbroken ministerial successions of bishops in a church," it is "also often understood to refer in the substantive sense to the apostolicity of the church in faith."[91] It notes that Lutherans speak of this in connection with a *successio verbi* and that present-day Catholic theology is increasingly adopting the view "that the substantive understanding of apostolicity is primary."[92] Since the gospel has been entrusted to the church as a whole, "the whole church as the *ecclesia apostolica* stands in the apostolic succession. Succession in the sense of the succession of ministers must be seen within the succession of the whole church in the apostolic faith."[93] The document concludes the section on the apostolicity of the church by observing that since Catholics hold that "the episcopate as a whole is kept firm in the truth of the gospel,…Catholic doctrine regards the apostolic succession in the episcopal office as a sign and ministry of the apostolicity of the church."[94]

In John Burkhard's view, these first two documents failed to develop adequately the underlying ecclesiology of the claim for the apostolic succession of the church as a whole.[95] He finds a remedy in the ecclesiology of communion found in *Facing Unity*[96] and in *Church and Justification*. An ecclesiology of communion views the one church as a "communion (*communio*) subsisting in a network of local churches."[97] Lutherans and Catholics share community in faith, community in sacraments, and community in service.

The document notes that the bishop's vigilance with regard to the apostolicity of faith "is bound up with the responsibility for the faith borne by the whole Christian people." Thus, "apostlic succession is really to be understood not as a succession of one individual to another, but rather as a succession in the church, to an episcopal see and to membership of the episcopal college, as shown by the lists of bishops."[98] The office of *episcopé* is exercised not in isolation, but "in concert with the community of believers." Thus *Facing Unity* describes the church as a communion and situates the bishop's ministry within that communion, the communion itself being in succession with the apostles in faith, sacraments, and service. The teaching of *Dei Verbum* about the church handing on to every generation all that it is and all that it believes in its teaching, life, and worship echoes this same idea of the church as a whole embodying apostolicity. This does not negate the apostolicity of ministry, but rather places the apostolic succession of ministers in its ecclesial context.

This perception of apostolicity as being predicated of the church as a whole should help Catholics recognize how the essential continuity of church and ministry can be preserved even when a succession of episcopal consecration is broken. The absence of an episcopal ministry in apostolic succession need not in itself preclude the recognition of Lutheran communities as apostolic and therefore as properly churches. This is especially true insofar as the Lutheran intent was never to undermine oversight. Presbyteral ordinations were a matter of historical factors and exigency rather than an attack on the episcopal office. In the past, Catholics have tended to justify the apostolicity of a church on the basis of its apostolic ministry, but developments in the theology of apostolicity suggest that the two concepts, apostolic church and apostolic ministry (defined as an apostolic succession going back to the beginning), need not be as inseparable as once thought. Since Lutherans and Catholics agree that the church is apostolic because it is founded upon the apostles' witness to the gospel and because it continuously professes the apostolic and evangelical faith, we recognize in both our ecclesial communities the attribute of apostolicity.

KEEPING THE CHURCH IN THE TRUTH OF THE GOSPEL

Teaching the truth necessary for salvation ranks among the necessary and significant activities of the church. Even though Lutheran churches have no universal teaching office understood as an institutional structure or individuals authorized to issue binding judgments, doctrine plays a major role in Lutheran life. The authoritative sources for this doctrine are first of all Scripture as the normative expression of the apostolic gospel, then the early ecumenical councils, especially in their christological and trinitarian formulations, and the Apostles', Nicene, and Athanasian creeds. Most Lutherans hold as binding doctrine the confessions and confessional documents of *The Book of Concord*, with the churches of the Lutheran World Federation privileging among its documents the Augsburg Confession of 1530 and Luther's Small Catechism.[99]

Lutherans realize the teaching ministry primarily in the ordained ministry through the activity of preaching, but also through the collaboration of those who are not ordained, often through synodical structures. Bishops exercise oversight of pastors, assuring correct teaching by them. They examine candidates for ordination, who promise to carry out their teaching ministry in agreement with Scripture according to its interpretation in the Reformation-era confessions of faith, and conduct regular oversight of pastors and their congregations. An ordained minister who publicly and obstinately goes against Scripture and the Lutheran confessions may be subject to a doctrinal disciplinary process and possible removal from ministry. The Lutheran World Federation, under the mandate of its member churches, has increasingly assumed a teaching role that reaches beyond regional church boundaries. The LWF exercised this role in 1984 in Budapest, when the LWF World Assembly suspended from membership the white churches of southern Africa that had not ended apartheid; in 1999, when the LWF confirmed the consensus of member churches and signed the *Joint Declaration on the Doctrine of Justification* with the Catholic Church; and 2010 in Stuttgart, when the LWF Assembly asked the Mennonites for forgiveness and reconciliation. Finally, Lutheran theologians have traditionally played an important role in the teaching ministry of Lutheran churches. For Lutherans, none of these ecclesial structures guarantee per se that the churches persevere in the apostolic message of salvation. They look to the Holy Spirit for this even as pastors exercise their teaching responsibilities.[100] Their criticism of the Catholic Church has been that the responsibility and inerrancy promised to the whole church was concentrated too fully in the teaching ministry of bishops and popes. Their corrective of this perceived imbalance is to measure all teaching against the gospel alone and have the church's ministry and its decisions as a matter of principle be open to examination by the whole people of God.[101]

The teaching office of the Catholic Church developed extensively during the years of separation after the Reformation, culminating in the definition of the possibility of papal teaching with the charism of infallibility at the First Vatican Council in 1870 and the development of the teaching on episcopal collegiality at the Second Vatican Council (1963–65). The teaching office is exercised by the Bishop of Rome and by the bishops in union with the Bishop of Rome. As the *Dogmatic Constitution on Divine Revelation* (*Dei Verbum*) declares, "This teaching function is not above the word of God but stands at its service, teaching nothing but what is handed down, according as it devotedly listens, reverently preserves and faithfully transmits the word of God, by divine command and with the help of the holy Spirit" (§ 10). The Bishop of Rome exercises an extraordinary universal magisterium of teaching doctrine protected from error by the charism of infallibility when teaching doctrinal matters essential to faith and morals that come from God's revelation and when speaking *ex cathedra* (literally "from the chair," meaning when acting officially with the intention to teach infallible doctrine).[102] The college of bishops can define doctrine when meeting in an ecumenical council. This means that the content of the teaching is irreformable and irrevocable even though the expression of the teaching may need to change in order to more accurately reflect the content of the teaching as language and usage historically evolve.[103] No single bishop other than the Bishop of Rome possesses the charism of infallibility.

More commonly, the pope and bishops exercise an ordinary magisterium of teaching authentic, but not infallible, doctrine. The pope does this through letters, encyclicals, apostolic exhortations, and apostolic constitutions, as well as in his addresses and homilies. Bishops may also issue non-infallible teaching collectively when issuing conciliar documents. For instance, the bishops expressly decided not to issue infallible teaching at the Second Vatican Council, so those documents represent authentic but non-infallible teaching except where they cite previous conciliar statements that do have that quality. Thus, meeting as an ecumenical council, bishops may determine whether or not they are teaching infallibly. Individually, bishops exercise their ordinary magisterium through their teaching and preaching in their own dioceses. Vatican II provided an ecclesial context for the teaching of the pope and the bishops. It situated the teaching office of the pope within episcopal collegiality and that of both the pope and bishops "within the witness given by the whole people of God in its prophetic role."[104]

The Catholic tradition also affirms a role for the whole church in the process of teaching and its reception even though this is both carried out and weighted differently when compared to the Lutheran tradition. Synodical forms of teaching, especially with the participation of the laity, have not developed in the Catholic tradition as extensively as they have among Lutherans. Nevertheless, since the whole people of God is graced with the charism of the "sense of faith" (*sensus fidei*) (*Lumen Gentium* § 12), the teaching of the magisterium finds "an echo in the faith of the church and call[s] forth assent."[105] This sense of the faith gives believers the ability to recognize the Word of God in what is taught even as they grow in understanding such that "the faithful constitute an indispensible means toward maintaining the church in the truth."[106] In this way, the teaching office "remains anchored in the life of faith of the whole people of God, who share in the discovery of and in witnessing to the truth."[107]

Magisterial formulations of truth have their limitations. While they establish lines of demarcation in clarifying the boundaries of doctrine, they do not express the truth in its fullness. They may settle doctrinal controversies, but in doing so may focus on one aspect of doctrine, failing to situate that within a broader context. The result may be a "one-sided fixation on the contrary of what was seen to be erroneous."[108] Finally, to be truly effective, magisterial teaching must be received by the faith of the church through the work of the Holy Spirit and pass into the belief and practice of the whole church.

While at first glance the exercise of teaching in the Lutheran and Catholic traditions appears to be quite different, both traditions place church teaching under the norm of the gospel. Both traditions affirm that the heart of the New Testament is God's saving action in Christ and that "our new life is solely due to the forgiving and renewing mercy that God imparts as a gift and we receive in faith."[109] The church bears the responsibility to continue to proclaim Christ's saving deeds by Word and Sacrament, to proclaim his gospel, and "to preserve in continuous succession God's word of saving truth."[110]

Within this deep commonality, significant differences exist in the teaching structures and processes of both traditions. While both Lutherans and Catholics entrust bishops with oversight of apostolic teaching with the accompanying responsibility of supervising pastors and priests, Lutherans locate the ministry of teaching primarily in the local congregation. Lutheran bishops exercise their oversight in the context of church synods, which include the participation of laypeople. No single minister is responsible for church teaching.[111] Within Lutheran churches, teaching and discernment of truth occur within a dynamic network of interactions of officeholders, church members, and theologians.

In the Catholic tradition, the "magisterium," or teaching office, is exercised by the episcopal college, the pope, and by individual bishops in communion with each other and the Bishop of Rome, although ordained priests and deacons share the responsibility for preaching and catechizing in service of the gospel. Since Vatican II, large numbers of laypeople participate in transmitting the faith through education and pastoral work, but they do not have a significant role in decision making in the church.

This account of the church in Catholic and Lutheran theology has shown that many of the differences once thought to be intractable are more permeable than previously imagined. Both Catholics and Lutherans view the church as being the place of salvation, thus integrating the doctrine of justification and the theology of the church. A renewed appreciation for eschatology reframes issues of the sinfulness or holiness of the church as well as the question of its hiddenness or visibility. Sacraments viewed as visible words along with the renewal of the rites to include more robust attention to the use of Scripture dissolves the issue of whether the church is a creature of the Word or constituted by the sacraments. Apostolicity viewed as an attribute of the whole church places the apostolic succession of its ministers within a broader ecclesial context. Both Lutherans and Catholics hold fast to Christ's promise to keep the church in the truth necessary for salvation. Nevertheless, significant differences remain regarding the church structures and the authority attributed to them for accomplishing this teaching.

The church is where many of the previous topics of dialogue are lived in the concrete historical circumstances of the time between Christ's presence on earth and the final reconciliation of all in Christ at the end of time. That is, the church is where the faith is professed, the Word is preached, the sacraments are celebrated, and teaching occurs. In this sense, the church is the culminating topic of ecumenical dialogue. This does not mean that the church is more important than the doctrine of God, Christ's saving redemption, or the Word of God, but it does mean that these other topics are interpreted and enacted within the church. The church bears within itself both the mystery of God's plan for salvation and the familiarity of home.

Part III

AN
ECUMENICAL
FUTURE

Chapter Seven

Looking Back—
Looking Forward

In ecumenical circles, Jesus' prayer to the Father recorded in John 17:11, 22, "that they may be one," often serves as the inspiration for modern attempts at repairing the broken unity among Christians. But in the phrase, "that they may be one," lurks several, often unexamined, perils. First, a prayer to God is not necessarily the same thing as a command to humanity. Indeed, one could argue that Jesus prays to the Father for unity precisely because he knows how impossible a task it is for Christians—as if to say, "You know how incapable my disciples are of establishing or maintaining unity, God, so you had better do it yourself." Second, reading John 17 as a command can sometimes confuse us into thinking that it is up to us to secure this unity—a sure invitation to some quite awful, Pelagian forms of works-righteousness that lead either to boasting about how good we are at establishing unity or to despairing that any unity is possible especially during an "ecumenical winter." Finally, the kind of unity for which Jesus is praying may not necessarily be simply an institutional unity and could even be taken as the mystical union of believers in the Body of Christ, where unity with Christ is more properly analogous to the unity of the Trinity.

In describing the growing convergence of Lutherans and Roman Catholics, however, a far better depiction may come from Ephesians 4:1–6. First, Paul, not simply as an apostle but as a "prisoner in the Lord," addresses his fellow believers. This lowly condition has far

181

more apostolic authority than any direct claim to apostleship. Second, he begs. Here we discover not an overwhelming command but a gentle invitation. Third, he connects leading a Christian life to "the calling to which you have been called." This calling, as the first three chapters of Ephesians makes clear, is one based upon the gospel of God's grace and mercy in Christ. Fourth, he describes the contours of such a calling: "with all humility and gentleness, with patience, bearing with one another in love." Here are all the ingredients of an ecumenical ethic (or, at least, etiquette), which in fact has marked Lutheran-Roman Catholic dialogue over the past fifty years.

The fifth phrase reveals Paul's reason for emphasizing these matters: "making every effort to maintain the unity of the Spirit in the bond of peace." Here it becomes clear that unity itself is not a human work but a gift of the Spirit—a gift that may be maintained, cherished, and nourished through our common calling to peace. The small liturgical exercise that marks the eucharistic liturgy—the exchange of peace—may reveal a daily and weekly call to the very bond of peace that now unites us in Christ and will unite us in the world to come.

Paul's final point outlines both the way the Spirit maintains peace and unity through us and, because it is written in the indicative, allows all ecumenical conversations and agreements to find their origin in God's gracious promise. "There is one body and one Spirit, just as you were called to the one hope of your calling, one Lord, one faith, one baptism, one God and Father of all, who is above all and through all and in all." This text especially makes the quest for unity and its maintenance into the chief Christian virtue, equally laid upon us all, *not* as an impossible command, but as a fruit of salvation itself. Whatever season of the ecumenical year, what motivates ecumenical conversation is precisely the unity we already have in the Trinity, in baptism, and in God's unfathomable mercy.

When commenting on this text (the appointed epistle for the eighteenth Sunday after Pentecost in the medieval lectionary), even Martin Luther could acclaim the "unity of the Spirit" as "the most necessary and beautiful grace that Christians possess."[1] He went on to bemoan division as a place where

Many are deceived; the masses immediately respond to new doctrine brilliantly presented in specious words by presumptuous individuals thirsting for fame. More than that, many weak but well-meaning ones fall to doubting, uncertain where to stand or with whom to hold.... Christians should feel bound to maintain the unity of the Spirit, since they are all members of one body and partakers of the same spiritual blessings. They have the same priceless treasures—one God and Father in heaven, one Lord and Savior, one Word, baptism and faith; in short, one and the same salvation, a blessing common to all whereof one has as much as another, and cannot obtain more. What occasion, then, for divisions or for further seeking? Here Paul teaches what the true Christian Church is and how it may be identified.[2]

Yet Luther was not the only sixteenth-century theologian to notice the ecumenical possibilities in these words. Johann Wild, OFM (1497–1554), the independent-minded court preacher for the archbishop of Mainz in the 1540s and 1550s, also preached on this text. He warned his listeners,

In sum, these four things must be present together: humility, so that one does not despise the other; meekness, so that one does not insult the other; patience, so that one bears and puts up with the other; and love, so that one helps the other. Where these four things are present, one walks in his or her Christian calling as is proper. And one can also say in truth: "We are one body and one Spirit, etc., have one God and Christ, faith and baptism." Where such things are absent, neither God nor Christ is present. Indeed, neither faith nor baptism helps. And let this cause us to open our eyes now. There is now a great conflict and quarrel about who are the true Christians. And if one looks at the matter properly, one finds that on neither side is there humility, meekness, patience or love. For this reason, there is no doubt that, should St. Paul still be preaching, he would recognize none of these people as true Christians. Let us consider what this means.[3]

This book's aim, therefore, has been to provide a simple outline for how, over the past half-century, Lutheran and Roman Catholic Christians have lived out their baptismal calling, empowered toward the unity by the Holy Spirit, as Ephesians describes it, and filled with the Spirit's gifts of humility, meekness, patience, and love.

THE COMMON TELLING OF HISTORY

As recounted in the first chapter, one of the first steps toward this unity occurs when Christians of different confessions strive to tell their story together, listening to each other's recounting and discovering in the process both areas of convergence and the truly church-dividing issues that remain barriers between them. History writing also involves a certain degree of surprise—for both reader and author. In this case, the oft-overlooked shock comes with the growing acknowledgment by historians that the Reformation, as we now call it, was unexpected and unplanned. When we replace icons of an angry young Martin Luther posting *Ninety-five Theses* on the church door in Wittenberg with pictures of a concerned teacher of the church posing questions about what he saw as an unclear and unhelpful church practice, a new avenue for ecumenical conversation opens—one where neither side dare begin by accusing the other of deliberately breaking the unity of the church.

But the history of the Reformation also reveals other surprising aspects of the events of the early sixteenth century. We learn that, while subsuming other authorities under the authority of Scripture, Luther and his colleagues never abandoned tradition, including the writings of the fathers and the decrees of the ecumenical councils, as a reliable witness to the gospel. The fact that a particular teaching is not word-for-word "in the Bible" does not *ipso facto* mean that it has no authority. Indeed, conversation with the past also marked theological conversation among Wittenberg's theologians and their allies. What some criticize as a "conservative" Reformation emanating from Wittenberg might better be understood as a proposal to the church catholic, where the conservation of good theology and practice for the sake of the gospel was its primary goal. Although this proposal, made concrete in the Augsburg Confession, was often cloaked in polemical language, what marked the early Reformation until well into the 1540s, and even beyond, was conversation—even and especially conversation between the Lutherans and their opponents. Thus, even the *modus operandi* for modern ecumenical conversations finds its roots in the events surrounding the Reformation.

CHARTING OUR ECUMENICAL CONVERSATIONS

The Doctrine of Justification

In 1541 at a religious colloquy held in Regensburg, Philip Melanchthon and Johann Eck, representing the Lutheran and Catholic sides respectively, came up with a common proposal on the doctrine of justification, which in the end, neither Wittenberg nor Rome accepted. The 1545 decree on justification by the Council of Trent and the article on justification in the 1576 Formula of Concord, written in part as a Lutheran response, set both confessions at odds with each other for the next four hundred years. Based both upon changing attitudes toward Scripture and Tradition and upon a more balanced approach to the history of the development of these doctrines during the Reformation, new steps toward reconciliation were possible after Vatican II. Beginning with the American dialogue and then taken up by the international conversations, it has become clear that on many issues connected to justification, Lutherans and Roman Catholics, despite centuries of polemic, shared broad areas of agreement.

This convergence in diversity was set down in the *Joint Declaration on the Doctrine of Justification*, formally signed in Augsburg in 1999 by representatives of the Lutheran World Federation and the Roman Catholic Church. In the first instance, the document involved a declaration of nonapplicability of condemnations by both sides, indicating that the condemnations of Trent and in the Lutheran Confessions did not apply to the doctrine as expressed in the joint agreement between the two communions. But the *Joint*

Declaration went much further by affirming both sides' confession that "by grace alone, in faith in Christ's saving work and not because of any merit on our part, we are accepted by God and receive the Holy Spirit, who renews our hearts while equipping and calling us to good works."[4] When some Lutheran critics of the agreement complain about the absence of the catchphrase "faith alone," they have overlooked certain historical nuances, used by Lutherans from the 1530s and summarized in the Formula of Concord, which insisted on the more general category of *"particulae exclusivae"* (exclusive clauses), indicated in the *Joint Declaration* by the words "not because of any merit on our part."[5]

Other differences, once thought church-dividing, also found reconciled diversity in the *Declaration*, especially the Lutheran insistence that a person is at the same time (*simul*) righteous and sinner. This statement did not mean that sin rules the justified but rather that the justified person lives only by God's mercy, and thus may not trust even the beginnings of righteousness and must acknowledge failings and sin while daily returning to God's promise of grace in baptism. This explanation converged with current Roman Catholic understanding of concupiscence, which remains in the justified but is not reckoned as sin.

The *Declaration* itself also marked an important first step forward in the relation between Rome and its "separated brothers and sisters," in that this joint statement did not require prior agreement on ecclesiology or ministry. This signaled Roman Catholic and Lutheran acknowledgment of this doctrine's centrality in the proclamation and mission of the church or, in the words of the *Declaration*, as "an indispensable criterion, which constantly orients all the teaching and practice of our churches to Christ."

Going forward, the principal task of both Lutherans and Catholics is to incorporate the agreement of the JDDJ into catechetical materials and preaching so that the teaching of the document is incorporated into the lived faith of congregations and parishes. Ecumenical agreements remain only documents until they become part of the living tradition of the churches. This task may be a bit more of a challenge for Catholics, more accustomed to hearing about sanctification than justification. Nevertheless, the agreement on justification is essentially the good news that we are saved by Christ alone by grace alone through faith. In this affirmation lies the core of the gospel message.

Scripture and Tradition

While a renewed telling of the history of the Reformation may help to break old stereotypes and provide glimpses of serious theological conversation, chapter 3 revealed just how certain modern trends also played their part, especially regarding the interpretation of Scripture and the understanding of Tradition. Taking different routes, both communions began investigating sixteenth-century events with an aim toward replacing old polemic with a renewed search for commonalities and the causes for church division. More dramatically, both also came to benefit from an approach to Scripture that did not downplay or ignore the historically conditioned context in which the biblical books arose or the literary forms their authors used.

On the one side, Lutheran theologians over the course of the nineteenth century came to reject the extremes of certain forms of Enlightenment and Liberal biblical interpretation in favor of rigorous historical and literary research coupled with the conviction that the Bible, as God's Word, contains God's living voice. On the Roman Catholic side, in reaction to some of the same intellectual forces dominating nineteenth-century European thought, a series of papal decrees during the twentieth century leading up to the Second Vatican Council opened the door to biblical scholarship that welcomed historical and literary insights while remaining committed to the Roman Catholic Church's proclamation of the gospel. Thus, serious dialogue between Lutherans and Roman Catholics, which began after Vatican II, could explore new approaches to traditional interpretive sticking points. On almost every biblical *crux interpretum*, new approaches helped to open up ecumenical conversations. Chapter 3 focused especially on two interpreters, John Reumann and Joseph A. Fitzmeyer, SJ, and their examination of righteousness and justification in Scripture, but the contribution of modern biblical interpretation has touched every aspect of our ecumenical conversations and invited both sides to abandon the polemic of the past for serious wrestling with the text of Scripture and its meaning for today.

The matter of Tradition and its relation to Scripture also underwent new scrutiny on both sides. On the one hand, Roman Catholic interpreters of Trent made clear that there were not two competing sources of authority in the church but rather one source, Jesus Christ. *Dei Verbum*, the decree on Scripture from the Second Vatican Council, seems also to imply that tradition itself must always be subject to the clear meaning of Scripture. On the other hand, the Lutheran use of the slogan *sola Scriptura* has been found to be a later dogmatic category, used only rarely by Luther and not at all by Philip Melanchthon. Moreover, a far more extensively used term was *solus Christus*. While Scripture has always been the first and true authority (*primum et verum*), Luther, Melanchthon, and their colleagues and followers never rejected other authorities, especially the church fathers and the ecumenical creeds. In all cases, these authorities are witnesses to Jesus Christ and his gospel.

These insights from both sides have resulted in some important steps toward rapprochement, so that the Lutheran-Roman Catholic Commission on Unity declared (par. 448), "Therefore regarding Scripture and Tradition Lutherans and Catholics are in such an extensive agreement that their different emphases do not of themselves require maintaining the present division of the churches. In this area, there is unity in reconciled diversity."

Baptism

On the question of baptism, the two communions have always maintained important areas of convergence. Already in 1530 at the Diet of Augsburg, the Roman Catholics accepted the article on baptism in the Augsburg Confession. Even earlier, in his first extensive work on the sacraments in 1520, the *Babylonian Captivity of the Church*, Luther praised God for having preserved the sacrament of baptism for the church. Both communions baptize infants and adults, use the trinitarian formula, confess the regenerative power and promise of the sacrament, and view it as the true entry point into the Christian life. In an emergency, both churches allow any baptized Christian, man or woman, to baptize. Both recognize the other church's baptism as valid. Modern liturgical renewal, with its reemphasis on this sacrament at all levels of Christian worship and life, matches the recent Lutheran "rediscovery" of the centrality of baptism in Luther's theology and practice. Roman Catholics, by rediscovering the catechumenate as the norm of a theology of initiation, have discovered conversion, renunciation of sin, and putting on of Christ in baptism as the pattern of Christian living.

However, differences remain. Lutherans view any renewal of God's promises of reconciliation and forgiveness as a return to baptism, a daily drowning of the old creature and raising up of the new. Roman Catholics emphasize God's work in the sacrament of reconciliation as a return to the condition created by baptism. Yet Lutherans also include in this return what they sometimes called the Sacrament of Absolution, a rite that early Lutherans never rejected and often counted as a sacrament.

Lutherans and Roman Catholics also distinguish the validity and efficacy of baptism somewhat differently. Against those who claimed that baptism required the commitment and faith of an adult, Lutherans insist, as do Roman Catholics, on the validity of the sacrament even for infants. For Roman Catholics, the efficacy of the sacrament depends upon its power to work through the performance of the rite (*ex opere operato*). On the other hand, for Lutherans, the promises of forgiveness and rebirth bestowed in baptism both effect and strengthen faith in the God who makes and keeps those promises through Christ by the power of the Holy Spirit. That is, baptism does not reach its goal until faith is present. Roman Catholics rightly worry that fiduciary faith, wrongly construed, could undermine the grace of God and make baptism dependent upon the human being, but they, too, hold baptism to be inseparable from faith, believing that baptism itself infuses the theological virtues of faith, hope, and charity and that proxy faith is present in the celebration of the sacrament through the faith of the parents and godparents as well as the assembled faith community.[6] Baptism is itself an act of faith since the baptismal rite includes a trinitarian profession of faith. Thus, both Lutherans and Catholics require faith for baptism, with Roman Catholics emphasizing the objective side (the faith of the church) and Lutherans the subjective (faith as trust).

Lutherans may worry that the emphasis on the *opus operatum* undermines the importance of faith (as trust in God's promises) and threatens to turn baptism into a rite effective by *mere* performance. This, however, fails to recognize that the Catholic principle of *ex opere operato* ("from the work worked") is correlated with another principle, *ex opere operantis* ("by the work of the person working or receiving the sacrament"). This correlation is not very different from what might be described as an objective offer of grace and its subjective reception in faith since both are conceptual means of distinguishing sacramental validity from sacramental efficacy. Sacramental activity involves both the work of God and human response to that work. Catholics express this with the principles of *ex opere operato* and *ex opere operantis*. Lutherans express this in terms of God's promise, which evokes faith in the baptized.

For both Lutherans and Catholics, baptism is not simply a human act performed in obedience to the divine command. Nor is it simply a sign of a profession of faith previously made and effecting nothing additional than that first act of faith. Both Lutherans and Roman Catholics insist on the power of baptism and reject all forms of Donatism, which would make sacraments dependent upon the holiness of the baptizer or of the one being baptized.

Both Lutherans and Catholics affirm baptism as an efficacious means of grace requiring faith either directly from the recipient of the sacrament or professed by proxy in the case of infants. The challenge for both Lutherans and Catholics is reconciling the requirement of faith for the sacrament in the case of the baptism of infants. Luther even posited the possibility of a *fides infantium*, infant faith. Practically speaking, since both Lutherans and Catholics baptize infants and both rely on proxy faith for the sacrament, the principle *ex opere operato* has functioned as something of a red herring in ecumenical relations, not representing as significant a difference between traditions as has sometimes been thought. Admittedly, the categories of discourse are quite different, Lutherans using the existential dynamic of direct address (promise received in faith) and Catholics using metaphysical categories, but in the end, both affirm baptism as a sacrament of faith.

A further sign acknowledging the mutual recognition of baptism by Lutherans and Catholics would be the adoption of a common baptismal certificate. Such a document would bear witness to the trinitarian formula used in the administration of baptism, since Catholics require that baptism be administered "in the name of the Father, and the Son, and the Holy Spirit" for validity.

Eucharist

Many more differences remain regarding the Sacrament of the Altar. But even here, the convergences are noteworthy. In the 1520 *Babylonian Captivity of the Church*, Luther complained about three "captivities" regarding this sacrament: withholding the cup from the laity, the doctrine of transubstantiation, and the sacrifice of the Mass. The first has found new common ground with certain decrees of the Second Vatican Council that once again allowed communion in both bread and wine by the laity. The second objection, which Luther held in common with some medieval theologians, notably Pierre d'Ailly, has been overcome by a reexamination of the origin of the term and its separation from Aristotelian physics. Moreover, although Lutherans reject using the term *transubstantiation*, over the centuries, they have fiercely defended Christ's real, substantial presence under the species of bread and wine without relying on philosophical explanations of the mystery.

The question of the sacrificial character of the Mass has been much more difficult an area to find agreement. Martin Luther and Philip Melanchthon both insisted that Christ's sacrifice for sin is, in the words of Hebrews, *eph-hapax* (once for all). The benefits of Christ's sacrifice are received efficaciously by all believers, and this reception issues in *eucharistia*, a sacrifice of praise and thanksgiving. While the Council of Trent continued to insist upon the sacrificial nature of the Mass as a sacrifice by Christ in the person of the priest on behalf of the church, Roman Catholic theology has emphasized that Christ's sacrifice on the cross is not repeated in the Supper. The one sacrifice of Christ is present liturgically under another modality. The Council of Trent spoke of this as "a bloodless offering" by which "the bloody sacrifice carried out on the cross should be represented, its memory persist until the end of time, and its saving power be applied to the forgiveness of sins."[7] As a result of the liturgical renewal, Catholics now speak of the sacramental representation of the once-for-all sacrifice through the category of *anamnesis*, the liturgical remembering that makes present a past historical event through the power of the Holy Spirit. This has allowed Lutherans and Roman Catholics to agree on the uniqueness and sufficiency of Christ's atoning life, death, and resurrection. Roman Catholics emphasize that in the Mass, the benefits of Christ's death are received and that the church joins itself to Christ's saving death before the Father by the power of the Holy Spirit. The church does not offer a sacrifice to God apart from Christ but rather, as the Body of Christ, it participates in his saving work.

Another neuralgic issue between Lutherans and Roman Catholics has been the propitiatory character of the Eucharist. If Christ's sacrifice is expiatory, that is, if this sacrifice is efficacious for the forgiveness of sin, then the sacramental modality of that same sacrifice carries the same efficacy and is therefore propitiatory. The resolution of the difference is achieved by uniting the concepts of *sacrificium* (sacrifice) and *sacramentum* (sacrament).

These significant steps forward still falter on the question of how the Eucharist may also play a role for those who have "died in the Lord." Here, a small step forward may be to understand the unity of believers in heaven and on earth, that is, in the church as the Body of Christ, where believers continually offer prayers for one another before God's throne. The US Lutheran-Catholic Dialogue developed this idea in Round XI, *The Hope of Eternal Life* (2010).[8]

Other differences also remain. Lutherans connect Christ's presence in the bread and wine with the action of the Lord's Supper itself—from the time the elements are presented at the altar until the benediction. Nevertheless, traditional practice (not always respected) gave special respect to any leftover consecrated elements and their disposal. To make practices of the churches consistent with ecumenical agreements on doctrine, the eucharistic elements need to be treated with appropriate care and reverence. Lutherans might consider returning to the practice of Luther and consuming the elements within the context of the service or immediately afterward.

Lutherans worried about worship of the elements apart from Christ's presence in the meal. Roman Catholics, who reserve the sacrament, do not find it contrary to the Supper to worship the continuing presence of Christ. Both parties continue to find ways to understand and respect the practices of the other—ways that emphasize Christ's real presence in the elements and the reception of those elements in the action of the meal.

Going forward, ecumenical dialogues on sacramental topics need to integrate sacramental theology with liturgical theology and practice. Liturgical texts should reflect ecumenical agreements, although another issue is how normative Lutheran books of worship are for individual pastors. If individual pastors take varying degrees of latitude in how the Lord's Supper is celebrated, the actual experience of any given liturgical celebration may not reflect the theology of either ecumenical consensus or even best Lutheran practice. Catholics recommend to Lutherans that they consider making the anaphora rather than the *verba nuda* of the words of institution an integral part of every liturgical service.

Ministry

Underneath the continuing conversations about the possibilities of eucharistic hospitality lurks the problem of recognition of ministries. Even if full agreement in the doctrine of the Eucharist were reached, the question of the validity of Lutheran ministries in Roman Catholic eyes remains. Here, too, substantial compatibility between the churches' teaching already exists. Both affirm that the public ministry is a divine institution; both ordain through the laying on of hands and invocation of the Holy Spirit; and both agree that ministry is subordinate to Christ who acts through it by the Holy Spirit and that its primary task is the proclamation of the gospel through Word and sacraments.

Differences remain. Lutheran churches do not all use bishops in ordination; Lutherans and Roman Catholics have different ways of relating the common priesthood of the baptized to public ministry, something that has also been a point of contention among Lutherans themselves; and Lutherans have not always been clear that the priest acts *in persona Christi*, despite the clear testimony of their own confessions. Part of the problem in these discussions has been the tendency to import categories used in one tradition to judge the language used in the other. This especially applies to questions about ontology versus functionality or about the apostolicity and validity of ministry. One neuralgic issue has focused on whether the public ministry has a sacrificial character. Another difficult, practical matter involves the ordination of women. Here, however, the care with which Roman Catholics have addressed the issue vis-à-vis growing Lutheran practice is itself a lesson in ecumenical conversation. This difference has not brought an end to ecumenical conversations and has even led to the recognition that ordained women are proper ministers within the context of the Lutheran communion. Whether this could lead to a differentiated consensus of some sort remains an open question.

An equally difficult matter has been the divergent ways in which Roman Catholics and Lutherans have expressed the unity of the ordained while acknowledging the various, usually threefold, offices (of bishop, priest, and deacon). Specifically, the Second Vatican Council recognizes the fullness of the ministerial office in the episcopate, while Lutherans, dependent in part upon statements by St. Jerome, argue that there is no essential difference between presbyter and bishop—even while (generally speaking) insisting that *episcopé* (especially ordinations and related oversight) is exercised by a distinct office. While Roman Catholic theology continues to elucidate the relation between priest and bishop, one hopeful step comes with the growing sense by both communions that the bishop represents his particular church in the communion of churches. At the same time, Lutherans have been involved in parallel debates on ordination, especially on the question of deacons and whether the term *ordination* is an appropriate term for consecration to their office.

The other major issue touches on apostolicity. Both churches agree both that the term primarily refers to faithfulness to the gospel, which is itself prior to the church, and that the ordained have been given the responsibility to maintain this apostolic witness. In their agreements with Anglicans, Lutherans have come to distinguish between the essence (*esse*) of the church and its well-being (*bene esse*) and connect this latter category to the continuity of apostolic succession of the ordained. What Lutherans do not have is a worldwide college of bishops, although exploration of what it means that the Lutheran World Federation is a *communion* of churches has led to increased importance of its decisions—including the *Joint Declaration* of 1999. To be sure, in Roman Catholic eyes, there are still "defects" or "deficiencies" in Lutheran ministries, but precisely what this means and the degree to which it is fundamentally church-dividing remains to be seen. The same is true in the continuing discussions about the primacy of the Bishop of Rome. Clearly, the

Second Vatican Council has provided new ways of viewing that primacy and its relation to collegiality, and subsequent popes have offered ways of understanding the decrees of Vatican I in a historical light.

Much work remains to achieve mutual recognition of ministries between Lutherans and Catholics. Recognition of ministry has traditionally been seen as either possible or not. Yet the nuanced and gradated understandings of apostolicity interpreted as both a ministerial and an ecclesial apostolicity raise the question whether recognition of ministries could also be achieved at least incrementally along the lines of an ecclesial recognition of imperfect communion. More broadly, topics of consensus regarding the church, including the issue of apostolicity, but also potentially the issue of the communion of churches, should be correlated with discussions of ministry. This would necessitate moving beyond categories of validity for a Catholic evaluation of Lutheran eucharistic celebrations, or at least reframing the juridical notion of validity within other theological categories such as communion and ecclesial apostolicity. Issues of ministry and ecclesiology cannot be addressed in isolation from each other.

Although the Reformers rejected the concept of the ministry as a sacrificial office as understood at the time of the Reformation, that issue has been reshaped by the contribution of the liturgical category of *anamnesis* to understandings of eucharistic sacrifice in clarifying that it is the one sacrifice of Christ sacramentally present in the Eucharist. Thus, it would appear that by correlating this agreement to the character of ministry, remaining differences in emphasis, vocabulary, and practice concerning sacrifice and its relationship to ministry may not be church-dividing.

Regarding the ordering of ministry, Lutherans do not reject the division of the one office into different ministries that has developed in the history of the church. Catholics and Lutherans agree that the ministry is exercised both locally in the congregation and regionally.[9] Both accept that the distinction between local and regional offices in the churches is "more than the result of purely historical and human developments, or a matter of sociological necessity," but is "the action of the Spirit."[10] Regarding the regional office, *Apostolicity of the Church* concluded that since "the supra-local visitations of the Reformation era did not happen by chance but emerged out of inner necessity. Thus Lutheran churches, too, have always been episcopally ordered in the sense of having a ministry which bears responsibility for the communion in faith of individual local congregations."[11] Moreover, the Augsburg Confession affirms the desire of the Lutheran reformers to preserve, if possible, the episcopal polity that they had inherited from the past.[12]

In contemporary practice, some Lutheran churches have "one three-fold ministry," while others do not.[13] While questions of order remain intensely discussed among Lutherans, there is no expectation of a single proper form, for the shape of ministry is not construed on the basis of a principle, but by the experiences the church has undergone.[14]

Both historical considerations of the circumstances and intentions at the time of the Reformation as well as current ecclesial practices suggest that the differences in Catholic and Lutheran polities should no longer be church-dividing. Much Lutheran polity distinguishes between bishops and pastors in terms of responsibilities of oversight and in terms of who is considered to be the appropriate minister of ordination. On the Catholic side, the question remains open as to whether the distinction between bishops and priests is of divine law. Thus, the beginning of canon 7 from the Council of Trent, "If anyone says that bishops are not of higher rank than priests, or have no power to confirm and ordain, or that the power they have is common to them and the priests," should be declared as non-applicable to Lutherans today.

The communal dimension of ministerial succession requires more ecumenical attention. Although many Lutheran churches have engaged the theology and practice of an episcopacy in apostolic succession, the implications of a communion ecclesiology in terms of the relationships among churches remain nascent in Lutheranism. Nor has a communion ecclesiology extended to either a theology or a practice of a corporate episcopacy. The international study on apostolicity noted that episcopal office is exercised "not only in personal contact with the congregation (personal dimension), in which it is essentially rooted (communal dimension), but also requires communion with the other bishops (collegial dimension)."[15] Thus a more collegial understanding of episcopal relationships by Lutherans is very desirable from an ecumenical point of view. An imperfect communion of churches implies an imperfect communion of ministers within a communion ecclesiology correlated with ministry. One can even ask whether there can be an imperfect implicit communion of Lutheran ministers with the episcopal college if the college is considered to be one as the church is one, a theological and spiritual reality, and not merely an administrative entity.

Since the communion of Lutheran churches in a worldwide framework is developing, the competency of leadership bodies above the level of the individual churches and the binding force of their decisions for these churches is variously regulated and insufficiently clarified. Views differ among Lutherans with regard to whether there ought to be an institutional exercise of a universal ministry of unity or how it should be structured. Furthermore, "there is a dispute about what intensity and what structure this relation to the universal church must have for the worshipping congregations and individual to be in accord with their apostolic mission."[16] Thus, Lutherans need to explore "whether the worldwide koinonia of the church calls for a worldwide minister of unity and what form such a ministry might take to be truly evangelical."[17] Catholics need to explore "how the universal ministry of the bishop of Rome can be reformed to manifest more visibly its subjection to the gospel in service to the koinonia of salvation."[18]

CHURCH

Standing behind many of the issues of ministry are the different, sometimes competing views on the nature of the church. The question underneath discussions of ecclesiology is whether such differences are complementary or church-dividing. It is clear that Luther never intended to create a separate church but rather to call the late-medieval church's attention to certain failings in teaching and preaching that hurt its pastoral work. The fact that Lutheran ecclesiology, such as it is, arose for the most part in reaction to differences with Rome and with other Reformed or Anabaptist ecclesiologies rather than as a result of independent reflection, may be both a weakness (in that this is a neglected area of Lutheran theology) and an ecumenical strength (in that, at many points, Lutheran and Roman Catholic understandings converge or are at least compatible).

Where progress has occurred, it especially centers on agreement on the trinitarian and christocentric origins of the church, its relation to God's Word, its role in receiving and proclaiming salvation, and its nature as the communion of saints. One important difference revolves around the notion of the universal church and its teaching office. Another involves the specific role of the laity in the church's teaching office. Then there are continuing questions about the relation between the reformability and holiness of the church.

One area of growing convergence has arisen out of what used to be seen as an unbridgeable gap. With many Protestant churches emphasizing preaching and, so they thought, the Word, and with Roman Catholics emphasizing the sacraments, especially the Eucharist, each side often assumed that the other had abandoned the apostolic tradition. But as Lutherans rediscovered the importance of the sacraments in Luther's thought as "visible words" (taking a concept from St. Augustine) and as Roman Catholics experienced a revival of interest in the oral proclamation of the gospel, most recently expressed in Francis I's *Evangelii Gaudium*,[19] it has become clear that church can only be defined as the place where Word *and* Sacrament conjoin.

While both churches confess the church as both recipient and instrument of salvation, differences remain particularly in the way in which they define the hidden and visible aspects of the church. When Luther insisted as early as 1519 that the church was properly speaking the assembly of all believers, his opponents immediately noticed that this definition undermined the certainty of the gospel that he was so eager to espouse. Since no one could see into a person's heart, they argued, no one could know for certain whether he or she was in the church or not. Luther responded by emphasizing that the church had certain visible characteristic markings (*notae*)—especially the proclamation of the Word and the administration of the sacraments—indicating its presence. While he sometimes could use this to dismiss his opponents' claims to be church, on occasion, he followed the logic of his argument and insisted that because his opponents also read the gospel, baptized, and celebrated the Mass, the church was also among them. In his most systematic exposition of the church in 1539, Luther expanded the marks to seven: proclamation of the Word, baptism, the Lord's Supper, absolution (in private and public confession), ordination, worship (especially prayer, praise, and instruction in the basics of the faith), and the cross.[20] Although later Roman Catholic scholars, such as Robert Bellarmine, provided an alternative list of the church's marks that included the councils and communion with the Bishop of Rome, the Second Vatican Council distinguishes between membership according to heart and membership according to body. This points to an important area of convergence that may help each church hear the real concerns of the other in the ways in which they construe ecclesiology. The fact that Lutherans often equate "church" with "assembly" of believers around Word and sacraments, and Roman Catholics now speak of the church as a "community" of faith, hope, and love, also points to an important narrowing of differences. It may be that a common rediscovery of the eschatological ground of the church will help in this process.

A related question touches on the question of *where* the church may be found. Already in the New Testament, the Greek word *ekklesia* is used in different ways to designate either the entire body of believers from all times and places ("upon this rock, I will build my church") or individual congregations ("to the churches of Galatia"). When Lutherans locate the fullness of the church in the local congregation, even while not necessarily limiting the church to individual congregations, and Roman Catholics tend to identify the fullness of church with the diocese, both communions are reflecting different aspects of the ancient practice: where bishops were pastors of a particular city where people regularly gathered for worship (the Lutheran emphasis) and where the bishop was seen as the central public representative of that worshiping community (the Roman Catholic emphasis). As dioceses became larger and more populous in the course of the Middle Ages, the intimate relation between bishop and people in individual congregations was largely broken, but the ecclesiological implications of this were not realized. In a world subject to "Balkanization" at so many levels, steps to reinvigorate the communal nature of the church at the local, regional, and worldwide levels will aid the very proclamation of the gospel in Word and Sacrament that God established for the church to do.

The question of apostolicity, which also arises in connection with ministry, has also shaped our mutual conversations. Both confessions agree that the church stands on the foundation of the apostles, while understanding the nature of that foundation differently—with the Lutherans emphasizing the apostolic continuity of proclamation and Roman Catholics emphasizing the succession of ministers. Only when these two definitions become mutually exclusive and focus almost solely on the problem of legitimacy, does the question of apostolicity become church-dividing. The Second Vatican Council's renewed emphasis upon the continuity of apostolic teaching and the Lutheran rediscovery of the reformers' commitment to *preserve* the entire range of apostolicity rather than destroy it have opened up new avenues for *rapprochement*, as indicated especially in the *Apostolicity of the Church*.

The question of apostolicity always brings with it issues related to the Petrine see. Here, again, the Second Vatican Council helpfully clarified certain aspects of the First Vatican Council, both by emphasizing that the Bishop of Rome exercises authority within the college of bishops and by making central the role of the Holy Spirit's guidance in proclamation. When this is combined with a renewed appreciation for an ecclesiology of communion and the centrality of a continuity of proclamation, then the differences in understanding become less daunting. The extent to which Lutherans and Roman Catholics share community in faith, sacraments, and service functions as a renewed mark of our churches' shared apostolicity.

Maintaining faithfulness to the gospel is of utmost concern to both churches. The Reformation itself was a debate over what constituted such faithfulness. For Lutherans, the question of maintaining that faithfulness was at first addressed in the context of the developing territorial churches. In the first instance, the event of presenting a confession of faith to the emperor in Augsburg in 1530 and the content of that confession seemed sufficient to mark such faithfulness. When differences arose among Lutheran churches that confessed the Augsburg Confession, further documents were written, culminating in the Formula of Concord of 1576, when the theological heirs of Martin Luther and Philip Melanchthon came to a differentiated agreement on the interpretation of the Augsburg Confession. Although only about two-thirds of the German-speaking churches subscribed to this document, it represented an important method of maintaining and building unity: through mutual conversations of theologians supported by the agreement of their territorial churches. This approach has, in one form or another, continued to play a role in Lutheran churches, where formal unification through a recognized hierarchy has been replaced by a variety of venues in which deliberation and consultation occur and which has always included both lay and ordained participants. This ability to come to theological decisions has slowly become a part of the Lutheran World Federation, as it has moved from a loose association into a communion of churches—able to make decisions about apartheid (1984) and justification (1999) and to ask forgiveness from the Mennonite World Conference (2000).

On the Roman Catholic side, by contrast, the role of papal infallibility as promulgated by the First Vatican Council has found useful clarification in the decree *Dei Verbum* at the Second Vatican Council, which insisted that the teaching function of the papal see is not above the Word of God but in service to it and that both the college of bishops and the entire church has a role to play in the process. That Lutherans and Catholics have developed different ways to maintain their churches' faithfulness to the gospel may thus present somewhat less of an obstacle to unity than had previously been imagined.

The sixth chapter showed how ecumenical dialogue has reconciled many of the differences between Lutheran and Catholics concerning the church. The question of the basic ecclesial unit, that which is necessary for a local expression to be fully church even if not the whole church, is largely reconciled insofar as different views of the meaning of a bishop and his relationship to a presbyter/pastor affect understandings of the identity of the local church. The historical views of St. Jerome, the fact that Lutherans include a necessary ministry of regional oversight and value regional expressions of the church, and that Catholics affirm the importance of the parish as the place where most Catholics encounter the church, show that Lutheran and Catholic views of the identity of the local church are complementary, both being necessary expressions of the church. Catholics and Lutherans alike affirm the necessity of Word, Sacrament, and ministry for what constitutes the church.

The question of the holiness and sinfulness of the church is largely resolved through a consideration of how eschatology has impacted both Lutheran and Catholic perceptions of the church. Catholics emphasize a real, but partial eschatology proleptically present in history and affirm the holiness of the church under its aspect of Body of Christ and temple of the Spirit. Nevertheless, while refraining from calling the church itself "sinful," they also describe the church as a pilgrim in history traveling on the way to perfection. Thus the church is "at the same time holy and always in need of purification" as it "pursues unceasingly penance and renewal" (*Lumen Gentium* § 8). Lutherans hold that no church office and decision is immune from error and sin, yet they, too, confess that the church on earth is holy, despite the presence of sin in it. Lutherans do not have a difficult time predicating the simultaneity of both sin and holiness of either a person or the church itself as the famous phrase *simul iustus et peccator* indicates. Both sides acknowledge the ongoing struggle against sin and error.[21]

Catholics refer to the church itself as analogously a "sacrament," while Lutherans refrain from doing so, largely on account of their definition of a sacrament as entailing a scriptural warrant for a sacrament, God's promise, and an audible or visible sign of that promise. The Catholic Church only began designating the church as a sacrament officially with the Second Vatican Council, and it is not a definition meant to cause a division from churches that would not acknowledge it. In Catholic theology, this concept has been helpful to describe the close relationship between Christ and the church as well as the difference between Christ and the church to correct an over-identification of the two through a description of the church as a prolongation of the incarnation.

Lutherans and Catholics both affirm that the church is (1) both a creature of the Word (*creatura verbi*) and servant of the Word (*ministra verbi*), (2) a sign of the universal saving will of God, (3) as Word and Sacrament, an instrument of grace, (4) essentially shaped by the reception of and administration of Word and Sacrament, and (5) constantly subject to the Lord. God imparts salvation as his gift even in the work of the church. Consequently, the document *Communio Sanctorum* concludes, "Where this is together taught, there is material agreement, even if different judgments exist about the analogous use of the term 'sacrament' in relationship to the church."[22]

The mechanisms for teaching and the binding character of that teaching perhaps constitute the greatest difference between Lutherans and Catholics with respect to the church. Both Lutherans and Catholics believe in the indefectibility of the church, that the church will be preserved in the truth necessary for salvation by the guidance of the Holy Spirit. Along with this, both traditions believe that the church has the responsibility to teach the gospel and to renounce error.[23] Both sides affirm the need for a ministry and office of teaching at various levels in the church (local, regional, and worldwide), exercised in the context of the whole church within a dynamic relationship with all the faithful who also have a charism for discerning truth and error.

Despite these agreements, Lutherans and Catholics deeply disagree about the certitude possible for church teaching and its binding character. Catholics hold that the papal and episcopal magisterium (teaching office) through the guidance of the Holy Spirit can express the truth of the gospel in doctrinal statements that express or interpret divine revelation. The various teachings of the magisterium can extend through a range of certitude and authority from authentic but fallible teaching to solemn teaching judged to be inerrant and infallible by the bishops gathered in ecumenical council or a pope teaching *ex cathedra* about faith or morals under certain exact, predetermined conditions. The kind of adherence required of the faithful varies according to the authority, object, and inerrancy of the teaching. This varies from simple assent to a response of faith, this last response only appropriate when the object of the teaching is a matter of divine revelation. Thus not all authentic Catholic teaching is infallible teaching. Nevertheless, "the religious assent of will and intellect" is to be given to all authentic teaching authority of the pope even when he is not speaking *ex cathedra* (*Lumen Gentium* § 25). Finally, all the faithful under the guidance of the Holy Spirit also cannot be mistaken in belief through "a supernatural sense of the faith in the whole people when 'from the bishops to the last of the faithful laity' it expresses the consent of all in matters of faith and morals" (§ 12). Thus, although teaching office is exercised by the magisterium, comprised only of the ordained, the reception of teaching in the inerrancy of belief extends to the whole church including the laity.

According to Lutheran understanding, the church fulfills its teaching office through "a many-layered process, aiming for consensus through the participation of various responsibility-bearers."[24] These include bishops whose responsibility it is to "judge doctrine and to reject doctrine that is contrary to the gospel,"[25] theologians, pastors, and members of congregations whose duty is "to test whether the proclamation offered to them accords with the gospel."[26] This process includes the ordained and the nonordained working together—that is, all the members of the church, contributing to a consensus ultimately tested by its relation to the continuity of the preaching and teaching tradition of the church.

The document *Communio Sanctorum* rightly observes that neither Lutherans nor Catholics can be expected to give up their faith positions on this matter, but that a way forward might be at least to diffuse the contradictions so that they are no longer church-dividing. For instance, both sides affirm the power of the Word of God to interpret itself. Catholics would need to show in theory and practice that the authentic and at times inerrant teaching office is also an instrument of God under the inspiration of the Holy Spirit and serves truth in the church, not standing against the power of Holy Scripture to interpret itself. Lutherans, on the other hand, would need to understand that the Catholic practice and understanding is not opposed to the Word of God interpreting itself.[27]

In addition, as the following section will show, a reconciled church has a certain latitude to allow for differing structures of decision making as long as there is communion among the episcopacy and with the Bishop of Rome. A reformed exercise of the papacy may allow more for structures of subsidiarity. Since the teaching office and its exercise involves both a theology and a practice of authority and those have changed and developed for both traditions in response to different historical pressures and necessities, they may continue to develop.

THE SHAPE OF A REUNITED CHURCH

Whether or not Lutherans and Catholics are able to reach the goal of the ecumenical movement—namely, full, visible unity—rests on the ecclesial implications of such a unity. A "return ecumenism," repudiated by *Unitatis Redintegratio* at Vatican II, remains a fear in the hearts of many separated Christians, for a "return ecumenism" implies a monolithic church with one culture, one structure, one history, one law, and one liturgy. In short, it implies that separated Christians simply reenter the one fold, assuming all the ecclesial structures of Roman Catholicism.

Communion ecclesiology potentially provides a lens for providing an alternative vision of what a relationship of full, visible communion might look like. Full communion need not imply that Lutherans lose their Lutheran identity and simply become Roman Catholic, that is, return to Rome. Potentially keeping their historical, cultural, liturgical, and doctrinal heritage, once church-dividing issues are transcended, these churches could potentially enter into communion with the church and Bishop of Rome. In some ways, this would be analogous to the way that Eastern Catholic Churches have their own Eastern code of canon law and their own liturgical rites, but are in a relationship of full communion with Rome.

Within this mode of ecclesiology, full communion does not imply a loss of history, culture, ecclesial structures of decision making, or specific liturgical rubrics. Five hundred years of growth and development cannot simply be erased, nor should it be. Within communion ecclesiology, church-dividing issues must be reconciled, which includes communion with the Bishop of Rome. However, Lutherans within the relationship of reconciled communion would retain the ecclesial identity forged since the Reformation. This kind of unity may echo the very proposal underlying the Augsburg Confession itself: acceptance of bishops in communion with Rome on the basis of freedom in the gospel, married priests, and communion in both kinds. Within such a communion, diversity enriches catholicity.

Up to now, ecumenical dialogues have concentrated on overcoming church-dividing issues, not by locating the lowest common denominator, as some mistakenly think, but by transcending differences through discovering overarching concepts, such as communion ecclesiology for envisioning church structures or *anamnesis* for resolving issues of eucharistic sacrifice. Perhaps now is the time for dialogue to concentrate its efforts on envisioning the shape of a reconciled church. The North American Orthodox-Catholic Theological Consultation engaged in such an exercise as one attempt to overcome an impasse over the issue of papal primacy.[28] The theological work between Lutherans and Catholics has matured to the point that such practical envisioning in light of the church's location in time and place may be the logical next step in dialogue. Just as Lutherans sought ecclesial solutions to their ecclesial situation at the time of the Reformation, so now new ecclesial solutions must be identified by both Lutherans and Catholics to reflect a reconciled relationship in the twenty-first century.

THE ECUMENICAL IMPERATIVE[29]

Perhaps the greatest ecumenical achievement of the twentieth century is the awareness of the need for Christian unity and the admission that the lack of unity wounds all ecclesial traditions. John Paul II, in his apostolic Letter *Tertio Millennio Adveniente* (1994) states,

> Among the sins which require a greater commitment to repentance and conversion should certainly be counted those which have been detrimental to the unity willed by God for his people. In the course of the 1,000 years now drawing to a close, even more than in the first millennium, ecclesial communion has been painfully wounded, a fact 'for which at times, people of both sides were to blame' (UR 3). Such wounds openly contradict the will of Christ and are a cause of scandal to the world (UR 1). (§ 34)

The task of mending division has a human face, so a primary goal of ecumenical dialogue consists in building relationships. In these relationships, dialogue partners learn to view Christian discipleship through the eyes of another and to recognize the integrity of the other's motivation and vision. Christian patterns of life, witness, and worship seen through the eyes of another become—in John Paul II's words—an ecumenical gift exchange (*Ut Unum Sint*, 28). In this exchange, each tradition receives the ethos of the other and those aspects of the Christian tradition that have been preserved in the tradition of the other.

Ecumenical dialogue does not establish uniformity as a criterion by which to measure ecumenical progress. The type of visible unity sought in full visible communion does not demand the sacrifice of that which is distinctive in various ecclesial traditions. The Roman Catholic *Directory for the Application of Principles and Norms on Ecumenism* states the goal of the ecumenical movement: "The [Vatican II] council affirms that this unity by no means requires the sacrifice of the rich diversity of spirituality, discipline, liturgical rites and elaborations of revealed truth that has grown up among Christians in the measure that this diversity remains faithful to the apostolic Tradition."[30] The diversity that must exist within full visible unity is not a concession to division but an expression of the very catholicity of the church. The *Ecumenical Directory* expands on this principle: "The unity of the Church is realized in the midst of a rich diversity. This diversity in the Church is a dimension of its catholicity. At times the very richness of this diversity can engender tensions within the communion. Yet, despite such tensions, the Spirit continues to work in the Church calling Christians in their diversity to ever deeper unity."[31]

Dialogue is neither a negotiating process toward a lowest common denominator of agreement nor simply a revisiting of past history to clear up misunderstandings. When dialogue partners encounter "binding positions" that seem to condemn the other, often the path forward through the difficulty is the identification of how that "binding position" was a means to preserve the gospel in a particular context.

Reception of the results of ecumenical dialogue remains a great challenge for both Lutherans and Catholics. At times, these results may be misinterpreted because other theologians or church officials may judge the results through the lens of the accustomed categories when, in fact, dialogue seeks to overcome old divisions through the use of new categories. For example, judgments concerning ecumenical agreements on ministry may be dominated by the juridical category of validity. Or, to cite another example, the category of communion rather than church membership allows for varying degrees of communion between Lutherans and Catholics rather than an all-or-nothing relationship.

One of the greatest challenges to ecumenical unity today may be the fear of losing one's ecclesial identity. Too often, members of a tradition define themselves contrastively by what someone else is not. There may be a fear that if differences are overcome, we may lose our identity as Lutherans or Catholics. As both traditions mine the same biblical and historical resources and together identify a new lens through which to view old divisions, they may find themselves appropriating each other's patterns of thinking and witnessing. Rather than something to be feared, this actually represents a fruit of ecumenical dialogue, the reception of a gift in the ecumenical gift exchange. To succeed ecumenically, we must be able to articulate our identity positively rather than oppositionally. Confessional identity as a sign of fidelity to faith must be distinguished from confessionalism as an ideology constructed in enmity to the other.

The world today requires the unity of Christians as never before. The need for a common Christian witness within a secular world is greater than the divisions within the churches. Seen from outside the walls of these churches, outside the commonality that labels these communities "Christian," belief in Christ and the Trinity is a much greater commonality than what appears from the outside to be intramural bickering about technical issues of which the common believer knows little.

Ecumenical efforts toward Christian unity provide a powerful witness to peace and reconciliation in a violent, war-torn world. As Vatican II's *Pastoral Constitution on the Church in the Modern World* states, "We are also mindful that the unity of Christians is today awaited and desired by many non-believers. For the more this unity is realized in truth and charity under the powerful impulse of the Holy Spirit, the more will it be a harbinger of unity and peace throughout the whole world" (*Gaudium et Spes* 92).

Abbreviations

BC   *The Book of Concord.* Edited by Robert Kolb and Timothy J. Wengert. Minneapolis: Fortress, 2000.

CA   Augsburg Confession.

DH   *Enchiridion symbolorum, definitionum et declarationum de rebus fidei et morum.* English and Latin. San Francisco: Ignatius Press, 2012.

JDDJ   *Joint Declaration on the Doctrine of Justification* (1999).

LW   *Luther's Works.* American Edition. Edited by Jaroslav Pelikan, et al. 55+ vols. Philadelphia: Fortress and St. Louis: Concordia, 1955–.

LWF   Lutheran World Federation.

MBW   *Melanchthons Briefwechsel.* Edited by Heinz Scheible, et al. 28+ vols. Stuttgart/Bad Cannstatt: Frommann/Holzboog, 1977–.

MPL   Migne, Jacques Paul. *Patrologia Latina.*

WA   *Martin Luthers Werke: [Schriften].* 61 vols. Weimar: Böhlau, 1883–1980.

WA Br   *Martin Luthers Werke: Briefwechsel.* 18 vols. Weimar: Böhlau, 1930–85.

Notes

Chapter One

1. Heiko Oberman, *Luther: Man between God and the Devil*, trans. Eileen Walliser-Schwarzbart (New Haven: Yale University Press, 1989), 13–206.

2. LW 48: 43–49.

3. LW 31: 17–33.

4. See, most recently, Joachim Ott and Martin Treu, *Luthers Thesenanschlag—Factum oder Fiktion* (Leipzig: Evangelische Verlagsanstalt, 2008). See also Volker Leppin and Timothy J. Wengert, "Sources for and against the Posting of the Ninety-Five Theses," *Luther Quarterly* 29 (2015): 373–98.

5. See Peter Fabisch and Erwin Iserloh, eds., *Dokumente zur Causa Lutheri (1517–1521)*, Part 1: *Das Gutachten des prierias und weitere Schriften gegen Luthers Ablaßthesen (1517–1518)* (Münster: Aschendorff, 1988), 377.

6. See Martin Brecht, *Martin Luther: His Road to Reformation 1483–1521*, trans. James Schaaf (Philadelphia: Fortress, 1985), 205.

7. LW 31: 77–252, here p. 80.

8. *Dokumente*, 33–201.

9. Charles Brockwell and Timothy J. Wengert, eds., *Telling the Churches' Stories: Ecumenical Perspectives on Writing Christian History* (Grand Rapids, MI: Eerdmans, 1995), 19.

10. Whether Luther himself published a first edition in Wittenberg (Grunenberg's printing press was after all in the basement of the Augustinian cloister where Luther lived) is also disputed, especially by those who question whether the *Theses* were ever posted. In any case, no Wittenberg printing has survived.

11. See, for example, Heiko Oberman's reconstruction of Johannes

Eck's dispute over usury in his *Werden und Wertung der Reformation: Vom Wegestreit zum Glaubenskampf*, 2nd ed. (Tübingen: Mohr [Siebeck], 1979), 161–200. For Tetzel and Wimpina's theses, see *Dokumente*, 310–37.

12. LW 31: 77–252.

13. No printed copy of such a translation exists, and it may well be that what they sent to Luther was a manuscript. The earliest translation of *The Ninety-five Theses* into German appeared after Luther's death, when they were included in a volume of his German works.

14. WA 1: 243–46. For the English translation, see *The Annotated Luther*, vol. 1: *The Roots of Reform*, ed. Timothy J. Wengert (Minneapolis: Fortress, 2015), 56–65.

15. *Dokumente*, 337–63.

16. For example: "Furthermore, so that I may instruct you correctly, please note the following. If you want to give something, you ought above all else (without considering St. Peter's building or indulgences) give to your poor neighbor. When it comes to the point that there is no one in your city who needs help (unless God deigns it, this will never happen!), then you ought to give where you want: to churches, altars, decorations or chalices that are for your own city. And when that, too, is no longer necessary, then first off—if you wish—you may give to the building of St. Peter's or anywhere else." Or, on the question of uncertainty: "Eighteenth, whether souls are rescued from purgatory through indulgences, I do not know and I also do not believe it, although some new doctors [of the church] say it. But it is impossible for them to prove it, and the church has not yet decided the matter. Therefore, for the sake of greater certainty, it is much better that each of you prays and works for these souls. For this has more value and is certain."

17. See Scott Hendrix, *Luther and the Papacy: Stages in a Reformation Conflict* (Philadelphia: Fortress, 1981), 44–70. The encounter between the two men also led Cajetan to research and write on indulgences. He produced one of the most complete treatments of the doctrine and practice from this time. See Bernhard Alfred R. Felmberg, *Die Ablasstheologie Kardinal Cajetans (1469–1534)* (Leiden: Brill, 1998).

18. LW 31: 100: "To be sure, the person who is absolved must guard himself very carefully from any doubt that God has remitted his sins, in order that he may find peace of heart."

19. LW 31: 274–75.

20. See Christopher Spehr, *Luther und das Konzil* (Tübingen: Mohr Siebeck, 2010).

21. See Bernhard Alfred R. Felmberg, *Die Ablasstheologie Kardinal Cajetans (1469–1534)* (Leiden: Brill, 1998).

22. Luther had in mind the councils of Nicea and Carthage, as

his account of the Leipzig debate shows. See WA 2: 398–99 and Spehr, *Luther und das Konzil,* 168f.

23. Luther dismissed extreme unction (the anointing of the sick) as having no command from Christ and, like all of his contemporaries, had no idea about confirmation's connection to baptism. By the 1530s, confirmation would be reinstated as a time of instruction in the faith. In the *Apology of the Augsburg Confession,* Philip Melanchthon treated penance as the "Sacrament of Absolution" and argued that ordination could also be a sacrament if no longer seen as a rite to set aside people to say private Masses for the dead.

24. Berndt Hamm, "Luther's *Freedom of a Christian* and the Pope," *Lutheran Quarterly* 21 (2007): 249–67.

25. We know from his private audience with the archbishop of Trier, which took place a few days later, that the chief problem was still the Council of Constance.

26. LW 32: 112. The appeal to conscience, which so fascinated historians of the Enlightenment and beyond, was actually part of an ongoing medieval discussion about canon law and would have been so understood by Luther's contemporaries.

27. Hendrix, *Luther and the Papacy,* 87–89. For Philip Melanchthon, see Peter Fraenkel, *Testimonia Patrum: The Function of the Patristic Argument in the Theology of Philip Melanchthon* (Geneva: Droz, 1961).

28. LW 32: 133–260.

29. For a partial translation of the *Weihnachtspostille,* see LW 52. A fuller translation is found in *The Sermons of Martin Luther,* trans. John Lenker, 8 vols. (Reprint: Grand Rapids, Baker, 1984), vols. 1 & 6. For *On Monastic Vows,* see LW 44: 243–400. Prefaces to the New Testament may be found in LW 35: 255–411. Luther disguised himself as a knight (Junker Jörg) and let his tonsure grow out. Upon his return to Wittenberg, he again took up the cowl and tonsure, not abandoning it until 1524. See Heiko Oberman, "Martin Luther *contra* Medieval Monasticism: A Friar in the Lion's Den," in *Ad fontes Lutheri: Toward the Recovery of the Real Luther: Essays in Honor of Kenneth Hagen's Sixty-Fifth Birthday,* ed. Timothy Maschke et al. (Milwaukee: Marquette University Press, 2001), 183–213.

30. LW 51: 67–100.

31. LW 31: 371–77.

32. Quite surprising for people used to equating all Protestants with iconoclasm is the main altar of the cathedral church in Aarhus, Denmark, which is graced at its pinnacle by a statue depicting the crowning of Mary by God the Father.

33. A fact emphasized in the Augsburg Confession, art. XXIV.

34. See Martin Brecht, *Martin Luther: The Preservation of the Church 1532–1546*, trans. James Schaaf (Minneapolis: Fortress, 1993), 51.

35. For details, see Karl Klüpfel, "Philipp von Hessen," in: *Real-Encyklopädie für protestantische Theologie und Kirche*, vol. 11 (Gotha: Besser, 1859), 519.

36. See LW 40: 263–320, where the title (*Unterricht der Visitatoren an die Pfarrherren*) is inaccurately rendered *Instructions for the Visitors of Parish Pastors in Electoral Saxony*. In 1538, the revised document was published using a title page containing the coats of arms of all five of Wittenberg's theologians.

37. Its Latin version, however, influenced (among others) John Calvin in his first edition of *The Institutes of the Christian Religion*.

38. See "Tetrapolitan Confession," in OER 4: 148–49. The chief hallmark of this confession was its more symbolic understanding of Christ's presence in the Lord's Supper.

39. Throughout this chapter, the word *Evangelical* designates those committed to Wittenberg's understanding of the gospel and corresponds with the word still used in German and other languages as the self-designation for Lutherans. Other terms are often anachronistic. *Lutheran* was sometimes a designation for a broader group of parties opposed to Rome and could be said best to define Evangelicals after 1580, with the publication of *The Book of Concord* (see below). *Protestant* was a technical term for the estates of the Empire who, after the second diet of Speyer, filed an official appeal of the imperial diet's decision, called a *protestatio*. It later came to denote a wide variety of groups opposed to Rome, especially Reformed churches and theology, and (at least in the United States) is a far cry from the general trends of Lutheran theology and practice.

40. At certain points, especially in the Augsburg Confession (henceforth CA) IX and XVI, the document distanced its signers from "Anabaptists," who were directly condemned by the second diet of Speyer in 1529 and thus stood under the ancient Roman imperial rescripts that named rebaptisms a capital crime. This rejection of the Anabaptists also had an "ecumenical" purpose, vis-à-vis the Roman party, in proving the catholicity of Evangelical theology and practice. For recent developments in the relations between the heirs of Anabaptists and Lutherans, see *Healing Memories: Reconciling in Christ: Report of the Lutheran–Mennonite International Study Commission* (Geneva: Lutheran World Federation and Strasbourg: The Mennonite World Conference, 2010).

41. See, especially, Robert Kolb, *Confessing the Faith: Reformers Define the Church, 1530–1580* (St. Louis: Concordia, 1991), 38–42.

42. Luther saw this as a fulfillment of Psalm 119:46, a verse that then graced the title page of every printing of the Latin version. See CA

(Latin), trans. Eric Gritsch, in *The Book of Concord* (henceforth BC), ed. Robert Kolb and Timothy J. Wengert (Minneapolis: Fortress, 2000), 31.

43. LW 51: 237–38.

44. BC 343–44.

45. Solid Declaration of the Formula of Concord, Binding Summary, 5, trans. Robert Kolb, in BC 527.

46. See LW 37: 151–372, especially 360–72 (*Confession Concerning Christ's Supper*, 1528); LW 40: 263–320 (*Instruction of the Visitors*, 1528); and for the remaining texts, Robert Kolb and James A. Nestingen, eds., *Sources and Contexts of the Book of Concord* (Minneapolis: Fortress, 2001), 83–104.

47. CA (German), Conclusion to Part One, par. 1, in BC 58. The Latin and German versions were both presented on June 25, 1530, with the German (the official language of the Empire) being read out at the diet. The Latin (the official language of the church) was given to the archbishop of Mainz. They are held in equal esteem by Lutherans today.

48. CA (Latin), Conclusion to Part One, par. 1, in BC 59. The German version elucidates the meaning of the word *writers* by adding, "the writings of the Fathers." They were thinking of the four doctors of the western church (Ambrose, Jerome, Augustine, and Pope Gregory I) as well as other early writers such as Hillary, Pope Leo I, or later writers like Bernard of Clairvaux, whom Luther referred to as the last of the church fathers.

49. Some of the language of CA III, on Christ's person and work, also set up later rejection of the sacrifice of the Mass by emphasizing the once-for-all nature of Christ's sacrifice on the cross.

50. CA IV.1 in BC 38 and 40.

51. CA V when combined with CA XII (on penitence) also defined the Evangelical insistence on distinguishing law (a Word that condemns sin and accuses) from gospel or faith (a Word that forgives sin and comforts the terrified). See also CA XX.

52. CA VI.1 (German), in BC 40.

53. CA VI.3 (German), in BC 40: "For Ambrose says, 'It is determined by God that whoever believes in Christ shall be saved and have forgiveness of sins, not through works but through faith alone, without merits.'" This fifth-century commentary on the Pauline epistles is now known as having been written by pseudo-Ambrose or, in line with the designation by Erasmus of Rotterdam, Ambrosiaster.

54. CA XX.9 (Latin), in BC 55: "To begin with…our works cannot reconcile God or merit grace and forgiveness of sins, but we obtain this only by faith when we believe that we are received into grace on account

of Christ, who alone has been appointed mediator and atoning sacrifice through whom the Father is reconciled."

55. CA XX.26 (Latin), in BC 57.

56. Wilhem Maurer, *Historical Commentary on the Augsburg Confession*, trans. H. George Anderson (Philadelphia: Fortress, 1986), 59–101.

57. CA XXVIII.34 (German), in BC 96.

58. See his *Exhortation to All Clergy Assembled at Augsburg* (1530), in LW 34: 3–61, especially 38–52.

59. *Melanchthons Briefwechsel*, vol. 4/1: *Texte 859–1003a (Januar–Juli 1530)* and vol. 4/2: *Texte 1004–1109 (August–Dezember 1530)*, ed. Johanna Loehr (Stuttgart-Bad Cannstatt: Frommann-Holzboog, 2007), nos. 921 and 1002 (to Archbishop Albrecht), 955 and 1010 (to Luca Bonfio), 952, 953, 990, and 1012 (to Lorenzo Campeggio).

60. See Heinz Scheible, "Melanchthon und Luther während des Augsburger Reichstags 1530," now in Heinz Scheible, *Melanchthon und die Reformation: Forschungsbeiträge*, ed. Gerhard May and Rolf Decot (Mainz: von Zabern, 1996), 198–221.

61. CA, Conclusion of Part One, 2 (German), in BC 60. The introduction to CA XXII–XXVIII, however, contained reference to the defense for civil disobedience as well: "Your Imperial Majesty may recognize that we have not acted in an unchristian or sacrilegious manner. On the contrary, we have been compelled by God's command (which is rightly to be esteemed higher than all custom [cf. CA XV.1–4 and XVI.6–7]) to permit such corrections."

62. See, especially, Heiko Oberman, "Dichtung und Wahrheit: Das Wesen der Reformation aus der Sicht der Confutatio," in *Confessio Augustana und Confutatio: Der Augsburger Reichstag 1530 und die Einheit der Kirche*, ed. Erwin Iserloh (Münster: Aschendorff, 1980), 217–31. Members of the Roman party, especially some bishops, were not especially supportive of the *Confutatio*, first published in 1559.

63. Christian Peters, *Apologia Confessionis Augustanae: Untersuchungen zur Textgeschichte einer lutherischen Bekenntnisschrift (1530–1584)* (Stuttgart: Calwer, 1997), especially 118–297. The German translation of the second edition is still the only version included in the German *Book of Concord* of 1580.

64. Its language was revived in the 1960s when it served as the basis for rapprochement between Lutheran and Reformed churches in Germany (the Leuenberg Agreement). This agreement was later used extensively by the Evangelical Lutheran Church in America in its agreements of full communion with the Presbyterian Church, USA, the Reformed Church in America, the United Church of Christ, and the United Methodist Church.

65. See CA, preface, 15–24, in BC 32–35.

66. Because of its stronger language regarding Christ's presence in the Lord's Supper, Melanchthon saw to it that some signers of the Wittenberg Concord, especially Martin Bucer, and the princes and cities of the Smalcald League avoided having to subscribe. See BC 326–28, for the signers.

67. Smalcald Articles, trans. William Russell, pt. III, in BC 310–26.

68. Because of its language on the Lord's Supper, later Lutherans downplayed its significance and preferred the "Unaltered" Augsburg Confession (the printed version of 1531).

69. WA Br 9: 406–10 (no. 3616). Their negative reaction is sometimes mistakenly construed as an "official" rejection of the document, as if Luther functioned as the final adjudicator for theological issues among the Evangelicals. It was instead a memorandum requested by the prince, not some sort of authoritative decree. Thus, in responding to this letter, Melanchthon did not deny the problems and countered that he expected the princes gathered for the diet to improve on the language (MBW 2699, in MBW T10: 199–201, dated May 19, 1541).

70. The letter emphasized the difference between Romans 3:21–28 and Galatians 5:6.

71. See Timothy J. Wengert, "The Day Melanchthon Got Mad: A Study in Lutheran Ecclesiology," *Lutheran Quarterly* 6 (1991): 419–33.

72. Maximillian Weber, "The Nature of Charismatic Authority and Its Routinization," in *Theory of Social and Economic Organization*, trans. A. R. Anderson and Talcott Parsons (New York: Oxford University Press, 1947), 363–85.

73. The word *superintendens* was already used by Augustine of Hippo as the equivalent Latin term for the Greek *episcopos*. For purely political reasons (since bishops of the Holy Roman Empire were also territorial princes), Evangelicals of the Empire could not generally use the word *bishop*. This contrasted to the kingdoms of Denmark, Finland, and Sweden where bishops remain to this day. Before being defeated in the Smalcald War, Elector John Frederick even oversaw the election and installation of two Evangelical bishops in his territories: Naumburg and Merseburg. They were deposed after the war.

74. See James Estes, *Christian Magistrate and Territorial Church: Johannes Brenz and the German Reformation*, 2nd ed. (Toronto: Centre for Reformation and Renaissance Studies, 2007).

75. When Melanchthon's memorandum to Elector Maurice was published in the summer of 1548, it resulted in his almost being declared a *persona non grata* by the imperial court in Austria. See Timothy J. Wengert, "'Not by Nature *Philoneikos*': Philip Melanchthon's Initial Reactions to

the Augsburg Interim," in *Politik und Bekenntnis: Die Reaktionen auf das Interim von 1548*, ed. Irene Dingel and Günther Wartenberg (Leipzig: Evangelische Verlagsanstalt, 2007), 33–49.

76. Chief among them Nicholas von Amsdorf, Matthias Flacius, and Nicholas Gallus.

77. John Frederick was released from captivity and retired to his ancestral lands, ducal Saxony, where he founded a new Evangelical university in Jena.

78. See Irene Dingel, ed., *Der Adiaphoristische Streit (1548–1560)*, vol. 2 of *Controversia et Confessio* (Göttingen: Vandenhoeck & Ruprecht, 2012), 3–25, and the forthcoming volumes in this series. Many of these disputes had already surfaced during Luther's lifetime. Thus, in 1527–1528, Johann Agricola and Philip Melanchthon crossed swords over the nature of contrition. Ten years later, Agricola and Luther debated the related question of the role of the law in the so-called first antinomian controversy, which ended when Agricola left for Berlin in the middle of the night. Tensions over the question of Christ's presence in the Lord's Supper continued throughout the period, with Melanchthon more worried about bread worship and Luther about Christ's absence. As a result of the publication of the second edition of Melanchthon's systematic magnum opus, the *Loci communes theologici* [chief theological topics], Nicholas von Amsdorf and Conrad Cordatus complained about the heightened role given to good works as a *sine qua non* for salvation.

79. Timothy J. Wengert, *Defending Faith: Lutheran Responses to Andreas Osiander's Doctrine of Justification* (Tübingen: Mohr Siebeck, 2012).

80. See Wengert, *Defending Faith*, 65–67.

81. See Wim Janse, "Joachim Westphal's Sacramentology," *Lutheran Quarterly* 22 (2008): 137–60; and more recently, Irene Dingel, "The Creation of Theological Profiles: The Understanding of the Lord's Supper in Melanchthon and the Formula of Concord," in Irene Dingel, et al., *Philip Melanchthon: Theologian in Classroom, Confession and Controversy* (Göttingen: Vandenhoeck & Ruprecht, 2012), 263–81.

82. Lyle Bierma, General Introduction to Caspar Olevianus, *A Firm Foundation: An Aid to Interpreting the Heidelberg Catechism* (Grand Rapids, MI: Baker, 1995), xiii–xl.

83. Robert Kolb, *Andreae and the Formula of Concord: Six Sermons on the Way to Lutheran Unity* (St. Louis: Concordia, 1977).

84. BC 481–85.

85. BC 486.

86. Emperor Rudolf II, the archduke of Austria and, as King of Bohemia, elector, was a sworn upholder of the [Roman] Catholic faith and of course had nothing to do with this document.

87. See Irene Dingel, *Concordia controversa: Die öffentlichen Diskussionen um das lutherische Konkordienwerk am Ende des 16. Jahrhunderts* (Gütersloh: Gütersloher Verlagshaus, 1996). Outside the Holy Roman Empire, the kingdom of Denmark never accepted *The Book of Concord*, using only the Augsburg Confession and Small Catechism of Luther as their confessional documents. Sweden also did not accept it until the late seventeenth century when the Latin edition was printed. In the seventeenth century, more territories accepted the document as the proper "rule and norm" for its pastors' theology.

88. The Elector of the Palatinate refused to include this text in his territory's copies of *The Book of Concord*.

89. See the *Disputation against Scholastic Theology* of September 1517 (LW 31: 9–16).

90. He had drafted the Saxon Confession for the occasion, which was subsequently published in Basel and then elsewhere.

91. The ambiguous legal standing of Reformed Christians in the Holy Roman Empire was at least one of the causes of the Thirty Years' War (1618–48).

92. See *Healing Memories*, 60–64.

93. See *Healing Memories*, 64–72. Johannes Brenz was the lone exception on the Lutheran side, arguing steadfastly against capital punishment for Anabaptists. Lutheran princes, too, tended to be far less eager to resort to execution than some of their theologians. A good deal of the article on the Anabaptists in the Formula of Concord (art. XII) dealt with the Socinians and other anti-trinitarians, not simply the Anabaptists.

94. These three ecclesiastical electors, when combined with the vote of the King of Bohemia (the archduke of Austria and, thus, a Habsburg), assured that the Habsburgs would continue to rule the empire until its dissolution in 1806, always outvoting the Protestant electors of the Palatinate, Brandenburg, and Saxony. Already prior to the Smalcald War, the archbishop of Cologne, Hermann von Wied, was placed under virtual house arrest by the emperor because of his attempts to reform his archdiocese with the assistance of Martin Bucer and Philip Melanchthon. See Heinz Scheible, "Melanchthon und Bucer," in *Melanchthon und die Reformation*, 245–69, especially 263f.

95. For the colloquy at Montbéliard, see Jill Raitt, *The Colloquy of Montbéliard: Religion and Politics in the Sixteenth Century* (New York: Oxford University Press, 1993).

96. Reinhard Kirste, *Das Zeugnis des Geistes und das Zeugnis der Schrift: Das* testimonium spiritus sancti internum *als hermeneutischer-polemischer Zentralbegriff bei Johann Gerhard in der Auseinandersetzung*

mit Robert Bellarmins Schriftverständnis (Göttingen: Vandenhoeck & Ruprecht, 1976).

97. Heinrich Denifle, *Luther and Lutherdom from Original Sources*, trans. Raymond Volz (Somerset, Ohio: Torch Press, 1917); and Hartmann Grisar, *Martin Luther: His Life and Work*, adapted from the 2nd German edition by Frank J. Eble and ed. Arthur Preuss (Westminster, MD: Newman, 1954).

CHAPTER TWO

1. Jeffrey Gros, Eamon McManus, and Ann Riggs, *Introduction to Ecumenism* (New York: Paulist Press, 1998), 28.

2. See http://www.lutheranworld.org/content/ecumenical-relations.

3. LWF Report 19/20, 1985, p. 175. This text is also anthologized in *The Ecumenical Movement: An Anthology of Key Text and Voices*, ed. Michael Kinnamon and Brian E. Cope (Grand Rapids, MI: Eerdmans, 1996), 122.

4. See http://download.elca.org/ELCA%20Resource%20Repository/The_Vision_Of_The_ELCA.pdf.

5. Vision Statement of the Evangelical Lutheran Church, chap. 4 of the constitution, "Statement of Purpose," declares that the Evangelical Lutheran Church in America is committed both to Lutheran unity and to Christian unity (4.03.d. and 4.03.f.).

6. Cited by Walter M. Abbott, "Ecumenism," in *The Documents of Vatican II* (New York: America Press, 1966), 336.

7. John XXIII, *Humanae Salutis*, December 25, 1961. The official Latin text may be found in *AAS* 54 (1962): 5–13. An English translation is available at http://www.diocesecc.org/pictures/Vatican%20Documents/humanae-salutis.pdf. Pope John XXIII established the Secretariat for Promoting Christian Unity June 5, 1960, and appointed Augustin Cardinal Bea as its first president.

8. Paul VI, Speech at the beginning of the Second Session of Vatican Council II, September 29, 1963. This was delivered in Latin (http://www.vatican.va/holy_father/paul_vi/speeches/1963/documents/hf_p-vi_spe_19630929_concilio-vaticano-ii_lt.html). The English quotes are from "Pope Paul Sets Agenda as Council's Second Session Opens," http://vaticaniiat50.wordpress.com/2013/09/29/pope-paul-sets-agenda-as-councils-second-session-opens/.

9. John A. Radano, *Lutheran and Catholic Reconciliation on Justification* (Grand Rapids, MI: Eerdmans, 2009), 11–12.

10. Pius XII, *Mystici Corporis*, June 29, 1943.

11. Congregation for the Doctrine of the Faith, "Responses to Some Questions Regarding Certain Aspects of the Doctrine of the Church," *Origins* 37 (2007): 134–36.

12. John Courtney Murray, "Religious Freedom," in *The Documents of Vatican II*, ed. Walter M. Abbott (New York: America Press, 1966), 672–73.

13. Ibid., 673.

14. Assertion of the doctrinal commission, *Acta Synodalia* III/2, 335.

15. In addition to Pesch, Jared Wicks signals Vinzenz Pfnür's investigation of the Augsburg Confession and the response to it by Catholic apologists: *Einig in der Rechtfertigungslehre?* (Wiesbaden, 1970). Jared Wicks, "Joint Declaration on the Doctrine of Justification: The Remote and Immediate Background," in *Justification and Sanctification in the Traditions of the Reformation*, ed. Milan Opocensky and Paraic Reamonn (Geneva: World Alliance of Reformed Churches, 1999), 129–36.

16. Otto Hermann Pesch, *Die Theologie der Rechtfertigung bei Martin Luther und Thomas von Aquin. Versuch eines systematisch-theologischen Dialogs* (Mainz: Matthias Grünewald Verlag, 1967).

17. Otto Hermann Pesch, "Kleiner 'Werkstattbericht' über die Arbeit am Teildokument 'Die Rechtfertigung des Sünders,' in *Lehrverurteingungen-Kirchentrennend*, vol. 2: *Materialien zu den Lehrerurteilungen und zur Theologie de Rechtfertigung* (Göttingen: Vandenhoeck and Ruprecht, 1989), 326–62. For an analysis of Pesch's contribution, see Pieter de Witte, *Doctrine, Dynamic and Difference: To the Heart of the Lutheran-Roman Catholic Differentiated Consensus on Justification* (New York: T & T Clark, 2012), 36–60.

18. Otto Hermann Pesch, "Existential and Sapiential Theology: The Theological Confrontation between Luther and Thomas Aquinas," in *Catholic Scholars Dialogue with Luther*, ed. Jared Wicks (Chicago: Loyola University Press, 1970), 61–81, 182–93.

19. de Witte, *Doctrine, Dynamic and Difference*, 59.

20. Wicks, "Joint Declaration on the Doctrine of Justification," 132–33.

21. Tuomo Mannermaa, *Christ Present in Faith: Luther's View of Justification*, trans. and ed. Kirsi Stjerna (Minneapolis: Fortress Press, 2005). For an overview of dissertations written by Mannermaa's students, see Tuomo Mannermaa, "Why Is Luther so Fascinating: Modern Finish Luther Research," in *Union with Christ*, ed. Carl E. Braaten and Robert W. Jenson (Grand Rapids, MI: Eerdmans, 1998), 1–20.

22. de Witte, *Doctrine, Dynamic and Difference*, 62.

23. See Simo Peura, "Christ as Favor and Gift: The Challenge of Luther's Understanding of Justification," in *Union with Christ*, 42–69.

24. de Witte, *Doctrine, Dynamic and Difference*, 63, referring to the work of Risto Saarinen, *Gottes Wirken auf uns: Die tranzendentale Deutung des Gegenwart-Christi-Motivs in der Lutherforschung* (Veröffentlichüngen des Instituts für europäische Geschichte Mainz, 137; Stuttgart: Franz Steiner, 1989).

25. de Witte, *Doctrine, Dynamic and Difference*, 63.

26. *The Gospel and the Church, Malta*, 1972, § 26, cited from *Growth in Agreement*, ed. Harding Meyer and Lukas Vischer (New York: Paulist Press, 1984), 174.

27. "Roman Catholic/Lutheran Relations," *Information Service* 14 (1971): 9–10.

28. *Church and Justification: Understanding the Church in the Light of the Doctrine of Justification* (Geneva: Lutheran World Federation, 1994), 7. See John Radano's comments regarding the reservations expressed by four participants, *Lutheran and Catholic Reconciliation on Justification*, 41n8.

29. *Growth in Agreement*, 243f.

30. *Justification by Faith: Lutherans and Catholics in Dialogue VII*, ed. H. George Anderson, T. Austin Murphy, and Joseph A. Burgess (Minneapolis: Augsburg Publishing House, 1985).

31. Lutheran-Roman Catholic Joint Commission, foreword to *Church and Justification* (Geneva: Lutheran World Federation, 1994), 9.

32. Ibid, 10.

33. Cited in Karl Lehmann and Wolfhart Pannenberg, eds., *The Condemnations of the Reformation Era: Do They Still Divide?* trans. Margaret Kohl (Minneapolis: Fortress Press, 1990), 3.

34. Lehmann and Pannenberg, *The Condemnations of the Reformation Era*. Although only the first volume was translated into English, the original German publication consisted of four volumes: Karl Lehmann and Wolfhart Pannenberg, eds., *Lehrverurteilungen-Kirchentrennend?* vols. 1–4 (Freiburg im Breisgau: Herder; Göttingen: Vandenhoeck & Ruprecht, 1986). For a negative Lutheran critique of this study, see Faculty of Theology, Georgia Augusta University, Göttingen, *Outmoded Condemnations? Antitheses between the Council of Trent and the Reformation on Justification, the Sacrament, and the Ministry—Then and Now*, trans. Oliver K. Olson with Franz Posset (Fort Wayne, IN: Luther Academy, 1992). For the Catholic evaluation of the study, see PCPCU, "Evaluation for the Pontifical Council for Promoting Christian Unity of the Study Lehrverurteilungen—kirchentrennend?" (Study Document, Centro Pro Unione Library, 1992). For the evaluation of the Protestant Churches of Ger-

many, see Arnoldshainer Konferenz, Vereinigte Evangelisch-Lutherische Kirche Deutschlands, and Lutheran World Federation, *Lehrverurteilungen im Gespräch: Die ersten offiziellen Stellungnahmen aus den evangelischen Kirchen in Deutschland* (Göttingen: Vandenhoeck & Ruprecht, 1993). For the evaluation of the German Conference of Catholic Bishops, see Deutschen Bischofskonferenz, *Stellungsnahme der Deutschen Bischofskonferenz zur Studie "Lehrverurteilungen—Kirchentrennend?"* (Bonn: Sekretariat der Deutschen Bischofskonferenz, 1994).

35. We will not be dealing with the last two sections of the study on ministry and sacraments.

36. Lehmann and Pannenberg, *The Condemnations of the Reformation Era*, 30–31.

37. Ibid., 42–43.

38. Ibid., 31–32.

39. Ibid., 45.

40. Ibid., 46.

41. Ibid., 32–33.

42. Ibid., 47. Italics in the original.

43. Ibid., 46.

44. Ibid., 33.

45. Ibid., 48.

46. Ibid., 49.

47. Ibid. Italics in original.

48. Ibid., 33–34.

49. Ibid., 50.

50. Ibid., 52.

51. Ibid., 53.

52. Ibid., 34–35.

53. Ibid., 53–56.

54. Ibid., 35.

55. Council of Trent, Decree on Justification, canons 2 and 3, DS 1552 and DS 1582.

56. Lehmann and Pannenberg, *The Condemnations of the Reformation Era*, 66–68.

57. Ibid., 68.

58. Ibid., 47. Italics in the original.

59. Ibid., 52–53.

60. Ibid., 66–68.

61. de Witte, *Doctrine, Dynamic and Difference*, 159.

62. Ibid., 160.

63. Radano, *Lutheran and Catholic Reconciliation on Justification*, 118.

64. *Strategies for Reception: Perspectives on the Reception of Documents Emerging from the Lutheran-Catholic International Dialogue*. Working Paper Presented to the Joint Staff Group Pontifical Council for Promoting Christian Unity, Lutheran World Federation, October 1991. *Information Service* 80 (1992): 42–43, and Geneva: Lutheran World Federation, Office of Ecumenical Affairs. Hereafter *Strategies*.

65. *Strategies*, no. 9.

66. Ibid., no. 10.

67. See de Witte, *Doctrine, Dynamic and Difference*, 158–64, for a more detailed account of the drafting history.

68. The Lutheran World Federation and The Roman Catholic Church, *Joint Declaration on the Doctrine of Justification*, English Language Edition (Grand Rapids, MI: Eerdmans, 2000).

69. Harding Meyer, "Consensus in the Doctrine of Justification," *Ecumenical Trends* 26, no. 11 (1997): 5/165.

70. "LWF on Joint Declaration—A. Background 3 & 4—Responses," *Lutheran World Information*, June 24, 1998, 3a–c.

71. "Response of the Lutheran World Federation," *Lutheran World Information*, June 23, 1998, 15–22; *Information Service* 98 (1998): 90–93.

72. Ibid., no. 32.

73. Ibid., no. 37.

74. See Johannes Wallmann, "Der Streit um die 'Gemeinsame Erklärung zur Rechtfertigungslehre,'" *Zeitschrift für Theologie und Kirche (Beiheft 10)* 95 (1998): 207–51; Theodore Dieter, "Zum Einspruch gegen die 'Gemeinsame Erklärung': Hermeneutik—Konsequenzen—Kritik der Kritik," in *Zitterpartie "Rechtfertigungslehre*, ed. A. P. Kustermann and A. Esche (Stuttgart-Hohenheim: Akademie der Diözese Rottenburg-Stuttgart, 1998), 63–76.

75. Protestant Professors of Theology, "Kein Konsens in der Gemeinsamen Erklärung," *Frankfurter Allgemeine Zeitung* (January 29, 1998), Politik 4; "Stellungsnahme theologischer Hochschullehrer zur geplanten Unterzeichnung der Gemeinsamen Offiziellen Feststellung zur Rechtfertigungslehre," *Frankfurter Allgemeine Zeitung* (September 25, 1999), 67. For a summary of the various critiques of the JDDJ, see Jakob K. Rinderknecht, "Seeing Two Worlds: The Eschatological Anthropology of the Joint Declaration on the Doctrine of Justification" (dissertation, Marquette University, 2015), 15–39.

76. Congregation for the Doctrine of the Faith and the Pontifical Council for the Promotion of Christian Unity, "Response of the Catholic Church to the Joint Declaration of the Catholic Church and the Lutheran World Federation on the Doctrine of Justification," *Information Service* 98 (1998): 93–95.

77. Cardinal Edward Cassidy, "Press Conference Statement," *Origins* 28, no. 8 (July 16, 1998): 128–30.

78. "Official Catholic Response to Joint Declaration," *Origins* 28, no. 8 (July 16, 1998): 130–32. This is titled "Response of the Catholic Church to the Joint Declaration by the Catholic Church and the Lutheran World Federation on the Doctrine of Justification," on the Vatican Web site: http://www.vatican.va/roman_curia/pontifical_councils/chrstuni/documents/rc_pc_chrstuni_doc_01081998_off-answer-catholic_en.html. Hereafter "Catholic Response."

79. "Catholic Response," § 5.

80. For a Lutheran assessment of the "Catholic Response" that asserts that the Catholic critique largely misrepresents Lutheran teaching, see David S. Yeago, "Interpreting the Roman Response to the Joint Declaration on Justification," *Pro Ecclesia* 7, no. 4 (1998): 404–10.

81. Cited in Radano, *Lutheran and Catholic Reconciliation on Justification*, 153.

82. "Reflection of Dr. Ishmael Noko, LWF General Secretary, June 25, 1998," *Information Service* 98 (1998): 97–98; *Lutheran World Information*, July 9, 1998, 7–8.

83. See "Letter of Cardinal Cassidy to LWF, July 30, 1998," *Information Service* 98 (1998): 98–100.

84. See note 39 in Radano, *Lutheran and Catholic Reconciliation on Justification*, 163.

85. Radano, *Lutheran and Catholic Reconciliation on Justification*, 164.

86. Cited by ibid., 164.

87. The World Methodist Council and its member churches affirmed their doctrinal agreement with the JDDJ on July 23, 2006. See the "The World Methodist Council Statement of Association with the Joint Declaration on the Doctrine of Justification at http://www.vatican.va/roman_curia/pontifical_councils/chrstuni/meth-council-docs/rc_pc_chrstuni_doc_20060723_text-association_en.html.

88. For this account of the achievement of the JDDJ, I am indebted to David S. Yeago, "Lutheran-Roman Catholic Consensus on Justification: The Theological Achievement of the Joint Declaration," *Pro Ecclesia* 7, no. 4 (1998): 449–70.

89. Yeago, "Lutheran-Catholic Consensus on Justification," 452.

90. Ibid.

91. Norman P. Tanner, ed., *Decrees of the Ecumenical Councils*, vol. 2 (Washington, DC: Georgetown University Press, 1990), 674.

92. Council of Trent, session 6 (January 13, 1547), Decree on Justification, chap. 8, "How justification of the sinner freely granted through faith is to be understood": "And we are said to receive justification as

a free gift because nothing that precedes justification, neither faith nor works, would merit the grace of justification; for *if it is by grace, it is no longer on the basis of works; otherwise* (as the same Apostle says) *grace would no longer be grace.*" Tanner, *Decrees of the Ecumenical Councils*, 674.

93. In this spirit, already article 5 of the Augsburg Confession stated, "To obtain such [justifying] faith God instituted the office of preaching [Latin: ministry], that is, giving the gospel and the sacraments. Through these, as through means, he gives the Holy Spirit who produces faith, where and when he wills, in those who hear the gospel. It teaches that we have a gracious God, not through our merit but through Christ's merit, when we so believe."

94. Yeago, "Lutheran-Roman Catholic Consensus on Justification," 456.

95. Ibid., 458.

96. *Joint Declaration on the Doctrine of Justification: A Commentary by the Institute for Ecumenical Research, Strasbourg* (LWF Office of Communication Services, n.d.), 30–31.

CHAPTER THREE

1. Josef Lortz, *Die Reformation in Deutschland*, 2 vols. (Freiburg: Herder, 1949); trans. Donald Walls as *The Reformation in Germany*, 2 vols. (New York: Herder & Herder, 1968).

2. Iserloh is perhaps best known for his questioning of the posting of the *Ninety-five Theses*, but his books *Luther und die Reformation: Beiträge zu einem ökumenischen Lutherverständnis* (Aschaffenburg: Pattloch, 1974) and *Geschichte und Theologie der Reformation im Grundriss* (Paderborn: Bonifacius, 1980) are important milestones in Roman Catholic Reformation research. Peter Manns wrote several books on the Reformation as well: *Martin Luther: "Reformator und Vater im Glauben"* (Stuttgart: Steiner, 1985) and *Martin Luther: Leben—Glauben—Wirkung* (Freiburg: Herder, 1982), trans. Michael Shaw as *Martin Luther: An Illustrated Biography* (New York: Crossroad, 1983).

3. See, for example, Jared Wicks, *Man Yearning for Grace: Luther's Early Spiritual Teaching* (Washington, DC: Corpus Books, 1968) and Wicks, *Luther and His Spiritual Legacy* (Wilmington, DE: Glazier, 1983); John O'Malley, "Luther the Preacher," in *The Martin Luther Quincentennial*, ed. Gerhard Dünnhaupt (Detroit: Wayne State University Press, 1984); Harry McSorley, *Luther: Right or Wrong? An Ecumenical-Theological Study of Luther's Major Work, The Bondage of the Will* (New York: Newman Press, 1968).

4. Heiko A. Oberman, *The Harvest of Medieval Theology: Gabriel Biel and Late Medieval Nominalism* (Cambridge, MA: Harvard University Press, 1963). He also wrote an influential biography of Luther, *Luther: Man between God and the Devil*, trans. Eileen Walliser-Schwarzbart (New Haven: Yale University Press, 1989). His students include, among others, Stephen Ozment, David Steinmetz, Berndt Hamm, and Christoph Burger. In a similar vein, Helmar Junghans, the Leipzig church historian, addressed the role of humanism in Luther's thought. See his *Der junge Luther und die Humanisten* (Weimar: Böhlau, 1984).

5. Karl Holl, *Gesammelte Aufsätze zur Kirchengeschichte*, vol. 1: *Luther* (Tübingen: Mohr Siebeck, 1921); Gerhard Ebeling, *Luther: An Introduction to His Thought*, trans. R. A. Wilson (Philadelphia: Fortress, 1970); Oswald Bayer, *Promissio: Geschichte der reformatorischen Wende in Luthers Theologie* (Göttingen: Vandenhoeck & Ruprecht, 1971); Berndt Hamm, *The Early Luther: Stages in a Reformation Reorientation*, trans. Martin Lohrmann (Grand Rapids, MI: Eerdmans, 2014). On the related question of Luther's relation to the papacy, see Scott Hendrix, *Luther and the Papacy: Stages in a Reformation Conflict* (Philadelphia: Fortress, 1981), who argues persuasively for a slow progression in Luther's thought from 1517 to 1520.

6. A similar reassessment of the Council of Trent by Lutheran scholars remains a desideratum. See, however, the work of the Jesuit scholar John O'Malley, *Trent: What Happened at the Council* (Cambridge, MA: Belknap, 2013).

7. Timothy J. Wengert, *Law and Gospel: Philip Melanchthon's Debate with John Agricola of Eisleben over "Poenitentia"* (Grand Rapids, MI: Baker, 1997).

8. One of the most avid collectors of differing interpretations was the late-medieval exegete Dennis the Carthusian whose commentaries often piled up various interpretations of the biblical text.

9. Even in the debate over the Lord's Supper, where Luther, in defending the real presence of Christ in the Eucharist, famously challenged Ulrich Zwingli to wrest the words "this is my Body" from him, the point was not so much that there was only one verse of Scripture in favor of the real presence but that in theological debate, one could not insist on a particular (in this case metaphorical) interpretation of a verse without proving that all alternative interpretations were false.

10. For an example of this rich tradition among Lutherans, see Robert Kolb, *The Wittenberg School of Exegesis* (forthcoming).

11. Erik Heen, "The Distinction 'Material/Formal Principles' and Its Use in American Lutheran Theology," *Lutheran Quarterly* 17 (2003): 329–54.

12. As one example from Martin Luther among many, see his preface to the German translation and commentary on Jonah (LW 19: 36): "Furthermore, Jonah is also an object of comfort for all who administer the Word. It teaches them not to despair of the fruit of the Gospel."

13. For an outline of these techniques, see Timothy J. Wengert, *Human Freedom, Christian Righteousness: Philip Melanchthon's Exegetical Dispute with Erasmus of Rotterdam* (New York: Oxford University Press, 1998).

14. Timothy J. Wengert, "A Note on 'Sola Scriptura' in Martin Luther's Writings," *Luther- Bulletin* 20 (2011): 21–31; see also Wengert, *Reading the Bible with Martin Luther: An Introductory Guide* (Grand Rapids, MI: Baker, 2013), 16–21. For Philip Melanchthon, see Peter Fraenkel, *Testimonia Patrum: The Function of the Patristic Argument in the Theology of Philip Melanchthon* (Geneva: Droz, 1961).

15. See, for an example of these authorities, CA art. XX.9–18, in BC 54–55.

16. For the complexity in Lutheran Orthodoxy, see Heinrich Schmid, *The Doctrinal Theology of the Evangelical Lutheran Church*, 3rd ed., trans. Charles A. Hay and Henry E. Jacobs (Reprint, Minneapolis: Augsburg, 1961), 38–92.

17. See Heen, "The Distinction 'Material/Formal Principles,'" and "A Lutheran Response to the New Perspective on Paul," *Lutheran Quarterly* 24 (2010): 263–91. The classic, though flawed work is by Robert Preus, *The Inspiration of Scripture: A Study of the Theology of the Seventeenth-Century Lutheran Dogmaticians* (Edinburgh: Oliver and Boyd, 1955).

18. Hans Frei, *The Eclipse of Biblical Narrative: A Study in Eighteenth- and Nineteenth-Century Hermeneutics* (New Haven: Yale University Press, 1974).

19. Timothy J. Wengert, "Philip Melanchthon's 1522 Annotations on Romans and the Lutheran Origins of Rhetorical Criticism," in *Biblical Interpretation in the Era of the Reformation*, ed. Richard A. Muller and John L. Thompson (Grand Rapids, MI: Eerdmans, 1996), 118–40.

20. Timothy J. Wengert, "Georg Major (1502–1574): Defender of the Wittenberg's Faith and Melanchthonian Exegete," in *Melanchthon in seinen Schülern*, Wolfenbütteler Forschungen, 73, ed. Heinz Scheible (Wiesbaden: Harrassowitz Verlag, 1997), 129–56.

21. See Timothy J. Wengert, *Reading the Bible with Martin Luther* (Grand Rapids, MI: Baker, 2013).

22. See, for example, the complete text of his hymn, "Built on the Rock the Church Doth Stand," trans. C. Doving, in *The Lutheran Hymnary* (Minneapolis: Augsburg, 1913), no. 132, especially v. 6: "Here stands the

font before our eyes / Telling how God did receive us: / Th'altar recalls Christ's sacrifice / And what His table doth give us; / Here sounds the word that doth proclaim / Christ yesterday, today the same, / Yea, and for aye our Redeemer." Another hymn by Grundtvig, "God's Word Is Our Great Heritage" (no. 137), set to the tune of Luther's "A Mighty Fortress," praises the Word as light, guide, and stay and ends with "Lord grant, while worlds endure, / We keep its teachings pure / Throughout all generations."

23. For example, see Albrecht Ritschl, *The Christian Doctrine of Justification and Reconciliation: The Positive Development of the Doctrine*, trans. H. R. Mackintosh and A. B. Macaulay (Edinburgh: Clark, 1900).

24. The tension among the Lutheran churches in the United States is well reflected by the collection of articles in John Reumann, ed., *Studies in Lutheran Hermeneutics* (Philadelphia: Fortress, 1979), in which members of the various church bodies share reflections on biblical hermenuetics.

25. Heinrich Denzinger, *Compendium of Creeds, Definitions, and Declarations on Matters of Faith and Morals: Latin—English*, 43rd ed., ed. Peter Hünermann (San Francisco: Ignatius, 2012), § 3280, p. 655, citing *De doctrina christiana* III, 4, no. 8 (MPL 34: 68). (Hereafter DH).

26. DH 3286. See also Leo XIII's apostolic letter, *Vigilantiae Studiique* of October 30, 1902.

27. DH 3825. Another important, earlier encyclical is that of Benedict XV from September 15, 1920, *Spiritus Paraclitus*.

28. DH 3826.

29. DH 3829.

30. DH 3830, citing Thomas Aquinas, *In Heb.*, c. 1, lect. 4.

31. DH 4205, quoting canon 7 of the second Synod of Orange as cited in Vatican Council I, *Dei Filius*. The canons of the Synod of Orange were particularly important for the convergence expressed in JDDJ.

32. DH 4206, quoting Vatican Council I, *Dei Filius*, chap. 2.

33. DH 4211.

34. DH 4218.

35. DH 4220, quoting John Chrysostom, *In Gen* 3, 8 (hom. 17, 1).

36. DH 4228–35.

37. DH 4233.

38. DH 4407.

39. For the twists and turns of American Roman Catholic biblical interpretation, see Gerald P. Fogarty, *American Catholic Biblical Scholarship: A History from the Early Republic to Vatican II* (San Francisco: Harper & Row, 1989).

40. *The Jerome Biblical Commentary*, ed. Raymond E. Brown, SS, et al. (Englewood Cliffs, NJ: Prentice-Hall, 1968), viii.

41. One of the "Background Papers" in *Justification by Faith: Luther-*

ans and Catholics in Dialogue VII, ed. H. George Anderson, et al. (Minneapolis: Augsburg, 1985), 77.

42. John Reumann with Joseph A. Fitzmyer and Jerome D. Quinn, *"Righteousness" in the New Testament: "Justification" in the United States Lutheran—Roman Catholic Dialogue* (Philadelphia: Fortress, 1982). Readers familiar with more recent Pauline scholarship may notice the absence of the "New" perspective on Paul. In fact, however, Reumann certainly knew of many of the chief aspects of this argument. As a result, he rejects a subjective reading of *pistis tou Christou* [the faith *of* Christ] in favor of "faith in Christ." He emphasizes the problem of using covenant language (championed now by James Dunn and N. T. Wright), and he rejects a severely introspective understanding of the term (either in Paul or among Lutherans). In fact, this "new" school is actually a recapitulation of old approaches found in Jerome and championed by Erasmus of Rotterdam. Thus, Luther and Melanchthon—to say nothing of Fitzmyer and Reumann—knew the contours of this (mis)reading of Paul and rejected it. For Reumann's explicit rejection of an important forerunner of this "new" perspective, championed by E. P. Sanders, see *"Righteousness,"* 120–23.

43. Reumann, *"Righteousness,"* 21–22, citing Henning Graf Reventlow, *Rechtfertigung im Horizont des Alten Testaments* (Munich: Kaiser, 1971).

44. Reumann, *"Righteousness,"* 25, citing Eberhard Jüngel, *Paulus und Jesus: Eine Untersuchung zur Präzisierung der Frage nach dem Ursprung der Christologie* (Tübingen: Mohr Siebeck, 1962).

45. Reumann, *"Righteousness,"* 39.

46. Ibid., 41f.

47. Ibid., 48.

48. Joseph Fitzmyer, "The Letter to the Galatians," in *The Jerome Bible Commentary*, 49:18 (p. 240 of the New Testament portion).

49. Reumann, *"Righteousness,"* 56, citing Hans Dieter Betz, *Galatians: A Commentary on Paul's Letter to the Churches in Galatia* (Philadelphia: Fortress, 1979).

50. Reumann, *"Righteousness,"* 60.

51. Ibid., 64.

52. Ibid., 76, citing Ernst Käsemann, *Commentary on Romans* (Grand Rapids, MI: Eerdmans, 1980), 92–96.

53. Ibid., 77, citing Käsemann, *Romans*, 92, 95, 96.

54. Reumann, *"Righteousness,"* 108.

55. Ibid., 116–19.

56. Ibid., 183, citing James C. Turro and Raymond E. Brown, "Canonicity," *The Jerome Biblical Commentary*, 67:97 (p. 533).

57. Reumann, *"Righteousness,"* 184.

58. Ibid., 185.

59. Ibid.

60. Ibid., 195, citing *The Gospel and the Church* from that report.

61. Ibid., 196, citing the Epitome of the Formula of Concord, III.11.

62. Reumann, *"Righteousness,"* 196–97.

63. Ibid., 205.

64. Ibid., 208. Fitzmyer may not have known that the early reformers (notably Luther, Philip Melanchthon, and Johannes Brenz) argued the point in terms of where one put one's faith: in the word of acquittal or in its effects. In comments on Rom 3:21–31 (p. 211), Fitzmyer also states, "I am most sympathetic to [Reumann's] treatment of the efficacious character of God's forensic declaration of justification."

65. Reumann, *"Righteousness,"* 210.

66. Ibid., 213–14.

67. Ibid., 215–16, where the citation is from Ernst Käsemann.

68. Ibid., 220.

69. Ibid., 227.

70. This was indeed done in the dialogue. See the background papers by Jerome D. Quinn, "The Scriptures on Merit," and Joseph A. Burgess, "Rewards, but in a Very Different Sense," both in *Justification by Faith*, 82–110.

71. *Justification by Faith*, § 4, p. 16. Even more broadly, see §§ 161–65, p. 73f.

72. Ibid., §§ 122–49, pp. 58–68.

73. JDDJ, § 8.

74. Ibid., § 12.

75. Ibid., §§ 15–17.

76. Section 18 of JDDJ has an even stronger statement: "Lutherans and Catholics share the goal of confessing Christ in all things, who alone is to be trusted above all things...." There are other examples scattered throughout the document. Even the "Annex to the Official Common Statement," which engendered some difficulty, also shows this intense listening. Thus, while remaining faithful to the Tridentine decrees and rejecting a certain understanding of the justified as sinner (par. A 2, p. 43), it goes on to insist that (par. A 2, p. 44): "Lutherans and Catholics can together understand the Christian as *simul iustus et peccator*, despite their different approaches to this subject." Similarly, biblical interpretation affected other parts of the Annex (note especially the citation of Rom 6:12–14, 3:28, and the like).

77. See Harold C. Skillrud et al., eds., *Scripture and Tradition: Lutherans and Catholics in Dialogue IX* (Minneapolis: Augsburg, 1995), 35.

78. *The Fourth World Conference on Faith and Order: The Report from Montreal 1963*, P. C. Rodger and Lukas Vischer, eds. (New York: Association Press, 1964), par. 39, p. 50. The report goes on to insist (par. 45) that Christians "exist as Christians by the Tradition of the Gospel (the *paradosis* of the *kerygma*) testified in Scripture, transmitted in and by the Church through the power of the Holy Spirit."

79. See, for example, *Scripture and Tradition*, § 4.

80. See *Teaching Authority & Infallibility in the Church: Lutherans and Catholics in Dialogue VI*, ed. Paul C. Empie, et al. (Minneapolis: Augsburg, 1978/1980). See, for example, the essay by Robert B. Eno, "Some Elements in the Pre-History of Papal Infallibility," 238–58, and the Common Statement, "Teaching Authority and Infallibility in the Church," 11–68.

81. *Apology of the Augsburg Confesssion*, trans. Charles Arand, VII/ VIII.31, in BC 179.

82. See CA (Latin), trans. Eric Gritsch, XX.11–18, in BC 55. This shift is reflected in *Scripture and Tradition*, §§ 35–41.

83. The translation is from *Decrees of the Ecumenical Councils*, vol. 2, ed. Norman P. Tanner (Washington, D.C.: Georgetown University Press, 1990), 663.

84. Joseph Ratzinger, "Revelation Itself," in *Commentary on the Documents of Vatican II*, vol. 3, ed. Herbert Vorgrimler (New York: Herder and Herder, 1969), 193. See also the interventions of Cardinal Meyer of Chicago, ibid., 185.

85. William Henn, "With Equal Feelings of Devotion and Reverence: Trent and Vatican II on Catholic Attitudes towards Scripture and Tradition" (unpublished manuscript), 1–11.

86. The Lutheran World Federation and the Pontifical Council for Promoting Christian Unity, *The Apostolicity of the Church* (Minneapolis: Lutheran University Press, 2006), 190–92, §§ 442–48.

CHAPTER FOUR

1. See *Babylonian Captivity of the Church* (1520) where, in the beginning, Luther identifies penance as a sacrament, but at the end, identifies only baptism and the Lord's Supper as sacraments. Cf. LW 36, 18 with 127.

2. Luther's conviction of the need for a personal response of faith was problematic with respect to infant baptism. His answer to the problem varied. At times, he viewed baptism as the prime example of the

absolute gratuity of salvation. At another time, he believed that the community of believers needed to be present, allowing faith to be vicariously present. On yet other occasions, he suggested that infants were capable of faith. He vigorously defended infant baptism against the Anabaptists.

3. *Apology of the Augsburg Confession*, XIV, 68.

4. Augustine, *Tractates on the Gospel of St. John* 80, 3, on John 15:3 (*MPL 35:1840; NPNF, ser. 1, 7:344*).

5. *Catechism of the Catholic Church*, second edition (Liberia Editrice Vaticana, 1997), § 1084. Hereafter, *Catechism*.

6. Karl Rahner, "What Is a Sacrament?" in *Theological Investigations*, vol. 14, trans. David Bourke (London: Darton, Longman & Todd, 1976), 135–60 at 138.

7. Ibid.

8. Louis-Marie Chauvet, *Symbol and Sacrament*, 221.

9. Ibid.

10. Ibid., 222.

11. LW 26, 37.

12. Paul C. Empie and William W. Baum, eds., *Lutherans and Catholics in Dialogue II: One Baptism for the Remission of Sins* (New York: USA National Committee for Lutheran World Federation and the National Catholic Welfare Conference, 1966), 85. Also available in Joseph A. Burgess and Jeffrey Gros, eds., Ecumenical Documents IV, *Building Unity: Ecumenical Dialogues with Roman Catholic Participation in the United States* (New York: Paulist Press, 1989), 90.

13. Large Catechism, Fourth Part, 84–86. Translation from BC 466–67.

14. Large Catechism, IV, 75.

15. Ibid., 77.

16. *Catechism*, § 1214, citing 2 Cor 5:17; Gal 6:15; cf. Rom 6:3–4; Col 2:12.

17. Ibid., § 1215, citing Titus 3:5; John 3:5.

18. Ibid., § 1262;

19. Ibid., § 1128.

20. Ibid., § 1128.

21. Ibid., § 1129.

22. *Apology of the Augsburg Confession*, XII, 32.

23. *The Condemnations of the Reformation Era*, 77.

24. LW 51: 186, cited by John Tonkin, op. cit., 100. See also Large Catechism, 66.

25. Small Catechism, The Sacrament of Holy Baptism; The Large Catechism, Fourth Part.

26. *Catechism*, §§ 1266, 1992.

27. *Apology of the Augsburg Confession*, IV, 103.

28. Convergence was reached on concupiscence in the *Lutheran-Roman Catholic Joint Declaration on Justification* insofar as Lutherans consider that concupiscence is not a sin that "rules" in the same way as other sin.

29. *Apology of the Augsburg Confession*, II, 35. See also Luther's marginal notes on Lombard's Sentences [1509/10], WA 9: 74–75. See the JDDJ, § 29.

30. JDDJ, § 29.

31. *Catechism*, § 1253.

32. Ibid., § 1253.

33. Ibid.

34. Ibid., § 1124.

35. *Presbyterorum Ordinis*, § 4, par. 1, 2. Cited in *Catechism*, § 1122.

36. *Catechism*, § 1123.

37. Large Catechism, 28–31.

38. Rite of Baptism for Children, § 2.

39. Ibid.

40. CA IX, 3; *Apology of the Augsburg Confession*, IX, 1; *Smalcald Articles*, 5.4; *The Baptismal Booklet*, 1; The Large Catechism, Fourth Part, 47ff. On the topic of Lutheran perspectives on infant baptism, see Edmund Schlink, *The Doctrine of Baptism*, trans. Herbert J. A. Bouman (St. Louis: Concordia Publishing House, 1972), 130–66; Eero Huovinen, "Martin Luthers Lehre vom Kinderglauben: Fides infantium als reale Gabe Gottes und reale Teilhabe an Gott," 27–48, and "Fides infantium—fides infusa? A Contribution to the Understanding of the Faith of Children in Luther," 29–66 in *Baptism, Church and Ecumenism* (Helsinki: Luther-Agricola-Gesellshaft, 2009).

41. This point is made by Henri de Lubac in *La foi chrétienne: Essai sur la structure du Symbole des Apôtres* (Paris: Aubier-Montaigne, 1970), 217–34.

42. *Catechism*, § 1121. For a Lutheran interpretation, see Eero Huovinen, "Die unverlierbare Gabe der Taufe ("character indelebilis") in der Theologie Martins Luthers," in *Baptism, Church and Ecumenism* (Helsinski: Luther-Agricoa-Gesellshaft, 2009), 15–26.

43. Lutheran-Roman Catholic Joint Commission, *Church and Justification* (Lutheran World Federation/Pontifical Council for Promoting Christian Unity, 1994), § 69.

44. Ibid., § 35.

45. Some of the material on Lutheran and Catholic theologies of the Eucharist that follows was included in Susan K. Wood, "Die Eucharistie: Ökumenische Errungenschaften und bleibende Unterschiede,"

Ökumenische Rundschau 4 (Oktober–Dezember 2012): 389–410. This article discusses ecumenical agreements reached with Lutherans, Anglicans, Methodists, and the Reformed.

46. Formula of Concord, Solid Declaration, VII. 38; LW 37: 299ff. First the Solid Declaration used the phrases "in the bread," "with the bread," and "under the bread," which later Lutherans shortened to "in, with, and under" the bread.

47. CA (German), art. 10.

48. Council of Trent, session XIII, chap. IV; also canon 2.

49. For reference to this work of the Holy Spirit for the Lutheran-Catholic dialogue, see *Ministry*, §§ 21, 22, 23.

50. For discussion of the Eucharist in ecumenical theology, see Geoffrey Wainwright, *Doxology: The Praise of God in Worship, Doctrine and Life* (New York: Oxford University Press, 1980), 272ff.; Risto Saarinen, *Faith and Holiness: Lutheran-Orthodox Dialogue 1959–1994* (Göttingen: Vandenhoeck & Ruprecht, 1997), 110ff.

51. For Luther's thought on the subject, see *The Misuse of the Mass* (1521) in LW 36: 147; *The Smalcald Articles* (1538), II; *Babylonian Captivity* (1520), LW 36: 56; *Treatise on the New Testament, That Is, The Holy Mass* (1520), LW 35: 86–87.

52. DH 1740.

53. Karl Lehmann and Wolfhart Pannenberg, eds., *The Condemnations of the Reformation Era: Do They Still Divide?* trans. Margaret Kohl (Minneapolis: Fortress Press, 1990), 85.

54. Ibid. Canon 4: "If anyone says that after the consecration is completed, the body and blood of our Lord Jesus Christ are not in the admirable sacrament of the Eucharist, but are there only *in usu*, while being taken and not before and not after, and that the hosts or consecrated particles which are reserved or which remain after communion, the true body of the Lord does not remain, let him be anathema;" Lehmann and Pannenberg, *The Condemnations of the Reformation Era: Do They Still Divide?* 85.

55. Ibid., §§ 1354, 1362–72.

56. Ibid., § 1363.

57. Lutheran-Catholic Dialogue, *The Eucharist* (1978), § 36.

58. Ibid., § 56.

59. See *Lutherans and Catholics in Dialogue III: The Eucharist as Sacrifice* (New York: USA National Committee of the Lutheran World Federation and the Bishops' Committee for Ecumenical and Interreligious Affairs; Washington, DC: United States Catholic Conference, 1967), 189.

60. Ibid., 191.

61. Lowell G. Almen and Richard J. Sklba, eds., *Hope of Eternal Life: Lutherans and Catholics in Dialogue XI* (Minneapolis: Lutheran University Press, 2011), 91–117.

62. *The Eucharist* (1978), § 54.

63. In 1969, the Sacred Congregation for Rites split into the Sacred Congregation for the Sacraments and Divine Worship and the Sacred Congregation for the Causes of the Saints. Then, in 1975, the Sacred Congregation for the Discipline of the Sacraments and the Sacred Congregation for Divine Worship merged to form the Sacred Congregation for the Sacraments and Divine Worship.

64. Sacred Congregation of Rites, *Eucharisticum Mysterium* (May 25, 1967), 3.e.

65. See also Congregation for Divine Worship, *Eucharistiae Sacramentum*, "On Holy Communion and the Worship of the Eucharistic Mystery Outside of Mass" (June 1973), § 5.

66. *Eucharisticum Mysterium*, 3.f.

67. WA Br 10: 348–49. Cited by Mickey Mattox, "Offered and Received: Lutheran Theology and Practice of the Eucharist," *Lutheran Forum* 37, no. 2 (Summer 2003): 33–44, at 37. This article was written when Mattox was a research professor at the Institute for Ecumenical Research in Strasbourg, France, for the eleventh plenary session of the international Lutheran-Orthodox Joint Commission, meeting in Oslo, Norway, in October 2002, considering the topic "The Mystery of the Church: Mysteria/Sacraments as Means of Salvation."

68. WA Br 10: 348–49, cited by Mattox, 37.

69. *The Eucharist* (1978), § 55.

70. Ibid.

71. Ibid. For a Lutheran assessment of the practice of adoration, see George Lindbeck, "Augsburg and the *Ecclesia de Eucharistia*," *Pro Ecclesia* 12, no. 4 (2003): 405–14.

72. *The Eucharist*, § 76.

73. Paul F. Bradshaw and Maxwell E. Johnson, *The Eucharistic Liturgies: Their Evolution and Interpretation* (Collegeville, MN: Liturgical Press, Pueblo, 2012), 326.

74. For the history and interpretation of Luther's adaptations of the canon, see Bryan D. Spinks, *Luther's Liturgical Criteria and His Reform of the Canon of the Mass* (Bramcote: Grove Books, 1982); Spinks, "Berakah, Anaphoral Theory, and Luther," *Lutheran Quarterly* 3 (1989): 267–80; Frank Senn, "Martin Luther's Revision of the Eucharistic Canon in the

Formula Missae of 1523," *Concordia Theological Monthly* 44 (1973): 101–18, Bradshaw and Johnson, op. cit., 246–51.

75. Bradshaw and Johnson, *The Eucharistic Liturgies*, 327.

76. Louis Bouyer, *Eucharist: The Theology and Spirituality of the Eucharistic Prayer* (Notre Dame: University of Notre Dame Press, 1968), 441–42. Cited by Bradshaw and Johnson, *The Eucharistic Liturgies*, 328.

77. Bradshaw and Johnson, *The Eucharistic Liturgies*, 329.

78. See Oliver K. Olson, "Contemporary Trends in Liturgy Viewed from the Perspective of Classic Lutheran Theology," *Lutheran Quarterly* 26 (1974): 110–57. But see also the various responses to Olson's position in this same volume. On the question of the epiclesis, see Maxwell E. Johnson, "The Holy Spirit and Lutheran Liturgical-Sacramental Worship," in *The Spirit in Worship—Worship in the Spirit*, ed. Teresa Berger and Bryan Spinks (Collegeville, MN: Liturgical Press, Pueblo, 2009), 155–78.

79. Bradshaw and Johnson, *The Eucharistic Liturgies*, 329.

80. See Eucharistic Prayer I (Roman Canon).

81. Prosper of Aquitaine, *Patrologia Latina* 51, pp. 209–10, "obsecrationum quoque sacerdotalium sacramenta respiciamus, quae ab apostolis tradita, in toto mundo atque in omni catholica Ecclesia uniformiter celebrantur, ut legem credendi lex statuat supplicandi."

82. Wolfgang Simon, in "Worship and the Eucharist in Luther Studies," *Dialog* 47, no. 2 (Summer 2008): 143–56, analyzes Luther's texts for new possibilities for conceiving the sacrament in terms of thanksgiving and active response related to the notion of offering.

83. The Lutheran Church-Missouri Synod and the Wisconsin Synod are not members of the LWF and practice closed communion.

84. Pontifical Council for Promoting Christian Unity, *Directory for the Application of Principles and Norms on Ecumenism* (Washington, DC: United States Catholic Conference, 1993), §§ 129–31.

85. Ibid., § 131.

86. Ibid., § 132.

87. Randall Lee and Jeffrey Gros, eds., *The Church as Koinonia of Salvation: Its Structures and Ministries: Lutherans and Catholics in Dialogue X* (Washington, DC: United States Conference of Catholic Bishops, 2004), § 107.

88. Joseph Ratzinger, "Briefwechsel von Landesbischof Johananes Hanselmann und Joseph Kardinal Ratzinger über das Communio-Schreiben der Römischen Glaubenskongregation," *Una Sancta* 48 (1993): 348, cited in *Church as Koinonia of Salvation*, § 107.

CHAPTER FIVE

1. *The Gospel and the Church. Report of the Joint Lutheran-Roman Catholic Study Commission* (*Malta Report,* 1972), § 63. Hereafter, *Malta.*

2. *Malta,* § 64.

3. *The Eucharist. Report of the Lutheran-Roman Catholic Joint Commission,* § 65. Hereafter, *Eucharist.*

4. *The Apostolicity of the Church. Study Document of the Lutheran-Roman Catholic Commission on Unity* (Minneapolis: Lutheran University Press, 2006), § 276. Hereafter, *Apostolicity;* USA National Committee of the Lutheran World Federation and the Bishops' Committee for Ecumenical and Interreligious Affairs, *Eucharist and Ministry,* Lutherans and Catholics in Dialogue IV, 1970, § 18.

5. Lutheran-Roman Catholic Joint Commission, *The Ministry in the Church* (Geneva: The Lutheran World Federation, 1982), §§ 20, 23. Hereafter, *Ministry.*

6. *Malta,* § 50, *Ministry* § 23, *Apostolicity,* § 275.

7. *Ministry,* § 23.

8. *Apostolicity,* § 273.

9. *Apostolicity,* § 275.

10. *On the Councils and the Churches,* WA 50: 641, 16–19 (LW 41: 164). Timothy J. Wengert explains that, here, Luther used the word *priest* in its (for his time) traditional sense of "public minister of the gospel." Timothy Wengert, *Priesthood, Pastors, Bishops: Public Ministry for the Reformation and Today* (Minneapolis: Fortress Press, 2008), 121.

11. *On Councils and the Churches,* WA 50: 632, 35–633, 3. LW 41: 154.

12. *Ministry,* § 20, n23; *Apostolicity,* § 238.

13. From the Baptism of the Lord, *Roman Missal* (2011), 203.

14. Thomas Rausch, "Priest, Community, and Eucharist," in *Finding God in All Things: Essays in Honor of Michael J. Buckley, S.J.,* ed. Michael J. Himes and Stephen J. Pope (New York: Crossroads, 1996), 263.

15. Congregation of Rites, Instruction *Eucharisticum Mysterium, On Worship of the Eucharist,* May 25, 1967, § 12; COL 179, no. 1241.

16. See also General Instruction of the Roman Missal (1970), no. 60, DOL 208, no. 1450.

17. This material on the relationship between the ordained priesthood and the common priesthood is from Susan K. Wood, *Sacramental Orders,* 128–34.

18. WA 12: 179, 9–10 (LW 40: 18). Luther capitalized the first clause in the original. Cited by Timothy J. Wengert, *Priesthood, Pastors, Bishops: Public Ministry for the Reformation and Today* (Minneapolis: Fortress Press, 2008), 20.

19. Lutheran World Federation, "Episcopal Ministry within the Apostolicity of the Church," "The Lund Statement," § 36. http://www.lutheranworld.org/sites/default/files/Episcopal%20Ministry%20within%20Apostolicity%20of%20the%20Church.pdf.

20. Wengert, *Priesthood, Pastors, Bishops*, 20.

21. LW 44: 127; WA 6: 407, 10–15.

22. LW 35: 100–101; WA 6: 370, 7–11. In other places in Luther's writings, the common priesthood is equivalent to "the body of Christ."

23. Martin Luther, *Babylonian Captivity of the Church*, LW 36: 116; WA 6: 566; cited in *The Lund Statement*, § 36.

24. CA XIV.

25. Bernard Lohse, *Martin Luther's Theology* (Minneapolis: Fortress Press, 1999), 290.

26. Wengert, *Priesthood, Pastors, Bishops*, 12.

27. Lohse, *Martin Luther's Theology*, 293.

28. For this reason, Philip Melanchthon, in the *Apology of the Augsburg Confession*, art. VII/VIII.28 (in BC 178) refers to the officeholder speaking *in persona Christi* ("they represent the person of Christ").

29. Lohse, *Martin Luther's Theology*, 22.

30. *Eucharist and Ministry*, § 18.

31. *Apostolicity*, § 102.

32. *Apology of the Augsburg Confession*, 13, 9–13.

33. *Apostolicity*, § 241.

34. Karl Lehmann and Wolfhart Pannenberg, eds., *The Condemnations of the Reformation Era: Do They Still Divide?* (Minneapolis: Fortress Press, 1990), 152.

35. The Lund Statement, § 40. See John H. P. Reumann, "The Ordination of Women: Exegesis, Experience, and Ecumenical Concern," in *Ministries Examined: Laity, Clergy, Women, and Bishops in a Time of Change* (Minneapolis: Augsburg, 1987), 78–139. This essay was written for an intra-Lutheran study of the topic in 1968–1969. Supplementary comments at the end of the essay gives the Lutheran history of the question from 1969 up to the republication of the essay in this volume.

36. *Ministry*, § 24.

37. Congregation of the Doctrine of the Faith, "*Responsum ad Propositum Dubium*," October 25, 1995, http://www.vatican.va/roman_curia/congregations/cfaith/documents/rc_con_cfaith_doc_19951028_dubium-ordinatio-sac_en.html.

38. Until the revision of the rites of ordination in 1968, the three major orders were priest, deacon, and sub-deacon. The change is the result of the recognition of the episcopacy as an order in its own right and the suppression of the order of sub-deacon.

39. *Apostolicity*, § 218.

40. See George Dolan, *The Distinction between the Episcopate and the Presbyterate according to the Thomistic Opinion* (Washington, DC: The Catholic University of America Press, 1950), 82–83; and Seamus Ryan, "Episcopal Consecration: The Legacy of the Schoolmen," *Irish Theological Quarterly* 22 (1966): 3–38. This argument from Jerome was preserved in the Lutheran confessions. See the *Treatise on the Power and Primacy of the Pope*, 60–82 (BC 340–43).

41. *Apostolicity*, § 241.

42. For a history of the terms *in persona Christi* and *in persona ecclesiae*, see B.-D. Marliangeas, *Clés pour une théologie du ministère* (Paris: Beauchesne, 1978).

43. See US Lutheran-Catholic Dialogue, *Church as Koinonia of Salvation: Its Structures and Ministries* (2004), § 169.

44. Karl Rahner, "The Area Bishop: Some Theological Reflections," in *Theological Investigations* 17 (New York: Crossroad, 1981), 166.

45. The Catholic Church also ordains titular bishops who either serve the universal church, most often in a Roman dicastery, or serve as auxiliary bishops in larger dioceses. They are members of the episcopal college, but do not represent a particular church within the communion of particular churches.

46. A particular church is administratively a diocese.

47. Cited in *Apostolicity*, § 274.

48. The word *Pfarrer* (Pfarr-Herr: lord of a parish) is connected to pastoral care in modern German. In the sixteenth century, there were two offices, so to speak, one of pastor (*Pfarrer*) and one of preacher (*Prediger*). The reformers preferred the term *Minister* (servant) in Latin or *Predigtamt* (office of preaching) in German. See CA V.

49. *Eucharist and Ministry*, § 21.

50. *The Lund Statement*, § 39.

51. *Apostolicity*, § b265,

52. The two bishops he consecrated (the archbishop of Cologne having been put under house arrest) were stripped of their offices in the wake of the Smalcald War of 1547–48 with the defeat of the elector John Frederick of Saxony. Attempts to work with the Roman bishops who took their place came to naught with the revolt of the princes in 1551–52 and the consequent Treaty of Passau (1552) and Peace of Augsburg (1555), which made it illegal for a bishop to become Lutheran.

53. *Confessio Augustana*, 28; *Apology*, 14.1.

54. Denmark, which ruled Norway and Iceland, retained the episcopal office, but lost episcopal succession when the Roman Catholic bishops were dismissed and replaced by bishops consecrated by Johannes

Bugenhagen, an associate of Luther and General Superintendent from Wittenberg, who was a priest, not a bishop. Sweden, which ruled Finland, preserved both the episcopal office and the succession of bishops beyond the eighteenth century. Swedish and Finnish emigrants to North America did not preserve these. See Michael Root, "The Lutheran Churches," in *The Christian Church: An Introduction to the Major Traditions*, ed. Paul Avis (London: SPCK, 2002), 198–99, 206.

55. CA XXVIII.

56. CA XVIII.

57. CA XVIII.

58. See *Church as Koinonia of Salvation*, § 67.

59. Ibid., §§ 189–95.

60. Ibid., § 232.

61. Lutherans, for example, are in communion with Reformed churches in Europe (through the *Leuenberg Agreement* of 1973) and in the United States (through the *Formula of Agreement* of 1997) that do not have an episcopal structure. On the other hand, they are in communion with Anglicans in Europe (through the *Porvoo Common Statement* of 1993) and in the United States (through the *Called to Common Mission* of 1999), which committed Lutherans to entering into episcopacy in apostolic succession. Not all Lutheran churches, however, have an episcopal ministry.

62. See Augustine's commentary on Psalm 126, par. 3 (*Patrologia Latina* 37: 1669): "Nam ideo altior locus positus est episcopis, ut ipsi superintendant et quasi custodiant populum. Nam et graece quod dicitur episcopus, hoc latine superintentor interpretatur; quia superintendit, quia desuper videt."

63. See Timothy J. Wengert, *Priesthood, Pastors, Bishops: Public Ministry for the Reformation and Today* (Minneapolis: Fortress Press, 2008), 57.

64. *The Lund Statement*, § 39.

65. See *The Diaconal Ministry in the Mission of the Church*, LWF Studies 01/2006 for a statement and the main presentations from an international consultation on the diaconal ministry.

66. *Apostolicity*, § 271.

67. Ibid., § 270.

68. Ibid., § 182.

69. Ibid., § 95.

70. Ibid., § 222.

71. The *Porvoo Common Statement*, http://www.anglicancommunion.org/ministry/ecumenical/dialogues/lutheran/docs/pdf/porvoo_common_statement.pdf. The participating churches are named in the *Porvoo Declaration*, § 58, which is found at the end of the *Porvoo Common Statement*.

72. Thus the document from the Congregation of the Doctrine of the Faith, *Dominus Iesus* (June 12, 2000), § 17, states that ecclesial communities that have not preserved the valid episcopate (and thus the integral substance of the eucharistic ministry) are not churches in the proper sense. See http://www.vatican.va/roman_curia/congregations/cfaith/documents/rc_con_cfaith_doc_20000806_dominus-iesus_en.html. See also the same congregation's document, "Responses to Some Questions Regarding Certain Aspects of the Doctrine on the Church," (June 29, 2007), again identifying apostolic succession as an essential element of the church in whose absence a community can be called "church" in the proper sense (fifth question in the document), http://www.vatican.va/roman_curia/congregations/cfaith/documents/rc_con_cfaith_doc_20070629_responsa-quaestiones_en.html.

73. *Porvoo Common Statement*, § 53.

74. *Porvoo Declaration*, § 58.b.

75. *Called to Common Mission*, § 12, http://www.episcopalchurch.org/page/agreement-full-communion-called-common-mission.

76. *The Lund Statement*, § 50.

77. *Apostolicity*, § 19.

78. See http://www.papalencyclicals.net/Leo13/l13curae.htm.

79. The question of apostolic succession of some of the Nordic bishops, especially the Swedish and the Finnish bishops, is more complicated and ambiguous, as some may have retained apostolic succession after the Reformation.

80. Part of the difficulty with the translation may be traceable to two separate uses of the word *defectus* in classical Latin—one meaning "absence" and the other (as a participle from *deficio*) meaning "deficiency."

81. Walter Kasper, "Die apostolische Sukzession als ökumenisches Problem," *Lehrverteilungen-kirchentrennend?* III, 345, cited in *Church as Koinonia of Salvation*, § 108.

82. *Church as Koinonia of Salvation*, § 107. For a discussion of "validity" as applied to Lutheran orders, see John J. Burkhard, *Apostolicity Then and Now: An Ecumenical Church in a Postmodern World* (Collegeville, MN: Liturgical Press, 2004), 218–23; and Charles Wackenheim, "Validité et nullité des sacrements: Le problème théologique," *Revue de droit canonique* 26 (1976): 15–22, especially the comment on ordination on p. 18.

83. *Church as Koinonia of Salvation*, § 53.

84. Ibid., § 70.

85. *Church and Justification*, § 106.

86. See *Malta*, § 66.

87. Bilateral Working Group of the German Bishops' Conference and the Church Leadership of the United Evangelical Lutheran Church

of Germany, *Communio Sanctorum: The Church as the Communion of Saints*, trans. Mark W. Jeske, Michael Root, and Daniel R. Smith (Collegeville, MN: Liturgical Press, 2004), § 174.

88. *Malta*, § 66.

89. "Differing Attitudes," I, Common Statement, §§ 6–8, in *Papal Primacy*, 12–13.

90. *Communio Sanctorum*, § 185.

91. *Church as Koinonia of Salvation*, § 73.

92. *Ministry*, § 73, citing *Malta*, § 66.

93. *Communio Sanctorum*, § 189.

94. Paul C. Empie and T. Austin Murphy, eds. *Papal Primacy and the Universal Church*, Lutherans and Catholics in Dialogue V, (Minneapolis: Augsburg, 1974), 35–36.

CHAPTER SIX

1. The most recent English translation is Robert Kolb and Timothy J. Wengert, eds., *The Book of Concord* (Minneapolis: Fortress Press, 2000). "Some Lutheran churches do not recognize some of the Reformation Confessions, especially the Augsburg Confession and Luther's Small Catechism."

2. Risto Saarinen, "Lutheran Ecclesiology," in *The Routledge Companion to the Christian Church*, ed. Gerard Mannion and Lewis S. Mudge (New York: Routledge, 2008), 170–86 at 180.

3. Ibid., 181.

4. Robert Bellarmine, *Of Controversies of Christian Faith against Heretics of Today* (1586), III, ii.

5. *Malta*.

6. Lutheran-Roman Catholic Commission on Unity, *The Apostolicity of the Church* (Minneapolis: Lutheran University Press, 2006).

7. *Church and Justification*, § 11.

8. Ibid., § 32.

9. Ibid., § 73.

10. Ibid., § 149.

11. *Malta*, § 23, cited in *Church and Justification*, § 159.

12. *Church and Justification*, § 156.

13. Ibid., § 160.

14. Ibid., § 163.

15. Ibid., § 165.

16. Ibid., § 36. See CA VII.

17. *Malta*, § 48.

18. Ibid. Also cited in *Church and Justification*, § 38.

19. Council of Trent, session 5, June 17, 1546, Second Decree: On Instruction and Preaching; session 24, November 11, 1563, Decree on Reform, canon 4.

20. Karl Rahner, "What is a Sacrament?" in *Theological Investigations*, vol. 14, trans. David Bourke (London: Darton, Longman, & Todd, 1976), 136.

21. Ibid.

22. Ibid., 138.

23. Ola Tjørhom is a Lutheran theologian who converted to Catholicism on January 25, 2003.

24. Ola Tjørhom, *Visible Church—Visible Unity: Ecumenical Ecclesiology and "The Great Tradition of the Church"* (Collegeville, MN: Liturgical Press, 2004), 49.

25. Ibid.

26. *Apology*, XXIV, 1.

27. See http://download.elca.org/ELCA%20Resource%20Repository/The_Use_Of_The_Means_Of_Grace.pdf.

28. ELCA, *The Use of the Means of Grace: A Statement on the Practice of Word and Sacrament*, 35b.

29. Tjørhom, *Visible Church—Visible Unity*, 50.

30. *Catechism*, § 1253.

31. *Church and Justification*, § 107.

32. *Church as Koinonia of Salvation*, §§ 10–13.

33. *Church and Justification*, § 108.

34. Tjørhom, *Visible Church—Visible Unity*, 51.

35. Some of the material for this section was developed in Susan K. Wood, *One Baptism: The Ecumenical Implications of the Doctrine of Baptism* (Collegeville, MN: Liturgical Press, 2009), 183–87.

36. *Church and Justification*, § 108.

37. *Lumen Gentium* § 1 says, "Cum autem ecclesia sit in Christo *veluti* sacramentum seu signum et instrumentum intimae cum Deo unionis totiusque generis humani unitatis." (emphasis added). The force of *veluti* is that the church is "sort of" a sacrament, that is, a sacrament analogously.

38. Yves Congar, *Un peuple messianique: L'Eglise: Sacrement du salut, salut et libération* (Paris: Edition du Cerf, 1975), 31.

39. *Communio Sanctorum*, § 87.

40. Robert Bellarmine, *Of Controversies of Christian Faith against Heretics of Today* (1586), III, ii.

41. See Tjørhom, *Visible Church—Visible Unity*, 45–46, who suggests that Lutherans were originally reluctant to acknowledge the sacra-

mentality of the church out of fear of falsely identifying Christ and the church, while today, the greater danger is to tear them totally apart.

42. World Council of Churches, *The Nature and Mission of the Church: A Stage on the Way to a Common Statement*, Faith and Order Paper, no. 198 (Geneva: World Council of Churches, 2005), 29. See also the discussion in *Communio Sanctorum*, §§ 86–88.

43. Ibid., 30.

44. CA VII.

45. Roman Confutation, pt. 1, art. VII, cited in n237 of BC 174.

46. *Apology*, art. VII and VIII: The Church, § 3.

47. The first thesis of the Berne Reformation Mandate (1528) cited in "The *Notae Ecclesiae*: A Reformed Perspective," by Christian Link in *Toward the Future of Reformed Theology: Tasks, Topics, Traditions*, ed. David Willis and Michael Welker (Grand Rapids, MI: Wm. B. Eerdmans, 1999), 241.

48. Ibid., § 14.

49. WA 51: 507m 13ff; LW 41: 211; *Against Hanswurst*, 1541.

50. LW 41: 164; and Vítor Westhelle, *The Church Event: Call and Challenge of a Church Protestant* (Minneapolis: Fortress Press, 2010), 85.

51. *Church and Justification*, § 139. It also notes that Melanchthon, in the *Apology of the Augsburg Confession*, rejected a view of the church as kind of "Platonic republic," § 136, citing *Apology* 7, 20.

52. *Church and Justification*, § 141.

53. Ibid., § 142.

54. Ibid., § 144.

55. Ibid., § 147.

56. LW 41: 164. Luther adds the cross as the seventh mark of the church in 1539: "Seventh, the holy Christian people are externally recognized by the holy possession of the sacred cross."

57. Translation from Tanner, 853.

58. WA 20: 514m 27f. Cited by Westhelle, *The Church Event*, 162. See also Gordon W. Lathrop and Timothy J. Wengert, *Christian Assembly: Marks of the Church in a Pluralistic Age* (Minneapolis: Fortress Press, 2004), 88–93.

59. See WA 41: 700 and LW 6: 149; WA 40: 69–70.

60. *Church as Koinonia of Salvation*, § 21.

61. *Church and Justification*, § 85.

62. Ibid.

63. *Lumen Gentium* § 26 describes this as a "community of the altar, under the sacred ministry of the bishop."

64. *Church and Justification*, § 93–95.

65. Ibid., § 92–93.

66. See http://www.lutheranworld.org/content/about-lwf.

67. Risto Saarinen, "Lutheran Ecclesiology," in *The Routledge Companion to the Christian Church*, ed. Gerard Mannion and Lewis S. Mudge (New York: Routledge, 2008), 170–86 at 180.

68. Ibid.

69. Pope John Paul II, Address on September 12, 1987, in *Origins* 17:16 (October 1, 1987): 258. Here Pope John Paul II extends the assertion in *Lumen Gentium* § 8, that the Church of Christ subsists in the Roman Catholic Church to the relationship between the universal church and particular churches. See *Church as Koinonia of Salvation*, § 53.

70. *Malta*, § 52.

71. *Apostolicity of the Church*, § 75.

72. See Congregation for the Doctrine of the Faith, *Dominus Iesus*, August 6, 2000, § 17.

73. *Apostolicity of the Church*, § 73.

74. Ibid., § 62.

75. Ibid., § 67.

76. Ibid., § 69.

77. Ibid., § 98.

78. Ibid., § 95.

79. Ibid., § 97.

80. *Apostolicity of the Church*, § 99, citing Luther, *Concerning Rebaptism* (1528), WA 26: 146f, LW 40: 231f. Also, *Commentary on Galatians* (1535), WA 40/1: 69; LW 26: 24.

81. DH 1501; Council of Trent, session 4, April 8, 1546, First decree; Translation, Tanner, 663.

82. Ibid.

83. *Apostolicity of the Church*, § 105.

84. Also see *Christus Dominus*, § 12.

85. *Apostolicity of the Church*, § 110.

86. Margaret O'Gara, *No Turning Back: The Future of Ecumenism*, ed. Michael Vertin (Collegeville, MN: Liturgical Press, 2014), 95.

87. Conversations between the British and Irish Anglican Churches and the Nordic and Baltic Lutheran Churches, *The Porvoo Common Statement* (1992) (London: Council for Christian Unity of the General Synod of the Church of England, 1993), § 33.

88. Ibid., § 49.

89. O'Gara, *No Turning Back*, 97.

90. *Malta*, § 57.

91. Roman Catholic-Lutheran Joint Commission, *The Ministry in the Church* (Geneva: The Lutheran World Federation, 1982), § 59.

92. Ibid., § 60.

93. Ibid., § 61.

94. Ibid., § 62.

95. John J. Burkhard, *Apostolicity Then and Now: An Ecumenical Church in a Postmodern World* (Collegeville, MN: Liturgical Press, 2004), 182.

96. Roman Catholic-Lutheran Joint Commission, *Facing Unity* (Geneva: Lutheran World Federation, 1985).

97. *Facing Unity*, § 5.

98. Ibid., § 110.

99. In the Lutheran World Federation, only the Batak Church of Indonesia does not use the Augsburg Confession as its basic confession, due to its origins in the mission groups of the nineteenth century. Instead, the LWF found the church's own, relatively recent confession to suffice for entrance into the LWF.

100. *Apostolicity*, § 389.

101. *Church and Justification*, §§ 212–13.

102. This manner of teaching has only occurred twice: the definition of the Immaculate Conception of Mary in 1854 and again in 1950 with the definition of the Assumption of Mary into heaven.

103. An example of this is the use of the word *person* to describe the distinct relations in the Trinity.

104. *Apostolicity*, § 419. See *Lumen Gentium*, § 25.

105. *Apostolicity*, § 424.

106. Ibid., § 424.

107. *Church and Justification*, § 216.

108. *Apostolicity*, § 426.

109. Ibid., § 433.

110. Ibid.

111. Ibid., § 451.

CHAPTER SEVEN

1. Martin Luther, *Luther's Epistle Sermons*, trans. John Lenker, vol. 3 (Minneapolis: Luther Press, 1909; Reprinted in vol. 8 of *The Sermons of Martin Luther* [Grand Rapids, MI: Baker, 1989]), 288. Cf. WA 22: 292–300.

2. Ibid., 289–90.

3. Johann Wild, *Sommertheyl der Postill oder Predigbuchs Euangelischer warheyt und rechter Catholischer Lehr* (Mainz: Behem, 1556), 630v.

4. *JDDJ*, § 15.

5. See the Formula of Concord, Solid Declaration, art. III, par. 36, trans. Robert Kolb, in BC 568. This paragraph was originally drafted by Martin Chemnitz.

6. See Susan K. Wood, *One Baptism: Ecumenical Dimensions of the Doctrine of Baptism* (Collegeville, MN: Liturgical Press, 2009), 171–76.

7. Council of Trent, session 22, September 17, 1552, chap. 1 and 2.

8. Lowel G. Almen and Richard J. Sklba, eds., *The Hope of Eternal Life: Common Statement of the Eleventh Round of the Lutheran-Catholic Dialogue* (Minneapolis: Lutheran University Press, 2011).

9. *Apostolicity*, § 280.

10. *Ministry*, § 45.

11. *Apostolicity*, § 279.

12. CA 28; *Apology* 14.1.

13. *Episcopal Ministry within the Apostolicity of the Church*, The Lund Statement by the Lutheran World Federation, Lund, Sweden, March 26, 2007, § 39, https://www.lutheranworld.org/sites/default/files/Episcopal%20 Ministry%20within%20Apostolicity%20of%20the%20Church.pdf.

14. *Apostolicity*, § 265.

15. Ibid., § 19.

16. Ibid., § 287.

17. *Church as Koinonia of Salvation*, § 120.

18. Ibid., § 117.

19. Francis, Post-Synodal Apostolic Exhortation, *Evangelii Gaudium* (The Joy of the Gospel), November 24, 2013.

20. Martin Luther, *On the Councils and the Church* (1539), in LW 41: 148–78.

21. *Church and Justification*, § 153–55.

22. *Communio Sanctorum*, § 89.

23. *Church and Justification*, § 207.

24. *Communio Sanctorum*, § 66, citing *Kirchliches Leben in ökumenisher Verpflichtung*, ed. Hermann Brandt (Stuttgart: Calwer Verlag, 1989), 133.

25. Ibid., citing CA 28:21.

26. Ibid., citing CA 28:22F and Lehrordnung der VELKD vom 16.61956, no. 470.

27. Ibid., § 68.

28. See "Steps toward a Reunited Church: A Sketch of an Orthodox-Catholic Vision for the Future" (October 2, 2010), http://www.assembly ofbishops.org/news/scoba/towards-a-unified-church.

29. The ideas in this section are reformulated from Susan K. Wood, "Editorial: A Parable for the Ecumenical Movement Today," *Ecclesiology* 10 (2014): 285–91.

30. Congregation of the Doctrine of the Faith, *Directory for the Application of Principles and Norms on Ecumenism* (March 25, 1993), § 20. The *Directory* cites *Unitatis Redintegratio*, § 4 and §§ 15–16.

31. Ibid., § 16.

Index

249